STAR WARS BATTLEFRONT™

PRIMA OFFICIAL GAME GUIDE　　　　DAVID KNIGHT

Prima Games
A Division of Random House, Inc.

3000 Lava Ridge Court
Roseville, CA 95661
1-800-733-3000
www.primagames.com

The Prima Games logo is a registered trademark of Random House, Inc., registered in the United States and other countries. Primagames.com is a registered trademark of Random House, Inc., registered in the United States. Prima Games is a division of Random House, Inc.

Associate Product Manager: Mario De Govia
Editorial Supervisor: Christy Seifert
Design & Layout: Derek Hocking

All other trademarks are the property of their respective owners.

Important:
Prima Games has made every effort to determine that the information contained in this book is accurate. However, the publisher makes no warranty, either expressed or implied, as to the accuracy, effectiveness, or completeness of the material in this book; nor does the publisher assume liability for damages, either incidental or consequential, that may result from using the information in this book. The publisher cannot provide information regarding game play, hints and strategies, or problems with hardware or software. Questions should be directed to the support numbers provided by the game and device manufacturers in their documentation. Some game tricks require precise timing and may require repeated attempts before the desired result is achieved.

ISBN: 0-7615-4709-6
Library of Congress Catalog Card Number: 2004107125
Printed in the United States of America

04 05 06 07 LL 10 9 8 7 6 5 4 3 2 1

CONTENTS

Prima would like to thank Tim Moore, Chane Hollander, David Silverstein, Troy Sims, Jeffrey Gullett, Brianna Woodward, Xavier Rodriguez, Zak Huntwork, Seth Benton, James Morris, and Matt Rubenstein for their contributions to this guide.

combat training

Welcome to *Star Wars* Battlefront™! In this epic game you take an active role in some of the most famous battles from both the Clone Wars and the Galactic Civil War era. Do you have what it takes to stop the Techno Union ships at Geonosis or topple the AT-AT walkers on Hoth?

Before you don your gear and unholster your blaster, it's a good idea to brush up on the basics. Even if you're not new to the front lines, a refresher course never hurts. In this section, we cover the fundamental skills needed to stay alive on the treacherous battlefields you encounter. We also take a look at the various gameplay modes, including some useful hints and team-play considerations for heated multiplayer sessions. So set your helmet aside for now and read up! Who knows, you may learn something that will keep you from becoming bantha fodder.

MOVEMENT & COMBAT BASICS

Constant movement is a must to avoid getting picked off by snipers or other enemies looking for an easy kill. Whether attacking or defending, keep moving. Running is the most common form of movement and should always be used when speed is a factor—or no vehicle is available. But running isn't the only form of movement available to your troops.

STRAFING

While constant movement is important, running in a straight line can often get you killed. Throw some variation in your advance by making random lateral movements. This makes you harder to target, especially if a sniper has you in his sights.

Strafing is essential to survival in close-range combat. Instead of moving forward and backward, move left or right to dodge an opponent's incoming blasts. But keep your sights on the enemy, and return fire.

In multiplayer games, newbies tend to stand in one spot while firing their weapon. Drive them nuts by circle-strafing around them. Center them in your sights and simply move right or left. By keeping them centered and moving laterally, you maneuver around them in a circular path. Keep moving and firing until they drop.

CROUCHING

To lower your visible profile, crouch. This is useful when it's necessary to hide behind an object while sneaking around, or when defending a command post. Crouching also presents the enemy with a smaller, more compact target, making you harder to hit at long range.

It's possible to move while crouched, but your speed is significantly reduced. Reserve this form of movement for situations when you have some sort of cover. Stand up and run when crossing high-traffic areas with concentrations of enemy fire.

Cover vs. Concealment

Understanding the difference between cover and concealment can greatly increase your lifespan on the battlefield. The term *cover* is used to describe a solid object that protects you from incoming fire and obscures your location—a rock or wall, for example.

Concealment masks your position from the enemy, but isn't solid enough to block incoming blasts—high grass and shrubs, for example. Even if the enemy can't see you, they can fire into the area where they suspect you are and still hit you.

Always choose cover over concealment if possible, because it provides protection against energy and explosive attacks.

combat training

Prone/Crawling

Dropping prone reduces your visible profile dramatically, often concealing your position behind grass or other surrounding objects. This is the best stance for snipers, especially if they're positioned on a high elevation.

You can crawl while prone, but this mode of movement is extremely slow and useful only when you need to shift positions slightly. The lack of mobility also makes it extremely difficult to defend yourself if you're attacked at close range. Reserve this stance for instances when you're far away from the high-traffic areas of the battlefield and need to stay out of sight.

Jumping/Rolling

Obviously, jumping gives you access to certain areas that are otherwise out of reach because of the absence of stairs or ramps. You can also jump over certain low barriers like rocks and walls.

Jumping can also save your life in certain combat situations. For instance, if you come face to face with a droideka, instead of duking it out, simply jump on top of it and drop down behind it. From there you can attack or simply retreat as the slow unit attempts to rotate and get you back in its sights.

The Republic jet trooper and Imperial dark trooper take jumping to a whole new level with the use of their jet packs. Use these units to explore new areas and stage attacks from unexpected directions. These

are your commandos, so use them to optimize the element of surprise.

Rolling is also a critical maneuver, allowing you to somersault laterally. This is best used when diving out of the way of an incoming thermal detonator or when evading the incoming blasts of a turret or vehicle. Keep diving and rolling in one direction until you can seek some sort of cover. This is faster than strafing, but you won't be able to return fire while diving.

You can also try diving and rolling around blind corners. This is a good way to dodge incoming blasts from defenders lying in wait.

Vehicles

Vehicles are a huge asset. Before entering a battle, take some time to study the maps in the subsequent sections and locate all the vehicle spawn points. Knowing where the vehicles appear helps you determine which areas are likely to come under attack and from which direction.

For the most part, controlling vehicles is just as intuitive as controlling infantry. Some vehicles offer secondary weapons like missiles, so experiment with their offensive capabilities before rushing into the heat of the battle.

As expected, vehicles can take damage from a variety of ordnance. But pilots and repair droids can repair them. Pilots can either repair them from outside the vehicle or while riding inside. In fact, the more pilots on board a vehicle, the quicker it repairs itself. This is even more incentive to reserve your vehicles for the pilot units.

NAVIGATION

Finding your way around the battlefield can often be confusing, especially in the dense forests of Yavin IV and Endor. Fortunately, a small map in the bottom left corner of the screen keeps you oriented.

You can call up an even larger map for an instant big-picture analysis of the battlefield. The white arrow shows your current position while the circles represent command posts. Friendly units appear as small green arrows and enemy units show up as red arrows. Some battlefields have indigenous units like Tusken Raiders and Ewoks, represented on the maps by yellow arrows. Check the map periodically throughout the battle to monitor the ever-changing tactical situation.

NOTE

In multiplayer games you cannot see the position of enemy units on the map.

SQUAD COMMANDS

Issuing commands to AI-controlled bots is a great way to bring a sense of order to the battlefield. Get near a group and order them to follow. This is a good way to assemble an attack squad necessary to take control of enemy-controlled command posts.

You can also order a group of troops to stay put. This is very helpful in positioning defenders at command posts your team already controls. If your command posts aren't constantly defended, you end up assaulting the same territory over and over again.

WEAPONS

Although there are 20 units in the game, their weapons are quite similar in operation and use, particularly among classes. Take some time to experiment with each. For more detailed information on the individual classes and units, flip ahead to the next section.

The blaster pistol is the most common sidearm, carried by almost all units as a secondary weapon. This pistol fires semiautomatically, draining the power reserves with each shot fired. It also recharges itself after each shot, but the rate of fire can overwhelm the recharging capability. If this happens, the pistol becomes inoperable temporarily while it recharges. To avoid draining the pistol's energy reserves, fire slowly and watch the energy meter at the top left corner of the screen.

Blaster rifles are the bread and butter of the soldier class, capable of unleashing an automatic salvo of laser fire. Unlike the blaster pistol, the blaster rifle uses ammo, stored in individual clips. Once drained, the clip must be reloaded, requiring the operator to cease firing for a few seconds. To prevent running out of ammo at inopportune times, keep the rifle fully loaded at all times. Make a habit of loading a fresh clip after each engagement, and visit pilots and ammo droids to stock up on clips.

All heavy weapons units carry a missile launcher, useful for taking out vehicles and infantry. The missiles are capable of locking onto vehicles before launch, indicated as a shrinking red diamond on the screen. When the diamond stops shrinking, a lock is attained and the missile may be fired. This is useful for hitting fast-moving targets like speeders and starfighters. The launcher does not lock onto infantry units, but missiles are still very effective in dealing with such threat. Fire missiles at your enemy's feet to maximize the damage. The jet trooper's EMP launcher works like the missile launchers, but cannot lock on to enemy vehicles.

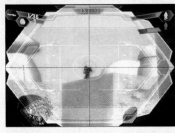

Sniper rifles are like high-powered versions of blaster rifles. But instead of firing multiple blasts automatically, it fires one high-intensity beam capable of killing with one hit—especially if it's a head shot. The amount of ammo a sniper rifle holds varies based on model, as does the magnification capability. These rifles are best used at long distances. Their rate of fire is extremely slow, making them difficult to use in close-quarters firefights.

Always aim for your target's head to maximize damage. Limb and torso hits cause equivalent amounts of damage, but head shots are often lethal. Of course, this depends on the power of the weapon being fired and the stamina of the target.

The Separatist and Imperial pilots use grenade and mortar launchers, as do the Rebel smugglers. These fire explosive shells in an arc-like trajectory. Each variation is capable of delayed detonation, so you can bounce the ordnance off walls and other surfaces to increase distance and enhance the weapon's ability to inflict indirect damage.

The Rebel pilot and dark trooper's blaster cannon is the equivalent of an energy-based shotgun, firing multiple bolts in a spread pattern. These weapons are devastating at close range, but virtually worthless at intermediate and long range. Use them for close-quarters assaults and defensive situations.

The Rebel smuggler's bowcaster and the clone pilot's bolt caster must be charged to produce optimal damage. You can do this by holding down the trigger for a few seconds, then releasing to fire. When fully charged, the bowcaster fires a devastating spread of lasers, similar to the previously mentioned blaster cannon. The bolt caster fires an equally devastating plasma bolt capable of frying any droid. Both weapons are most effective at close range.

Thermal detonators and concussion grenades are hand-tossed weapons carried by most infantry units. Thermal detonators are the most common. A slight delay before explosion allows you to bank the thermal detonator off walls and bounce it around corners. The concussion grenade is a little different. It's carried only by the soldier class and sticks to any vehicle it touches.

Mines are the cornerstone of any defensive strategy. These versatile, explosive discs are carried exclusively by heavy weapons units and can be placed on the ground or stuck to other surfaces. They only explode when an enemy unit or vehicle is nearby, making them relatively safe to use around friendly units. Experiment with them and compose wicked traps for your opponents. They can be destroyed if spotted, so keep them out of sight whenever possible.

GAMEPLAY CONCEPTS

The structure of gameplay is largely centered on capturing and defending key locations, putting more emphasis on cooperation than on individual skill. Victory conditions aren't solely based on a team's number of kills or deaths, but rather on how much territory is controlled throughout the course of the battle. Take a minute to glance over the game's unique concepts to better grasp the best path to victory.

REINFORCEMENT POINTS

Every reinforcement point is precious, so seek out medical droids to heal injuries.

Reinforcement points are your team's lifeblood. They represent the number of reserves your team has at any given time. This ever-fluctuating number is prominently displayed in the top of the screen—think of it as a way of keeping score. Every time you or a teammate dies, one ticket is drained from your team's total count. Basically, the side with the most reinforcement points at the end of the game wins.

When your team's point count reaches zero, the game ends, resulting in a victory for your opponent. But even if your team is lagging in points, you can still win the game by capturing all the command posts.

COMMAND POSTS

Each battlefield has a number of command posts, usually ranging from five to seven. In addition to serving as spawn points for infantry, some command posts are also capable of spawning vehicles. If that's not incentive enough to defend them, take into account that controlling the majority of the command posts causes your opponent's reinforcement points to slowly bleed away.

In other words, if a map has five command posts, your team must capture at least three to impose a reinforcement drain—the 50 percent plus one rule holds firm on all maps. The reinforcement drain should be the sole focus of your strategy; it's the quickest way to whittle away the enemy forces.

Stay within the command post's radius until it turns green—this means you've captured it.

Capturing a command post requires a friendly unit to be within its radius for a few seconds. The time differs based on the type of command post and the number of friendly units within the radius. Light command posts are the most common, taking only a few seconds to neutralize and capture.

Heavy command posts, usually positioned at certain strategic locations, take considerably longer, requiring the assistance of almost a small squad of friendly troops to capture.

COMMAND POST CAPTURE TIMES (1 UNIT)

Command Post Type	Time to Neutralize	Time to Capture
Light	11 seconds	11 seconds
Heavy	33 seconds	17 seconds

If it's an enemy-held command post, the first step is to neutralize it. During this phase, enemy troops may spawn nearby, presenting great danger to the attackers. The command post turns white once neutralized, but it's important to stay within the radius until the capture phase is complete.

Command posts cannot be captured if an enemy unit is also within the radius, so patrol the perimeter and blast any defenders attempting to keep your team from gaining control. Units in vehicles cannot capture command posts; they must alight before contesting the position.

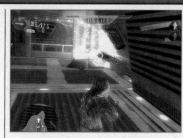

Destructible command posts must be demolished with explosives or other heavy weapons.

Some command posts can't be captured at all. These destructible command posts appear as diamonds on the map. Structures like the Shield Bunker on Endor serve as a spawn point for the Empire, but cannot be captured by the Rebels. Instead, the Rebels must destroy it to stop the Empire from spawning troops there.

The same is true of heavy-assault transports like the Republic AT-TE and the Empire's AT-AT—these are mobile spawn points. Destroying command posts reduces the total count on the map and should be taken account of in your overall assessment of how many command posts you need to hold.

SPAWNING

Study the map briefly before entering the battle.

Spawning is the process of choosing what class you want to play as and determining where you enter the battle. Don't take this process lightly. Before spawning, take a look at the map and determine where you're most needed. The first priority is occupying any undefended command posts. Next, look for friendly command posts under attack and spawn in with an appropriate unit. Finally, look for an unguarded enemy command post and devise a quick attack plan to reach it before the enemy realizes the mistake.

SINGLE PLAYER

The three single-player modes are a great way to get familiar with the game and its 16 battles. If you're looking forward to playing multiplayer, these single-player modes should be your first stop.

Devote some time to memorizing the significant features of each map, as well as the strengths and weaknesses of all the units and vehicles. The more time you spend in single-player modes, the better equipped you'll be to serve and possibly lead a multiplayer team.

combat training

Some units and vehicles are exclusive to the Historical Campaign, like these fambaas from Naboo.

In the Historical Campaign mode, you can choose between the Clone Wars or Galactic Civil War and play the conflicts in chronological order. In some instances, you see different characters and units than in the other game modes. For example, on Naboo you play as the CIS forces against the Gungan Grand Army, complete with shield generator-toting fambaas.

If you want to relive the battles as they appear in the movies, then this is the mode for you. Completing certain key battles also unlocks special features like planetary concept art and stills from the movies. See the table below to browse the special features and what's needed to unlock them.

UNLOCKABLE SPECIAL FEATURES

Special Feature	Requirement
Naboo Stills	Win at Naboo: Theed
Game Art	Win at Kashyyyk: Islands
Geonosis Stills	Win at Geonosis
Kamino Storyboards	Win at Kamino
Weapons & Units Stills	Win at Rhen Var: Harbor
Tatooine Concept Art	Win at Tatooine: Mos Eisley
Yavin Concept Art	Win at Yavin: Temple
Hoth Concept Art	Win at Hoth
Bespin Concept Art	Win at Bespin: Platforms
Endor Concept Art	Win at Bespin: Cloud City

GALACTIC CONQUEST

Galactic Conquest mode takes a more non-linear approach to dominance. In this mode you can select from eight campaigns spanning the Clone Wars and Galactic Civil War. Depending on which campaign you select, you have to fight your way across the galaxy as the Republic, CIS, Rebels, or Empire.

In the Clone Wars campaigns, the Republic uses Kamino as home base while the CIS uses Geonosis. Likewise, the Rebels use Hoth as their base and the Empire resides on Endor in the Galactic Civil War campaigns. This leaves the remaining six planets up for grabs.

Browse the planetary bonuses before making your first move.

You begin the campaign with the initiative. Decide where to attack first. Make your decision based on the planetary bonuses, listed in the table below. Kashyyyk is a good place to start. The extra reinforcements really come in handy for future battles. But the sabotage option at Bespin is a good start, too, at least before you engage the enemy in the vehicle-heavy battles.

Whatever the choice, you must win both battles at the planet before the bonus becomes available. If you lose the battle, the AI gains the initiative and keeps it until you win a battle. But if you keep winning battles and push the AI back to its home planet, you can defeat it there and win the campaign.

PLANETARY BONUSES

Planet	Bonus	Description
Bespin	Sabotage	Enemy vehicles come into play damaged.
Kashyyyk	Reinforcements	An extra garrison of troops are added to your reinforcement count.
Naboo	Bacta Tanks	Your units gain regeneration and heal over time.
Rhen Var	Orbital Sensors	Enemy sensors are jammed preventing them from seeing units on their minimap.
Tatooine	Jedi Hero	A Jedi hero fights alongside your troops in the next battle.
Yavin IV	Elite Training	Your troops receive advanced training and become more accurate.

Remember, the same planetary bonuses are available to the AI, so consider robbing them of the bonuses that are causing you the most difficulty. This makes Bespin an even more attractive planet for your first strike, because the AI is likely to play the sabotage bonus before vehicle-intensive battles. The last thing you want in these battles is for your vehicles to spawn in already smoking. Take some time to think over a grand strategy before striking out.

INSTANT ACTION

Choose the lineup of maps you wish to play before diving in.

Instant Action is the quickest way to jump into a game and start playing against the AI-controlled bots. This mode best reflects the way the battles appear in multi-player games, making it good for building experience and familiarity with the maps. Select a play list of battles and work your way through them, or simply load one and play it over and over till you know each command post and droid position by heart.

MULTIPLAYER

Once you're comfortable with the maps, consider going online to test your skills and tactics against human opponents. Better yet, join up with some friends and devise new strategies as a team. Playing as an effective team requires a tremendous amount of coordination as well as a sense of familiarity and intuition.

When possible, try to log a few hours playing with the same individuals until you form a sense of cohesion. In this section we'll discuss some general tactical considerations your team will want to address and rehearse before moving into action against human opponents.

Split Screen

If you don't have access to a LAN or online connection, plug in a second controller and play with a split screen. In this mode, the screen is split horizontally; one player controls the action on the top half and the other player controls the bottom half. Split screen allows you to play competitively or cooperatively with a friend in all three of the single-player modes.

Competitive play can make the Galactic Conquest mode much more exciting. Playing cooperatively allows you to try out new tactics or team up in a vehicle.

TEAM COMPOSITION

The soldier class is well-rounded and capable of dealing with a variety of offensive and defensive roles. Soldiers should make up the bulk of your team.

Determining which units your team should enter the battle with largely depends on the ever-changing tactical situation. For instance, early in the battle, pilots come in handy for constructing turrets while heavy-weapons units place mines around command posts and other key choke points. But after the opening moments of a battle, the action is extremely unpredictable and your team must respond by spawning the appropriate units at the right place and time.

Soldier units are the most versatile, capable of dealing with a variety of offensive and defensive circumstances. The majority of your team should be soldier units.

The remaining classes are more specialized and best deployed for specific tasks. If faced with enemy vehicles, spawn heavy-weapons units to attack with mines and missiles. Pilot units are useful for repairing droids and vehicles or dispensing health and ammo to teammates. Snipers can play a big role in defending command posts, but a recon droid is also effective for calling in devastating orbital strikes on enemy positions.

Each faction's special unit provides even more specialization, ranging from the aerial capabilities of the dark trooper and jet trooper to the amazing stamina and firepower of the droideka and Rebel smuggler.

Experiment with all the units in each faction and study their strengths and weaknesses.

Because of the fluid situation on the battlefield, all your teammates should be well acquainted with every unit—not just every unit within your chosen faction, but with every potential unit on the map. Being familiar with your unit's own strengths and weaknesses is just as important as knowing the enemy's.

Some units are evenly matched, but most aren't. Instantly analyzing the differences is important in determining whether attacking, retreating, or calling for help is the correct course of action. Spend some time experimenting with each unit in the game to get a better understanding of its capabilities.

combat training

ATTACK SQUADS

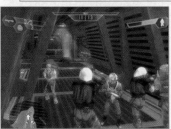

Mixed attack squads are the best way to overwhelm enemy positions.

On some maps your team can simply hold existing command posts and win the battle. But most maps require some sort of offensive effort to take additional command posts in an attempt to bleed the opposing team's reinforcements. The best way to stage attacks is to assemble one or two small squads whose main focus is capturing command posts.

If they aren't attacking, the rest of your team members should busy themselves with defending your team's existing positions. Your offensive squad(s) should be composed of the most experienced players who have mastered all classes and can hold their own in close-quarters fighting. These players must have a team-oriented attitude, willing to cover their team's backs instead of striving for their own statistical glory.

An attack squad should consist of no more than five players. Groups any bigger than this are likely to draw attention, eliminating any element of surprise. Plus, strictly limiting the size of your attack squads encourages more teammates to hold back and defend.

Most of your squad should consist of soldiers, especially if you're not expecting to run into any turrets or enemy vehicles. If vehicles or turrets pose a threat, bring along a heavy-weapons unit. Pilots make a nice addition to any squad, capable of replenishing teammates with health and ammo.

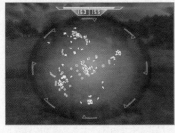

Before staging an attack, analyze the map to find the path of least resistance.

Once your squad is assembled, organize a plan of attack. This can be done over headsets or simply by designating one teammate as squad leader and allowing that person to devise a plan. Try to identify enemy command posts that are deep behind enemy lines. These are less likely to be defended, especially if intense fighting is occurring elsewhere on the map.

Before moving out toward the enemy command post, study the map and try to recognize and avoid the high-traffic areas. The most direct path to an enemy command post is often the most deadly. Instead, sweep out toward one of the command post's flanks. This is the best way to maintain an element of surprise, too.

While moving toward an enemy position, your squad members should keep a distance of several paces between each other. This prevents the entire squad from being taken out by a single thermal detonator, missile, or mine.

Take out defensive features like turrets before assaulting any command post.

Begin your attack by systematically dismantling any defensive features such as turrets or minefields. If turrets are in place, bring up the heavy-weapons squad member to take them out at long range. A sniper can do the same without damaging the turret. If needed, a sniper could also call in an orbital strike just before your assault to soften up defenses. But this must be carefully coordinated to prevent friendly-fire incidents. As soon as the command post's defenses are down, rush in with your soldiers and overwhelm any defenders with speed and firepower.

COMMAND POST CAPTURE

Capturing a command post is the most dangerous part of an assault. This requires your teammates to huddle around the command post so they're all within the radius needed to neutralize the position. The more teammates within the radius, the quicker the command post is neutralized.

Enemy units can still spawn in the area until the command post is neutralized, so your team needs to keep its eyes peeled for enemies suddenly appearing from all possible directions. Look for cover within the radius and attack any opposing units that suddenly appear. In a pinch, droids provide decent cover, and they're almost always next to a command post. Some command posts can also be contested from nearby rooftops or balconies. Think of the command post's radius as an invisible dome while testing its three-dimensional boundaries.

Stay on guard until the command post is neutralized. Enemy units may spawn in at any moment.

Once neutralized, the command post turns white and the enemy can no longer spawn fresh units. Keep your squad in place until the command post is completely captured. The enemy is informed when one of their command posts is lost, often prompting them to stage a counterattack.

Your attack squad suddenly needs to switch to a defensive frame of mind, turning to cover all possible entries and avenues of attack while staying within the command post's radius. If available, have teammates in vehicles patrol the area around the command post and engage any attackers.

As soon as the command post is captured, friendly troops may spawn at the newly captured position. Spawn or move defenders to the new command post while your attack squad prepares to assault another enemy-held position.

DEFEND! DEFEND! DEFEND!

Keep a few teammates at each command post your team holds.

All command posts held by your team must be defended at all times. Defenders should always keep an eye on the map to monitor the tactical situation. Be aware of which command posts your team holds. In multiplayer games, the fog of war comes into play, so you can't see where the enemy units are positioned.

By studying the map, you can see where your teammates are and determine which command posts under your team's control aren't defended. Further, it's possible to theorize which command posts are most likely to come under attack by searching for enemy spawn points near your positions.

Covering these unguarded command posts is the first priority for defenders. Even one defender can make a difference, especially if hidden within the command post's radius. A command post cannot be captured as long as one of your defenders is within its radius, but it can be neutralized. If defending alone, try to position yourself in a corner within the radius where you can see all entrances.

Sniper units may wish to defend from a greater distance, using the command post as bait. Defending from a distance is safer, but if multiple enemies rush a command post, it may be impossible to prevent it from being captured unless a fellow defender is within the radius.

When possible, take the high ground to get a tactical advantage.

Mines and turrets are defenders' best friends. Since pilots are needed to construct turrets and heavy-weapons units are needed to place mines, these classes are good to keep around a command post. Construct turrets as soon as possible to prevent rush attacks by the enemy. Place mines early, particularly around entrances and other narrow choke points likely to be traversed by enemy units.

For best results, try to hide mines by placing them around blind corners or sticking them onto walls. If the enemy discovers the mines, they can remove them quickly with blaster fire or explosives. A heavy-weapons unit can place only four mines, so pick your spots wisely and avoid placing mines close together unless defending against vehicle attacks or creating a highly visible minefield as a way of diverting enemy infantry attacks.

VEHICLE SUPPORT

Make sure your team's vehicles are manned at all times. Get your starfighters in the air quickly before they are destroyed or stolen by the enemy.

Vehicles play a huge role in *Battlefront* and great efforts must be taken to defend them and their spawn points. In most cases, vehicles are linked to command posts; if the enemy captures these positions, the vehicle spawn points are lost as well. Your team should lock down any command posts that spawn vehicles.

Even if you defend the command post well, it may not be enough to prevent the enemy from rushing in and stealing a vehicle; jet troopers and dark troopers are particularly proficient at such tactics. To prevent vehicle theft, place mines on the vehicle spawn points or on the vehicles themselves. Even better, make sure the vehicles are occupied as soon as they spawn.

Unless they're being used to stage a breakout assault, vehicles should always be manned by pilots. Every pilot in a vehicle contributes to its repair as it takes damage. In other words, the more pilots on board, the harder the vehicle is to destroy. For example, a Republic LAAT/I Gunship can hold up to five pilots. It's extremely tough to shoot down, because it repairs itself almost instantly as it takes hits.

Just as you would for your attack squads, set aside a number of pilot slots on your team to correspond with the number of vehicles under your control. Repair droids can also be used to repair your vehicles and restock them with missiles. Make sure your pilots memorize the locations of these droids, because they can also provide a serious boost during combat. Simply park a vehicle next to a repair droid to receive endless repairs.

combat training

Vehicles can't capture command posts, but they can be used to clear out defenses like turrets before the infantry moves in.

Despite their menacing presence on the battlefield, vehicles only provide a supporting role because they're incapable of capturing a command post themselves. While vehicles can be used to rush into a command post's radius, the conversion process doesn't begin until a teammate gets out. Use vehicles to suppress a command post's defenses and provide cover while your attack squads move in for the capture. Careful coordination between your vehicles and attack squads is essential in quickly overrunning an enemy command post.

Heavy-assault transports like the AT-TE and AT-AT are mobile spawn points capable of attacking command posts while continuously spawning troops on the enemy's front doorstep. If used properly, these devastating units demonstrate the beauty and horror of a combined infantry and vehicle assault. If available, use these transports to pound the opposing team into submission and gobble up their command posts one at a time.

KNOW THE MAP!

Although it may seem obvious, there is no better way to prepare for a multiplayer session than studying all the maps extensively. Knowing where all the command posts are is important, but so is knowing the location of vehicle spawn points, turrets, and droids. Identifying less obvious features like choke points and sniper positions is also extremely important.

Multiplayer games are often chaotic, offering little time to get your bearings. In most cases, if you stand still, you're dead. You need to hit the ground running to link up with your team and attempt some sort of coordinated strategy.

COMBAT TRAINING

units & weaponry

In battle, knowing your strengths and weaknesses is as important as knowing your enemy's. In this section we look at the units you encounter during your push for galactic conquest.

You'll find detailed information on all 20 units that make up the four factions, complete with background, rankings, and gameplay tips. We also provide overviews on the native inhabitants and Jedi heroes, detailing how they may help or hinder your advances. Finally, we look at resupply items and droids you find on the battlefield to restore your health and keep your weapons loaded.

Intra-Faction Rankings
In this section, each unit is ranked (1-5) among the other units in its faction. This helps you determine which unit is best for the varying tactical situations you encounter. Here's a breakdown of the criteria:

FIREPOWER: *The unit's total offensive capability, taking both primary and secondary weapons into account.*
STAMINA: *How hardy the unit is. The higher the ranking, the more hits the unit can take before dying.*
SPEED: *How fast the unit moves when running.*

SOLDIER CLASS

The soldier class is the centerpiece of each faction, attaining battlefield dominance through rapid firepower. Each soldier unit is equipped with a blaster rifle (or equivalent) capable of sustaining a high volume of fire. With the exception of the super battle droid, each unit also carries several thermal detonators and grenades.

Thermal detonators are best used against other infantry units. Try bouncing them off walls or around corners to gain a tactical advantage. The concussion grenades can stick to surfaces, making them most useful against vehicles when caught in a tight spot. However, soldier units should not seek out engagements with vehicles—this is best reserved for heavy-weapons units.

CLONE TROOPER

FACTION: *Republic Clone Army*
INTRA-FACTION RANKINGS
FIREPOWER: 4th
STAMINA: 2nd
SPEED: 4th

The clone troopers, perfect genetic creations, are the backbone of the Republic Army. Pure and simple, the clone troopers have been bred to be warriors. They have an unswerving

loyalty to the Republic and are fearless in battle. They are most effective against infantry units or vehicles when they attack in large, coordinated numbers.

EQUIPMENT

Weapon/Equipment	Ammo	Description
Republic DC-15 Blaster Rifle	60/180	The long-barreled DC-15 emits a powerful blue laser projectile, specially designed to shred infantry and vehicle units alike.
Republic DC-15s Blaster Pistol	N/A	An emergency sidearm, designed to be small, portable, and deadly. The DC-15s is useful in close-quarters combat, and makes a good backup.
Merr-Sonn V-6 Haywire Grenade	3	Clone troopers carry a small, hand-held haywire grenade. The device has been calibrated to cause massive electrical disruptions to droid circuitry.
SoroSuub LXR-6 ConcussionGrenade	2	Concussion grenades are not as common as thermal detonators, but are carried by all clone troopers. The blast field created by these grenades is effective against vehicles.

NOTE

Use clone troopers as the core of your attack squads. when multiplied by four or five units, their rapid rate of fire is truly devastating. back off when encountering droidekas. seek cover and wait for their shield to drop before attacking.

SUPER BATTLE DROID

FACTION: *CIS*
INTRA-FACTION RANKINGS
FIREPOWER: 4th
STAMINA: 3rd
SPEED: 4th

After the debacle at the Battle of Naboo, the Trade Federation ordered a stronger, more independent battle droid, officially designated the B2. Resembling hulking, reinforced battle droids, super battle droids are superior to their skeletal-looking counterparts. Their broad, looming frames make them less susceptible to battle damage, and their built-in firepower makes them a formidable threat to opposing armies.

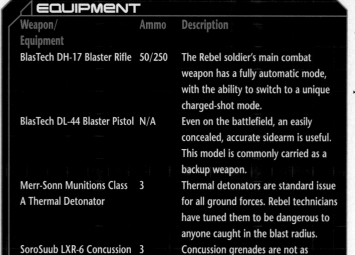

EQUIPMENT

Weapon/ Equipment	Ammo	Description
Wrist Blaster	55/220	A rapid-fire blaster has been mounted directly to the super battle droid's frame, reducing the risk of dropping the weapon, having it misfire, or being disabled by a Jedi Knight. The wrist blaster can also fire a volley of blaster bolts providing a more potent assault on a target.
Wrist Launcher	4	Super battle droids also come equipped with a limited supply of rockets. Fired from the wrist much like the blaster, the rockets are "dumb fired" at targets.

NOTE

In most cases, rapid fire is more important than the three-shot volley offered by the wrist blaster. The wrist launcher's ammo disappears quickly, so use these rockets sparingly. Aim at your target's feet to maximize the chance of a hit. Otherwise, your foe might sidestep an incoming rocket.

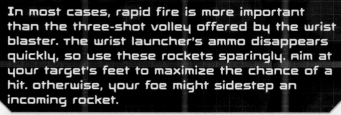

REBEL SOLDIER

FACTION: *Rebel Alliance*
INTRA-FACTION RANKINGS
FIREPOWER: 4th
STAMINA: 3rd
SPEED: 3rd

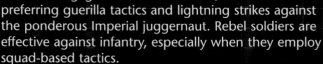

Rebel soldiers, who come from all walks of life, do not have the benefit of years of Imperial combat training. They are, however, unmatched in their will, enthusiasm, and devotion to their cause. They do not wear armor or engage in standard warfare, preferring guerilla tactics and lightning strikes against the ponderous Imperial juggernaut. Rebel soldiers are effective against infantry, especially when they employ squad-based tactics.

EQUIPMENT

Weapon/ Equipment	Ammo	Description
BlasTech DH-17 Blaster Rifle	50/250	The Rebel soldier's main combat weapon has a fully automatic mode, with the ability to switch to a unique charged-shot mode.
BlasTech DL-44 Blaster Pistol	N/A	Even on the battlefield, an easily concealed, accurate sidearm is useful. This model is commonly carried as a backup weapon.
Merr-Sonn Munitions Class A Thermal Detonator	3	Thermal detonators are standard issue for all ground forces. Rebel technicians have tuned them to be dangerous to anyone caught in the blast radius.
SoroSuub LXR-6 Concussion Grenade	3	Concussion grenades are not as common as thermal detonators but are carried by many Rebel soldiers. These grenades have powerful magnets, allowing them to stick to vehicles.

NOTE

Rebel soldiers have a huge advantage over Imperial units in forest settings, thanks to their green camouflage. While the stormtrooper's white armor is readily visible, the Rebel soldier blends into the forest. This makes staging ambushes and sneak attacks much easier, particularly in multiplayer games.

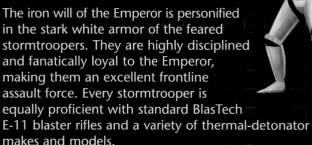

STORMTROOPER

FACTION: *Galactic Empire*
INTRA-FACTION RANKINGS
FIREPOWER: 3rd
STAMINA: 3rd
SPEED: 3rd

The iron will of the Emperor is personified in the stark white armor of the feared stormtroopers. They are highly disciplined and fanatically loyal to the Emperor, making them an excellent frontline assault force. Every stormtrooper is equally proficient with standard BlasTech E-11 blaster rifles and a variety of thermal-detonator makes and models.

UNITS & WEAPONRY

EQUIPMENT

Weapon/ Equipment	Ammo	Description
BlasTech E-11 Blaster Rifle	55/220	Standard rifle of the Empire's front line units, this weapon is reliable and deadly, but sacrifices accuracy for raw power.
BlasTech SE-14r Light Repeating Blaster Pistol	N/A	An ongoing Imperial contract with BlasTech yielded this semiautomatic blaster pistol, commonly used as a backup sidearm.
Baradium-Core Thermal Detonator	4	This is a hand-held explosive device effective against infantry. Unlabeled code keys prevent captured munitions from being used against Imperial forces.
SoroSuub LXR-6 Concussion Grenade	2	Concussion grenades are not as common as thermal detonators but are carried by all Imperial stormtroopers. The blast field created by these grenades is effective against vehicles.

NOTE

Group stormtroopers with dark troopers for assaults in close quarters. Together they can overwhelm most enemy positions. However, go easy on the thermal detonators—they're as deadly to you as they are to the enemy.

HEAVY-WEAPONS CLASS

When it comes to taking out vehicles, heavy-weapons units are what you want. Each is armed with a missile launcher capable of locking onto enemy vehicles. Use this function when targeting fast-moving or distant vehicles. To lock on a target, face an enemy vehicle and watch for a shrinking red diamond to appear. When the diamond stops shrinking, the lock is attained and the missile tracks the vehicle. You can also dumb-fire the missile launcher when speed or distance is less of a factor.

The use of mines is also unique to this class, making them a defensive necessity for undefended command posts. Try to conceal the location of mines by sticking them on walls or around blind corners. The better you conceal the mine, the more likely your trap will be successful.

PRIMAGAMES.COM

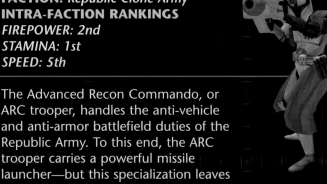

ARC TROOPER

FACTION: *Republic Clone Army*
INTRA-FACTION RANKINGS
FIREPOWER: 2nd
STAMINA: 1st
SPEED: 5th

The Advanced Recon Commando, or ARC trooper, handles the anti-vehicle and anti-armor battlefield duties of the Republic Army. To this end, the ARC trooper carries a powerful missile launcher—but this specialization leaves the trooper with fewer options in close combat, so he relies on his brethren to protect him. When threatened by vehicles, the ARC trooper's value becomes brutally apparent. Not only does he have the ability to engage vehicles directly with the missile launcher, but he can also create defensive perimeters with his mine dispenser.

EQUIPMENT

Weapon/ Equipment	Ammo	Description
Merr-Sonn PLX Missile Launcher	2/6	The Merr-Sonn PLX hand-held launcher is versatile; dumb-fire it or program it to fire the smart GAM (gravity-activated mode) guided missile specially designed for the weapon.
Republic DC-15s Blaster Pistol	N/A	An emergency sidearm designed to be small, portable, and deadly, the DC-15s is useful in close-quarters combat and makes a good backup.
Merr-Sonn V-1 Thermal Detonator	3	Clone troopers carry a smaller, battlefield version of the devastating thermal detonator. The device has been calibrated to maximize enemy casualties.
Conner Ship Systems HX2 Mine	4	With ARC troopers come proximity mines. Use them against those who don't watch their step.

NOTE

The ARC trooper is key to taking out the separatist AATS. Use a mix of mines and missiles to demolish these tanks before they overrun your command posts. The PLX missile launcher holds two missiles at a time for quick launching. However, the reloading process can take time, so seek cover while preparing a new salvo.

ASSAULT DROID

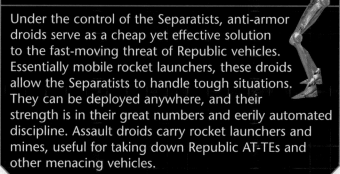

FACTION: *CIS*
INTRA-FACTION RANKINGS
FIREPOWER: 3rd
STAMINA: 2nd
SPEED: 5th

Under the control of the Separatists, anti-armor droids serve as a cheap yet effective solution to the fast-moving threat of Republic vehicles. Essentially mobile rocket launchers, these droids allow the Separatists to handle tough situations. They can be deployed anywhere, and their strength is in their great numbers and eerily automated discipline. Assault droids carry rocket launchers and mines, useful for taking down Republic AT-TEs and other menacing vehicles.

EQUIPMENT

Weapon/ Equipment	Ammo	Description
BAW E-60R Missile Launcher	7	Once the battle droid proved its ineffectiveness against the Republic's walkers, Baktoid Armor Workshop quickly produced this powerful anti-armor rocket launcher. Clone pilots have learned to fear its presence on the field.
Separatist Blaster Pistol	N/A	Due to the touchy political quagmire of producing weapons for an enemy of the Republic, the origin and manufacturer of this pistol remains anonymous. Those familiar with these types of weapons are fairly certain it is a BlasTech design, but BlasTech denies knowledge. Nevertheless the "Separatist" pistol remains a tried-and-true backup weapon for the droid armies.
Merr-Sonn V-1 Thermal Detonator	3	Merr-Sonn denies selling thermal detonators to the Separatists, yet many droids have been seen carrying V-1 thermal detonators on the battlefield. The device has been calibrated to maximize enemy casualties while minimizing friendly contact.
Conner Ship Systems HX2 Mine	4	Proximity mines are effective at catching those who aren't paying attention. Outdated, but cheap and still effective, the HX2 proximity mine is carried exclusively by assault droids.

NOTE

Remember, missile launchers aren't limited to targeting ground vehicles. The Republic's LAAT/i gunship poses a serious threat on several battlefields. Use the assault droid's missile launcher to lock on to it and blast it out of the sky. It takes several missiles to down it, so consider staying near an ammo droid to continuously supply ordnance.

REBEL VANGUARD

FACTION: *Rebel Alliance*
INTRA-FACTION RANKINGS
FIREPOWER: 2nd
STAMINA: 2nd
SPEED: 4th

Those looking to leave their mark on an Imperial walker can surely find a place in the Rebel Vanguard division. When asked why someone would want to do this line of work, the Vanguard's most common answer is: "So I can blow up Imperials!" Always given the tough assignments, Vanguards are called upon to punch holes in an Imperial vehicle brigade. The heavy weapons they carry provide the means to take down menacing enemy air and ground vehicles attempting to lay siege.

EQUIPMENT

Weapon/ Equipment	Ammo	Description
Golan Arms HH-15 Missile Launcher	2/8	It packs the punch needed to crack through a tough position. The hand-held missile launcher is prized among the Rebel Vanguards.
BlasTech DL-44 Blaster Pistol	N/A	Even on the battlefield, an easily concealed, accurate sidearm is useful. This model is commonly carried as a backup weapon.
Merr-Sonn Munitions Class A Thermal Detonator	3	Thermal Detonators are considered standard issue to all ground forces. Rebel technicians have tuned them to be dangerous to anyone caught in the blast radius.
Conner Ship Systems 3HX3 Mine	4	On the battlefield, every edge is needed, even when that edge is a highly explosive one. Mines are excellent as a backup weapon for the covert destruction of one's enemies.

NOTE

Unlike other missile launchers, the Golan Arms HH-15 fires two missiles at a time, making quick work of Imperial AT-STs. Be sure to lock on first, particularly when engaging vehicles at long range. If dumb-fired, the missiles are highly inaccurate and may even miss a stationary target.

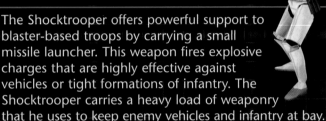

SHOCKTROOPER

FACTION: *Galactic Empire*
INTRA-FACTION RANKINGS
FIREPOWER: 2nd
STAMINA: 1st
SPEED: 5th

The Shocktrooper offers powerful support to blaster-based troops by carrying a small missile launcher. This weapon fires explosive charges that are highly effective against vehicles or tight formations of infantry. The Shocktrooper carries a heavy load of weaponry that he uses to keep enemy vehicles and infantry at bay.

EQUIPMENT

Weapon/ Equipment	Ammo	Description
MiniMag PTL Missile Launcher	7	Shocktroopers carry these hand-held missile launchers on the battlefield to take down Rebel vehicle brigades. Anyone caught in the blast radius may not live long enough to regret it.
BlasTech SE-14r Light Repeating Blaster Pistol	N/A	An ongoing Imperial contract with BlasTech yielded this semiautomatic blaster pistol. Commonly used as a backup sidearm.
Baradium-Core Thermal Detonator	3	This is a hand-held explosive device effective against infantry. Unlabeled code keys prevent captured munitions from being used against Imperial forces.
Golan Arms KE-6b Mine	4	The KE-6b proximity mine is a modified version of the KE-6 mine. A soldier drops the device at the desired location and watches destruction ensue as his enemies approach.

NOTE

Shocktroopers come in handy for escorting AT-ATs on Hoth, using their missiles to chase away attacking Rebel airspeeders. In addition to engaging vehicles, shocktroopers are also useful during infantry engagements. Position them near narrow corridors and other choke points and use mines and missiles to blast incoming troops.

TIP

In dire situations, consider sacrificing yourself for the greater good by rushing an enemy vehicle and tossing a mine underneath it. The resulting explosion kills you, but it may also take out the vehicle and save your teammates.

PILOT CLASS

Pilots are part combat engineer, part field medic, and part resupply clerk—a valuable asset on any battlefield. Their ability to repair vehicles is impressive enough, but they can also heal and resupply teammates as well as themselves. Pilots are also the only units who can construct gun turrets and repair droids, using their fusioncutter. But pilots are most valuable inside vehicles, instantly repairing damage. The more pilots on board, the quicker the damage is repaired. So fill your vehicles with as many pilots as possible. Increasing the lifespan of your vehicles enhances your chances of winning the battle.

CLONE PILOT

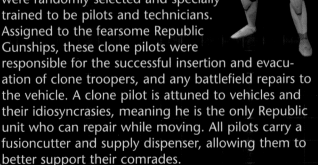

FACTION: *Republic Clone Army*
INTRA-FACTION RANKINGS
FIREPOWER: 5th
STAMINA: 4th
SPEED: 2nd

While the bulk of the Republic clones were trained for infantry duty, a few were randomly selected and specially trained to be pilots and technicians. Assigned to the fearsome Republic Gunships, these clone pilots were responsible for the successful insertion and evacuation of clone troopers, and any battlefield repairs to the vehicle. A clone pilot is attuned to vehicles and their idiosyncrasies, meaning he is the only Republic unit who can repair while moving. All pilots carry a fusioncutter and supply dispenser, allowing them to better support their comrades.

EQUIPMENT

Weapon/ Equipment	Ammo	Description
Drever Corp "DN Bolt Caster" Plasma Disruptor	N/A	Drever Corp originally created the "Phoenix II" plasma disruptor as a tool for customs agents and special forces commandos, for use in breaching locked doors. But soldiers began improvising with the tool, wielding it against battle droids and other enemies. Its effectiveness as a weapon was undeniable and prompted Drever Corp to develop the "DN Bolt Caster" plasma disruptor weapon. It's expensive but effective, especially against droid armies.
Republic DC-15s Blaster Pistol	N/A	An emergency sidearm designed to be small, portable, and deadly, the DC-15s is the clone pilot's primary weapon.
SoroSuub F-187 Fusioncutter	N/A	The fusioncutter is a general-purpose device. It can repair vehicles and buildings and construct unassembled battlefield equipment.
Health/Ammo Dispenser	5	A variety of inexpensive supplies, including various medicines, emergency care tools, and ammunition can be handed out with the supply dispenser. Perfect for those always on the go!

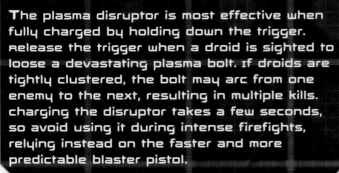

NOTE

The plasma disruptor is most effective when fully charged by holding down the trigger. Release the trigger when a droid is sighted to loose a devastating plasma bolt. If droids are tightly clustered, the bolt may arc from one enemy to the next, resulting in multiple kills. Charging the disruptor takes a few seconds, so avoid using it during intense firefights, relying instead on the faster and more predictable blaster pistol.

PILOT DROID

FACTION: *CIS*
INTRA-FACTION RANKINGS
FIREPOWER: 5th
STAMINA: 4th
SPEED: 2nd

Thius is a specific type of Trade Federation battle droid capable of piloting virtually every type of vehicle, including transports, AATs, and MTTs. Pilot droids have advanced specialization programming that allow them to easily understand the control systems of any vehicle. Pilot droids are adept at repairing vehicles and bringing supplies across the battlefield to keep the battle droid army pushing forward.

EQUIPMENT

Weapon/ Equipment	Ammo	Description
Merr-Sonn RD-4 Grenade Launcher	5/10	The versatile RD-4 grenade launcher lobs small grenades outward toward targets. The weapon can be configured to fire grenades that either bounce or explode on contact with the target.
Separatist Blaster Pistol	N/A	Due to the touchy political quagmire of producing weapons for an enemy of the Republic, the origin and manufacturer of this pistol remains anonymous. Those familiar with these types of weapons are fairly certain it is a BlasTech design, but BlasTech denies knowledge. Nevertheless, the "Separatist" pistol remains a tried-and-true backup weapon for the droid armies.
SoroSuub F-187 Fusioncutter	N/A	The fusioncutter is a general-purpose device. It can repair vehicles and buildings; it can also construct unassembled battlefield equipment such as gun turrets.
Health/Ammo Dispenser	5	A variety of inexpensive supplies including various medicines, emergency care tools, and ammunition can be handed out with the supply dispenser. Perfect for those always on the go!

NOTE

By holding down the trigger, you can delay the detonation of the grenade launcher's ordnance. The grenade bounces around before eventually exploding. Use this to increase the launcher's range by skipping grenades across the ground or bouncing them around corners. Pilot droids can also heal their fellow droids with the fusioncutter, making them a key component to any assaulting force.

REBEL PILOT

FACTION: *Rebel Alliance*
INTRA-FACTION RANKINGS
FIREPOWER: 5th
STAMINA: 4th
SPEED: 2nd

Rebel pilots don't always have the benefit of Imperial naval training, but dedication and resolve has gotten many Rebel pilots out of tough situations, both in and out of the cockpit. Pilots are capable at initiating repairs and helping with the construction of makeshift command posts. They are also the only class who can carry supplies for battle-weary Rebel troops.

EQUIPMENT

Weapon/ Equipment	Ammo	Description
Golan Arms CR-1 Blaster Cannon	30/90	After a cache of weaponry was stolen from a Golan Arms supply depot, these modified blaster cannons found their way into the hands of the Rebel Alliance. The CR-1 blaster cannon fires multiple blaster bolts per shot and is thesingle most brutal close-range anti-infantry weapon.
BlasTech DL-44 Blaster Pistol	N/A	Even on the battlefield, an easily concealed accurate sidearm can be quite useful. This model is commonly carried as a backup weapon.
SoroSuub F-187 Fusioncutter	N/A	The fusioncutter is a general-purpose device. It can repair vehicles and buildings and construct unassembled battlefield equipment.
Health/Ammo Dispenser	5	A variety of inexpensive supplies including various medicines, emergency care tools, and ammunition can be handed out with the supply dispenser. Perfect for those always on the go!

NOTE

While most pilots are best reserved to supporting roles, the Rebel pilot is capable of leading assaults, thanks to the devastating power offered by his blaster cannon. With each pull of the trigger, the blaster cannon fires five laser bolts in a shotgun-like spread. The weapon is unparalleled at close range, but its accuracy decreases dramatically at greater distances. So use the Rebel pilot for interior assaults where short-range engagements are likely.

IMPERIAL PILOT

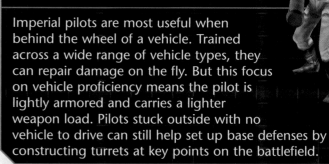

FACTION: *Galactic Empire*
INTRA-FACTION RANKINGS
FIREPOWER: 5th
STAMINA: 4th
SPEED: 2nd

Imperial pilots are most useful when behind the wheel of a vehicle. Trained across a wide range of vehicle types, they can repair damage on the fly. But this focus on vehicle proficiency means the pilot is lightly armored and carries a lighter weapon load. Pilots stuck outside with no vehicle to drive can still help set up base defenses by constructing turrets at key points on the battlefield.

EQUIPMENT

Weapon/ Equipment	Ammo	Description
Merr-Sonn V-6d Mortar Launcher	5/10	The versatile V-6d mortar launcher lobs small grenades outward toward targets. The weapon can be configured to fire grenades that either bounce or explode on contact with the target.
BlasTech SE-14r Light Repeating Blaster Pistol	N/A	An ongoing Imperial contract with BlasTech yielded this semiautomatic blaster pistol. Commonly used as a backup sidearm.
SoroSuub F-187 Fusioncutter	N/A	The fusioncutter is a general-purpose device. It can repair vehicles and buildings and construct unassembled battlefield equipment.
Health/Ammo Dispenser	5	A variety of inexpensive supplies including various medicines, emergency care tools, and ammunition can be handed out with the supply dispenser. Perfect for those always on the go!

UNITS & WEAPONRY

NOTE

Like the pilot droid, the imperial pilot can bounce grenades off surfaces with their mortar launcher. But they're more productive in vehicles, particularly the AT-AT. Since AT-ATS only have a pilot and co-pilot position, make sure both spots are occupied by imperial pilots to help offset the constant beating they take from Rebel vehicles and turrets.

SNIPER CLASS

Snipers are the masters of reconnaissance and precision attacks. Their sniper rifles are extremely powerful, capable of dropping an enemy with a single shot. But they fire and reload slowly, making them most useful in long-range engagements where retaliation is less of a threat. In close combat, the sniper is better off using a pistol. In fact, this is the weapon they should arm while moving around from one sniping position to the next.

All snipers are also equipped with a recon droid. These spherically shaped droids hover across the battlefield and can be used to spot distant units or call in an orbital strike on their own location. Orbital strikes are devastating against stationary positions, like turrets, or slow-moving vehicles, like the AT-TE or AT-AT. The recon droid can also defend itself with a very low-powered blaster. But they also have a limited energy supply, so they must be used quickly before they're rendered inoperable. Sniper units only carry one recon droid, and they have to visit an ammo droid to grab a new one.

TIP

Sniper rifles fire a narrow, high-intensity beam that can easily be traced back to its source. Snipers need to keep shifting locations to avoid being targeted.

CLONE SHARPSHOOTER

FACTION: *Republic Clone Army*
INTRA-FACTION RANKINGS
FIREPOWER: 1st
STAMINA: 5th
SPEED: 1st

Unlike a traditional army, where snipers are culled from the best of the best shooters, the clone troopers all possess the same characteristics regarding eyesight, accuracy, steadiness, and patience. However, the clone sharpshooter has received special "flash training," teaching him the intricacies of being a good sniper. He has also trained exclusively with the modified DC-15x Sniper Rifle and the Arakyd R-1 Recon Droid.

On the battlefield, the clone sharpshooter is responsible for one task: disrupting enemy infantry. His specialized conditioning provides him with the ability to gather intelligence, sit, wait, and methodically pick off enemy units one by one.

EQUIPMENT

Weapon/ Equipment	Ammo	Description
Republic DC-15x Sniper Rifle	6/36	The DC-15x is a modified version of the standard clone trooper rifle, with added sights and accuracy for long-range efficiency.
Republic DC-15s Blaster Pistol	N/A	An emergency sidearm designed to be small, portable, and deadly, the DC-15s is useful in close quarters combat and makes a good backup.
Merr-Sonn V-1 Thermal Detonator	3	Clone troopers carry a smaller, battlefield version of the devastating thermal detonator. The device has been calibrated to maximize enemy casualties.
Arakyd R-1 Recon Droid	1	The clone sharpshooter can deploy a remote recon droid to gather battlefield intelligence. The recon droid can call down an orbital strike, taking out any enemies nearby.

NOTE

The clone sharpshooter's rifle can fire six shots before reloading is necessary. This gives the sharpshooter a slight advantage over the assassin droid. But the DC-15x's scope only has one magnification zoom level. The sharpshooter should hold back at long distances and engage droidekas—their personal shield makes them easy to spot. Wait for the shield to drop before firing a couple of quick shots to eliminate these droids.

ASSASSIN DROID

FACTION: *CIS*
INTRA-FACTION RANKINGS
FIREPOWER: 2nd
STAMINA: 5th
SPEED: 1st

Its accurate sniper rifle, plus the ability to call for orbital strikes, makes this droid especially effective at dispatching targets from long range. Assassin droids are specifically programmed and designed with advanced targeting capabilities that allow them to take down targets at extreme range. The long-range sniper rifle is its weapon of choice, capable of killing any infantry unit with a single head shot.

EQUIPMENT

Weapon/ Equipment	Ammo	Description
BAW E-5s Sniper Rifle	4/36	Many organic snipers are given special sniper weapons, suited to their capabilities. Not so for the assassin droid, who is specially programmed to use the E-5s, an otherwise ordinary rifle, to its utmost capability.
Separatist Blaster Pistol	N/A	Due to the touchy political quagmire of producing weapons for an enemy of the Republic, the origin and manufacturer of this pistol remains anonymous. Those familiar with these types of weapons are fairly certain it is a BlasTech design, but BlasTech denies knowledge. Nevertheless, the "Separatist" pistol remains a tried-and-true backup weapon for the droid armies.
Merr-Sonn V-1 Thermal Detonator	3	Merr-Sonn denies selling thermal detonators to the Separatists, yet many droids have been seen carrying V-1 thermal detonators on the battlefield. The device has been calibrated to maximize enemy casualties while minimizing friendly contact.
Arakyd Mark IV Recon Droid	1	A small seeker droid can be deployed to gather intelligence while on the battlefield. This small, portable droid can also call down an orbital strike, taking out any enemies in the blast radius.

NOTE

The assassin droid's E-5s sniper rifle has two magnification levels, making it effective in picking off targets at extreme distances. But this comes at a cost—it has only four shots per clip. When the Republic uses AT-TEs, consider launching multiple orbital strikes against these slow-moving walkers. Simply fly the recon droid beneath the transport and initiate the strike.

REBEL MARKSMAN

FACTION: *Rebel Alliance*
INTRA-FACTION RANKINGS
FIREPOWER: 1st
STAMINA: 5th
SPEED: 1st

Rebel marksmen know what it means to "lead" a target. A highly motivated team of marksmen can turn a marching company of Imperial stormtroopers into one or two *fleeing* Imperial stormtroopers before they even get close to the Rebel base. The marksmen have the specialized task of finding and eliminating targets from a safe location. They are deadly accurate and can even the odds on the battlefield.

EQUIPMENT

Weapon/ Equipment	Ammo	Description
BlasTech E-17d Sniper Rifle	4/36	Effective over a great distance, sniper rifles are the preferred weapons of choice for those wishing to remain hidden from their target.
BlasTech DL-44 Blaster Pistol	N/A	Even on the battlefield, an easily concealed accurate sidearm can be quite useful. This model is commonly carried as a backup weapon.
Merr-Sonn Munitions Class A Thermal Detonator	3	Thermal Detonators are considered standard issue to all ground forces. Rebel technicians have tuned them to be dangerous to anyone caught in the blast radius.
Arakyd R-4 Recon Droid	1	The Rebel marksman can deploy a remote recon droid to gather battlefield intelligence. The recon droid can call down an orbital strike, taking out any enemies nearby.

NOTE

The Rebel marksmen's rifle is virtually identical to the assassin droid's, providing two magnification levels but only four shots per clip. Their recon droid's orbital strike is also extremely useful for whittling away at the thick armor of enemy walkers, like the AT-AT.

SCOUT TROOPER

FACTION: *Galactic Empire*
INTRA-FACTION RANKINGS
FIREPOWER: 1st
STAMINA: 5th
SPEED: 1st

Scout troopers use concealment, recon droids, and patience to target faraway enemies and eliminate them with their high-powered sniper rifles. The lightly armored scout is trained to advance well ahead of infantry divisions, or provide rear-guard cover for troops. Ever vigilant, the scout takes pride in his role, acting as the long arm of the Imperial law.

EQUIPMENT

Weapon/ Equipment	Ammo	Description
Modified BlasTech E-11s Sniper Rifle	6/36	The Modified E-11s is a single-shot, long-range rifle with a high-powered zoom. A carefully placed head shot with this rifle can make the difference between advancing and fleeing enemy troops.
BlasTech SE-14r Light Repeating Blaster Pistol	N/A	An ongoing Imperial contract with BlasTech yielded this semiautomatic blaster pistol. Commonly used as a backup sidearm.
Baradium-Core Thermal Detonator	3	This is a hand-held explosive device effective against infantry. Unlabeled code keys prevent captured munitions from being used against Imperial forces.
Arakyd R-4 Recon Droid	1	The scout trooper can deploy a recon droid to gather battlefield intelligence. The recon droid can also call down an orbital strike, taking out any nearby enemies in the blast radius.

NOTE

The scout trooper's rifle is similar to the clone troopers, with only one magnification level and six shots per clip. When attacking Rebel command posts, consider using scout troopers to pick off the operators of gun turrets. This is preferable to destroying them, because it allows your own troops to use them once they take control. The scout trooper's recon droid also plays a key role when targeting the shield generator at Hoth with orbital strikes.

SPECIAL UNITS

The special units defy categorization, offering unique skills to their respective factions. For the most part, their skills and capabilities are quite specialized, making them extremely effective in certain situations. But their specializations leave them with glaring weaknesses that can be easily exploited by the enemy. So use these units as the need arises.

JET TROOPER

FACTION: *Republic Clone Army*
INTRA-FACTION RANKINGS
FIREPOWER: 3rd
STAMINA: 3rd
SPEED: 3rd

Capitalizing on the "genetic memory" of Jango Fett, the jet trooper uses a limited-flight jet pack to cover great distances very quickly. The agility of the flying jet trooper makes him very hard to hit, and his EM pulse launcher can be a deadly weapon at close range.

EQUIPMENT

Weapon/ Equipment	Ammo	Description
Merr-Sonn EM Pulse Launcher	2/6	The EM pulse launcher fires an electromagnetic pulse outward toward targets. A blast from this weapon has been known to cause a massive electrical disruption capable of frying fragile droid circuitry.
Republic DC-17 Blaster Pistol	N/A	Jet troopers are often stuck in intense situations and carry better blaster pistols than most other soldiers. The DC-17 has a higher rate of fire than its predecessors and is extremely deadly.
Merr-Sonn V-1 Thermal Detonator	6	Clone troopers carry a smaller, battlefield version of the devastating thermal detonator. The device has been calibrated to maximize enemy casualties.

NOTE

Use the jet trooper's jet pack to reach new areas. Keep leapfrogging from one elevation to the next, allowing the jet pack to recharge after each jump. This can take you to some very advantageous positions on the battlefield. The EM pulse launcher is great for taking out droids at close range, but reloads slowly making it hard to use during intense firefights. Instead, use the DC-17 blaster pistol to rapidly dispatch enemies. It works the same way as other blaster pistols, but benefits from a much higher rate of fire. In multiplayer games, try assembling small squads of jet troopers to overwhelm the enemy with aerial assaults on command posts. Before setting down, saturate the landing zone with thermal detonators and EM pulse blasts.

DROIDEKA (DESTROYER DROID)

FACTION: *CIS*
INTRA-FACTION RANKINGS
FIREPOWER: 1st
STAMINA: 1st
SPEED: 3rd

Even feared by Jedi Knights, the crab-like droideka is equipped with a personal shield and two powerful repeating blasters instead of arms. The droideka is a highly effective firing platform because of its tripod design, but this effectiveness comes at the sacrifice of speed. To counter its lack of mobility, the droideka can transform into a wheel to cruise rapidly around the battlefield.

EQUIPMENT

Weapon/Equipment	Ammo	Description
Repeating Blasters	N/A	Twin high-energy blasters, mounted in its arms, serve as the droideka's main offensive weaponry. The blasters have a secondary fire mode allowing them to fire a salvo of blaster shots at a target.
Personal Shield	N/A	The droideka's personal shield deflects damage from all ordnance for as long as the shield is deployed. The shield cannot be activated when the droideka is rolling around the battlefield in its wheel form.

Weapon/Equipment	Ammo	Description
Transform	N/A	The droideka has two modes of locomotion. The first is the wheel form, which allows for quick travel, but no use of weaponry or shielding. The second is the walk state, in which the droideka can scuttle and reorient while firing and using its shield.

NOTE

The droideka is one of the most devastating units in the game, capable of spitting out a steady stream of blaster fire while sitting safely behind its personal shield. This makes them great for defending command posts, as well as rushing neutral positions early in the game. In their wheel form, the droideka can zip across the battlefield, but they're also vulnerable to attacks. While the droideka can deploy its shield for protection in its walk state, its movement is reduced dramatically, including its ability to rotate.

For this reason, droidekas are most effective when traveling in groups of two or three. This way they can cover all possible angles of attack, preventing flanking maneuvers. Deploy the personal shield only when a threat is present, to conserve its energy. Also, don't roll through deep water—the droideka explodes when it's waterlogged.

TIP

Team droidekas with pilot droids to provide constant repair. The pilot can hide behind the droideka's shield for cover while launching grenades.

units & weaponry

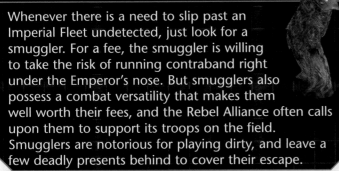

WOOKIEE SMUGGLER

FACTION: *Rebel Alliance*
INTRA-FACTION RANKINGS
FIREPOWER: 3rd
STAMINA: 1st
SPEED: 5th

Whenever there is a need to slip past an Imperial Fleet undetected, just look for a smuggler. For a fee, the smuggler is willing to take the risk of running contraband right under the Emperor's nose. But smugglers also possess a combat versatility that makes them well worth their fees, and the Rebel Alliance often calls upon them to support its troops on the field. Smugglers are notorious for playing dirty, and leave a few deadly presents behind to cover their escape.

EQUIPMENT

Weapon/ Equipment	Ammo	Description
Wookiee Bowcaster	35/175	The Wookiee bowcaster is less advanced than a blaster pistol, but it packs quite a powerful punch. Hand-built by the master weapon crafters of Kashyyyk, the bowcaster is the traditional weapon of the Wookiees.
Merr-Sonn HH-4 Grenade Launcher	5/10	The versatile HH-4 grenade launcher lobs small grenades outward toward targets. The grenades used by the launcher are similar to the larger hand-held thermal detonators soldiers carry.
Merr-Sonn TB-47 Time Bomb	3	Much like its predecessors, the TB-47 time bomb severely damages or destroys a target in a matter of seconds. Just drop the device next to a vehicle or building and the countdown to destruction begins.

NOTE

Its diverse arsenal of weapons makes the wookiee smuggler an offensive powerhouse. Plus, it's one of the hardiest units in the game, capable of taking heavy damage. The wookiee bowcaster can fire individual bolts or, when charged (by holding down the trigger), fire multiple bolts in a wide spread. But a fully charged spread eats up ammo quickly (seven per shot) and the bowcaster takes a few seconds to charge. This makes it difficult to use in fast-moving, close-quarters firefights.

The grenade launcher fires munitions with a delay, causing them to bounce around before exploding. This can make targeting a bit difficult, as the grenade bounces away from your enemy with anything less than a direct hit. It's the time bomb that really makes the wookiee smuggler useful in certain situations. This explosive device can be attached to virtually any surface, and detonates after a 10-second timer counts down to zero. Try attaching these bombs to the legs of walkers or gun turrets. The time bomb also plays a critical role in the demolition of the shield bunker on Endor. The wookiee smuggler's offensive capability comes at the cost of speed, however. It's one of the slowest units in the game.

TIP

In multiplayer games, opposing players can't see the time bomb's timer, thus creating a sense of paranoia as the bomb ticks down to detonation.

DARK TROOPER

FACTION: *Galactic Empire*
INTRA-FACTION RANKINGS
FIREPOWER: 4th
STAMINA: 2nd
SPEED: 4th

Dark troopers are the close-combat elite unit of the Imperial Forces. It is rumored that these troops are more than mere humans or clones. It is said that they are cyborgs, enhanced with machine parts that augment their physical and mental abilities. Dark troopers use their jet packs to jump to their targets. Once in position, they attempt to do as much damage as possible. Cyborgs or not, the dark trooper is deadly and fearsome.

EQUIPMENT

Weapon/ Equipment	Ammo	Description
Golan Arms Blast Cannon	30/180	The blast cannon fires a spread of lasers, like a shotgun. Multiple blaster bolts are discharged per shot. This is the single most brutal close-range anti-infantry weapon.
BlasTech SE-14r Light Repeating Pistol	N/A	An ongoing Imperial contract with BlasTech yielded this semiautomatic blaster pistol. Commonly used as a backup sidearm.
Baradium-Core Thermal Detonator	4	This is a hand-held explosive device effective against infantry. Unlabeled code keys prevent captured munitions from being used against Imperial forces.

NOTE

The dark trooper's jet pack provides the unit with an abrupt vertical boost, making it more useful for quick escapes than for travel. But with some practice, the jet pack can still be used to maneuver around the higher elevations of the battlefield. The trooper's blaster cannon is identical to the Rebel pilot's, firing the same buckshot-like blast.

The combination of this weapon and the dark trooper's aerial capability make this unit extremely effective in staging surprise attacks on enemy command posts at close range. For best results, assemble small squads and drop in on the enemy, seizing the element of surprise while blasting defenders. The dark trooper is best sticking to the air and rooftops. When moving around on the ground, the unit is extremely sluggish, presenting a slow-moving target to enemy troops.

TIP

Both the dark trooper and jet trooper are impervious to fall damage, allowing them to drop from high elevations without suffering a scratch. Use this to your advantage by flying over enemy positions in an aerial vehicle and dropping out over enemy command posts at high elevations.

UNIT RANKING CHARTS

NOTE

Remember, the units are ranked 1-5, with 1 being the highest.

REPUBLIC CLONE ARMY RANKINGS

Unit	Firepower	Stamina	Speed
Clone Trooper	4	2	4
ARC Trooper	2	1	5
Clone Pilot	5	4	2
Clone Sharpshooter	1	5	1
Jet Trooper	3	3	3

CIS RANKINGS

Unit	Firepower	Stamina	Speed
Super Battle Droid	4	3	4
Assault Droid	3	2	5
Droid Pilot	5	4	2
Assassin Droid	2	5	1
Droideka	1	1	3

REBEL ALLIANCE RANKINGS

Unit	Firepower	Stamina	Speed
Rebel Soldier	4	3	3
Rebel Vanguard	2	2	4
Rebel Pilot	5	4	2
Rebel Marksman	1	5	1
Wookiee Smuggler	3	1	5

GALACTIC EMPIRE RANKINGS

Unit	Firepower	Stamina	Speed
Stormtrooper	3	3	3
Shocktrooper	2	1	5
Imperial Pilot	5	4	2
Scout Trooper	1	5	1
Dark Trooper	4	2	4

NON-PLAYER CHARACTERS (NPCs)

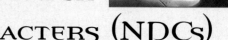

Non-player characters are AI-controlled units that occupy certain battlefields. In some instances, the native inhabitants take part in the battle, allying themselves with a particular faction. Take a quick look at the different NPCs and determine how they fit into your battle plan.

GUNGANS

HOME WORLD: *Naboo*
ALLIANCE: *Republic Clone Army/Rebel Alliance*
MAP: *Naboo: Plains*

The Gungan Grand Army takes part in the Naboo Plains battle in all variations of gameplay. In the Historical Campaign, you must face the Gungans while playing as the CIS forces. Gungans use spherical hand-tossed weapons called boomers. Upon contact, these spheres burst, releasing a lethal plasma shock to any nearby battle droids. In great numbers, these boomers can also be lethal to the Separatist AATs.

ROYAL PALACE GUARDS

HOME WORLD: *Naboo*
ALLIANCE: *N/A*
MAP: *Naboo: Theed*

The Royal Palace Guards of Theed only make an appearance in the Historical Campaign, waging the battle against the player-controlled battle droids. The guards comprise a few different classes including soldiers, heavy-weapons units, and pilots. They also have access to the Gian speeder, a vehicle that is also exclusive to the Historical Campaign.

WOOKIEES

HOME WORLD: *Kashyyyk*
ALLIANCE: *Republic Clone Army/Rebel Alliance*
MAP: *Kashyyyk: Islands and Kashyyyk: Docks*

During the two Kashyyyk battles, the Wookiees make a significant contribution to the defense of their home world. Armed with a mix of bowcasters and missile launchers, the Wookiees are a formidable group, capable of blasting both infantry and tanks. The attacking force should always seek the command post or posts where they spawn and capture it to remove them from the battle.

GEONOSIANS

HOME WORLD: *Geonosis*
ALLIANCE: *CIS*
MAP: *Geonosis: Spire*

These insectoid creatures aid the Separatists during the battle on Geonosis. They're armed with miniature versions of their turret-based sonic blasters. These rifle-sized weapons fire a blast of concussive energy that does minimal damage to its targets, but is fully capable of knocking its victim off his feet. Try to shoot Geonosians while they're on the ground, because they can be hard to hit while flying.

TUSKEN RAIDERS

HOME WORLD: *Tatooine*
ALLIANCE: *None!*
MAP: *Tatooine: Dune Sea*

Of all the NPCs, the notoriously territorial Tusken Raiders are the most dangerous. Unwilling to ally themselves with any faction, the Tusken Raiders strike out at both factions simultaneously, and are fully capable of capturing command posts and conquering a sizable portion of the map. Don't underestimate them: Their rapid-firing blaster rifles can inflict a great deal of harm on your units. Do your best to stay out of their way, letting your enemy deal with them instead.

SARLACC

HOME WORLD: *Tatooine*
ALLIANCE: *N/A*
MAP: *Tatooine: Dune Sea*

Even the mighty Tusken Raiders steer clear of the Sarlacc. This immobile carnivorous creature lives in the sand near the Cistern command post of the Dune Sea map, feasting on anything that moves within grasp of its long tentacles. When moving around this area, stay a good distance away from the Sarlacc. However, you can drive vehicles over it with no repercussions.

JAWAS

HOME WORLD: Tatooine
ALLIANCE: Neutral
MAP: Tatooine: Mos Eisley

Jawas are indifferent to the presence of strangers on their home world. In fact, they can help your faction in a number of ways. They're equipped with fusioncutters, and wander around the map constructing turrets as well as repairing droids. This can be a huge asset when playing the map as the Separatists. Don't lash out at them till they start helping the enemy.

EWOKS

HOME WORLD:
The Moon of Endor
ALLIANCE: Rebel Alliance
MAP: Endor: Bunker

These furry pint-sized creatures don't look dangerous, but their spears and rocks can inflict serious damage on the Empire's units. Ewoks have a tendency to attack in swarms, making them much more deadly. However, their attack range extends no more than a few feet. As long as the Imperials keep their distance, they're safe.

JEDI HEROES

A Jedi among your ranks can easily turn the tide of a battle.

The Jedi heroes appear in various stages of the single-player games, aiding a particular faction in battle. Although only armed with lightsabers, Jedi are often the deadliest participants on the battlefield. Their prowess with the lightsaber allows them to kill enemies with one swipe of the blade. They can also use their lightsaber to defend against projectile attacks, often redirecting the blasts back at the shooter.

The Jedi aren't invincible. They take damage like every other unit on the battlefield and can also be killed. Still, it isn't wise to seek the notoriety of being a Jedi killer—chances are you won't survive very long.

In the Galactic Conquest mode, the Jedi heroes are a planetary bonus. Win both battles at Tatooine to attain this option, then attack other worlds with a Jedi on your side. The era and your chosen faction determine which Jedi join you. See the following table for more details.

Don't get in a duel with a Jedi. It's a fight you're likely to lose.

AVAILABLE JEDI

Jedi	Era	Faction
Count Dooku	Clone Wars	CIS

Historical Campaign Appearance
Kashyyyk: Islands

Jedi	Era	Faction
Mace Windu	Clone Wars	Republic Clone Army

Historical Campaign Appearance
Geonosis: Spire

Jedi	Era	Faction
Darth Vader	Galactic Civil War	Galactic Empire

Historical Campaign Appearance
Tatooine: Mos Eisley

Jedi	Era	Faction
Luke Skywalker	Galactic Civil War	Rebel Alliance

Historical Campaign Appearance
Hoth: Echo Base

TIP
Jedi cannot capture command posts, but they can help clear out the defenders.

DROIDS & ITEMS

Expending ammo and taking damage is part of the battlefield experience. Fortunately you can heal and resupply using a variety of resources. Droids are the best way to get your supply fix; they provide an endless inventory of health and munitions. But other supply items can be found to help keep your team on the move.

MEDICAL DROID

Medical droids slowly heal any injured units within their operational radius. Fully healing at a medical droid can take a while, so make sure the surrounding area is secure. Sometimes snipers use medical droids as bait, picking off unsuspecting units when they feel most secure.

AMMO DROID

Ammo droids replenish all forms of ammo—from rifle clips and mines to recon droids. Fully restoring your ammo takes slightly less time than healing, but you still need to hang out next to the droid while stocking up. Ammo droids can be used as bait by snipers, but they can also be booby-trapped by slyly sticking a mine to its side. Approach ammo droids cautiously, especially when behind enemy lines.

REPAIR DROID

While it's possible to repair vehicles using the pilot's fusioncutter, repair droids can do the job much faster. They're also the only way to replenish vehicles' missiles. Repair droids are less common than the medical and ammo droids, so memorize their locations, especially if you're piloting vehicles.

Repair droids can also help out in combat situations. Try parking a combat speeder or AAT next to one of these droids while dueling an enemy vehicle. The repair droid helps offset the damage you take, giving you a clear advantage. But enemies may try this same tactic. So if you keep hitting an enemy vehicle and it's taking no damage, look for a repair droid nearby and destroy it before continuing your duel.

TIP

Droids help your enemy as well. Take them out wherever they may benefit the enemy.

BACTA TANK

Dead units randomly drop these cylindrical tanks, instantly restoring 25 percent of your health. Grabbing these tanks on the run is much easier and safer than camping near a medical droid.

AMMO CANISTER

Like the bacta tank, dead units randomly drop ammo canisters. This is a quick way to replenish some ammo, increasing your munitions by a full clip. For more details on specific ammo distribution, see the table below.

HEALTH/AMMO DISPENSER

Health/ammo dispensers are carried exclusively by pilot units, and can be distributed to teammates for quick healing and ammo replenishment. Although this combo pack looks similar to the standard bacta tank and ammo canister, these dispensers provide twice the healing power and supplies, increasing your health by 50 percent and your ammo by two full clips. A pilot who runs out of these dispensers can load up on more only at an ammo droid. Picking up another dispenser or ammo canister won't work. For more details on specific ammo distribution, see the table below.

AMMO DISTRIBUTION

Class/Unit	Ammo Canister	Health/Ammo Dispenser
Soldier	1 clip, 1 thermal detonator, 1 concussion grenade	2 clips, 2 thermal detonators, 2 concussion grenades
Heavy Weapons	2 missiles, 1 mine, 1 thermal detonator	4 missiles, 2 mines, 2 thermal detonators
Pilot	1 clip/5 grenades	2 clips/10 grenades
Sniper	1 clip, 1 thermal detonator, 1 recon droid	2 clips, 2 thermal detonators, 1 recon droid
Jet Trooper	2 EMP rounds, 1 grenade	4 EMP rounds, 2 grenades
Super Battle Droid	1 clip, 1 rocket	2 clips, 2 rockets
Wookiee	1 clip, 5 grenades,	2 clips, 10 grenades,
Smuggler	1 time bomb	2 time bombs

vehicles & turrets

Vehicles offer more than a way to get from one side of the map to the other. Their speed and destructive firepower are the deciding factor in every battle in which they appear. Each faction has an arsenal of vehicles with unique attributes and capabilities. In this section, we take a detailed look at every vehicle as well as the turrets.

SCOUT VEHICLES

This type of ground vehicle is fast and light. It can zip across the battlefield at great speed, but is not meant for heavy combat. Scout vehicles are armed, but only lightly armored for minimal protection. Use these vehicles as transports. Snipers can use them to reach remote areas and monitor enemy troop movements.

74-Z SPEEDER BIKE

Length: 4.4 Meters
Max Speed: 500 KPH
Crew: Pilot
Armament: 1 Laser Cannon
Faction: Republic, Galactic Empire, Rebel Alliance

Developed by the Aratech Repulsor Company, the 74-Z military speeder bike is compact, flies low to the ground, and presents a small profile. Speeder bikes are capable of speeds up to 500 kilometers an hour and are maneuverable, making them the vehicle of choice for reconnaissance missions. You can scout a battlefield's perimeter or zip away from a scuffle with relative ease on an Aratech speeder bike.

NOTE

The speeder bike is the fastest ground vehicle available, capable of zooming across the map in seconds. With its immense speed comes the potential for disaster. Even at moderate speeds, the speeder bike explodes on contact with any solid object. However, you can use it to run down enemy units—this is often preferable to shooting them with the bike's slow-firing laser cannon, mounted beneath the frame.

STAP

Height: 2 Meters
Max Speed: 400 KPH
Crew: Pilot
Armament: 2 Blaster Cannons
Faction: Separatists

The STAP is a military version of a civilian craft known as the Airhook. Designed to carry a single soldier, the STAP is a slender low-atmosphere repulsorlift reconnaissance vehicle manufactured by the Baktoid Armor Workshop and used by the Separatist droid army. As a light and fast reconnaissance craft, the STAP is an excellent craft to use for scouting targets along the battlefield and providing support for ground troops.

TIP

The STAP has more offensive capability than the speeder bike, armed with dual blaster cannons. This makes the vehicle useful for staging rush attacks on lightly defended command posts. Circle the position until the defenders are neutralized, then zoom toward the command post to capture it.

MEDIUM ASSAULT VEHICLES

These vehicles have heavier weapons and armor, and are slower than the scout craft, but they pack more power and durability. They make up the bulk of your assault force. Learn to coordinate them with infantry to overwhelm enemy command posts.

COMBAT LANDSPEEDER

Length: 5.7 Meters
Max Speed: 227 KPH
Crew: Pilot,
Main Gunner
Armament: 2 Blaster Cannons, Missiles (4/115),
1 Blaster Cannon Turret
Faction: Rebel Alliance

The combat landspeeder is a military landspeeder concept that never came to fruition. After a bad night at the Sabaac tables, a SoroSuub designer sold the design blueprints to the Rebellion to pay off debts. The combat landspeeder is fast, maneuverable, and equipped with reinforced hull plating. Rebellion officers have found the vehicle to be effective when used for lightning strikes against military targets.

vehicles & turrets

TX-130S Fighter Tank (IFT-X)

Length: 8.2 Meters
Max Speed: 193 KPH
Crew: Pilot, Main Gunner
Armament: 2 Blaster Cannons, Missiles (2/98), 1 Beam Cannon
Faction: Republic

The Republic fighter tank is a specially designed repulsor craft developed to counteract the strong ground forces of the Separatist droid armies. Its repulsorlifts are specially tuned for quick maneuvering, yet they carry a heavy payload of firepower. Clone troopers fighting alongside these tanks have a much easier time advancing.

TX-130T Fighter Tank (IFT-T)

Length: 8.2 Meters
Max Speed: 193 KPH
Crew: Pilot, Main Gunner
Armament: 2 Blaster Cannons, Missiles (2/98), 1 Beam Cannon
Faction: Galactic Empire

The Imperial Department of Military Research modified Rothana Heavy Engineering's TX-130S fighter tank. The new TX-130T maintains many features of the old design, but packs more punch than its predecessor. The TX-130T's repulsorlifts are much better tuned for quick maneuvering, while adding a more impressive weapons layout to the old design. The TX-130T is well suited for pushing the front lines forward.

AAT (Armored Assault Tank)

Length: 9.75 Meters
Max Speed: 55 KPH
Crew: Pilot, Main Gunner
Armament: 2 Laser Cannons, 1 Laser Blaster
Faction: Separatists

Intended for frontal assaults, the AAT is one of the most heavily armed and armored vehicles produced by the now-defunct Baktoid Armor Workshop. As the Separatist movement grew, the Trade Federation added the battle-hardened AATs to the ranks of the Separatists' Droid Army for use as frontline assault tanks.

TIP

Both the pilot and gunner positions in the AAT need to be manned to maximize this tank's offensive potential. If piloting the tank alone, switch to the gunner position to fire the main gun, then jump back in the pilot's position to use chassis-mounted laser cannons while the main gun recharges. Group the AATs in pairs and use their impressive firepower to rush command posts before infantry assaults.

HAILFIRE DROID

Height: 8.5 Meters
Max Speed: 45 KPH
Crew: Pilot
Armament: 1 Laser Cannon, Hailfire Missiles (5/155)
Faction: Separatists

Haor Chall Engineering developed the hailfire for the InterGalactic Banking Clan to protect its holdings on outlaw worlds. The hailfire is light, mobile, and uses a missile system designed for rapid strikes. When the InterGalactic Banking Clan joined the Separatist movement, they "loaned" the hailfires to the Separatists as a heavily armed response tank in the droid army.

TIP

Hailfire droids are important in the battle on Geonosis, playing a key role in demolishing the Republic's AT-TEs. Attack the AT-TEs from the sides where their fore and aft laser cannons can't hit you. The hailfire's rockets are also effective when tilted skyward to engage the Republic gunships.

ASSAULT WALKERS

These vehicles are more heavily armed and armored, and are used at the front of most assaults. Like the medium assault vehicles, use these walkers to soften the enemy's defenses, concentrating on destroying turrets and other vehicles. Watch out for heavy-weapons units, too—trace missile smoke trails to their source and blast these troops before they inflict heavy damage.

SPIDER WALKER

Height: 7.32 Meters
Max Speed: 90 KPH
Crew: Pilot
Armament: 1 Beam Cannon, 1 Laser Cannon
Faction: Separatists

Before its dissolution, Baktoid Armor Workshop sold the spider walker design to the Commerce Guild. Considered an artillery unit, the spider walker houses a homing laser that can be maintained for periods of time. Wielding this devastating weapon, the spider walker has been known to bore through armored vehicles and cut down platoons of foot soldiers on the battlefield.

TIP

In addition to its homing laser, the spider walker is armed with a faster-firing laser cannon. Use this weapon to suppress enemy troops while the homing laser recharges. The homing laser is most effective against enemy vehicles, but can be used against infantry, too. Sweep it across the enemy ranks to cut down multiple targets with one swipe.

AT-ST (All-Terrain Scout Transport)

Height: 8.6 Meters
Max Speed: 90 KPH
Crew: Pilot, Co-Pilot
Armament: 2 Blaster Cannons, 2 Light Blaster Turrets
Faction: Galactic Empire

After making modifications recommended by the Imperial Department of Military Research, Kuat Drive Yards redesigned the Old Republic's AT-PT and prototype AT-XT walkers and created the AT-ST. The AT-ST is a fast and maneuverable patrol and reconnaissance walker valued by Imperial tacticians for its ability to make swift attacks against ground troops and repulsorlift vehicles.

vehicles & turrets

TIP

For a walker, the AT-ST is fast and agile, capable of rushing the front lines and maneuvering through difficult terrain with ease. But its forward-facing weapons make it vulnerable to flanking attacks. Keep the enemy in front of this walker. On Hoth, use the AT-STs to help escort the AT-AT walkers to the Rebel shield generator.

Heavy Assault Transports

These lumbering behemoths can unload devastating amounts of firepower on a target, and can serve as mobile command posts. Use these huge walkers to assault enemy command posts at close range, spawning troops on the enemy's front doorstep. But these transports draw plenty of fire, so make sure pilots are on board to maintain the vehicle's health. Unlike any other vehicle, the heavy assault transports contribute to the map's total number of command posts. The destruction of one of these vehicles reduces the number of command posts, and thus changes the balance of power on the battlefield. Determine ahead of time how many command posts your team needs to hold to maintain a reinforcement drain on the enemy in the event one of these vehicles falls.

AT-TE (All Terrain Tactical Enforcer)

Size: 5.02 Meters Tall,
12.4 Meters Long
Max Speed: 60 KPH
Crew: Pilot, Co-Pilot,
Main Gunner
Armament: 4 Laser
Cannons (fore), 2 Laser
Cannons (aft), 1 Projectile Cannon
Faction: Republic

The four-legged AT-TE is a multipurpose assault vehicle developed by Rothana Heavy Engineering and produced at Kuat Drive Yards. The Enforcers carry a lot of firepower that lays waste to anything in their way. It also has a large crew compartment for hauling troops from one side of the battlefield to another.

TIP

Although heavily armed, the AT-TE is vulnerable to side attacks. Therefore, the main gunner must watch these angles to prevent enemy infantry and vehicle attacks. Better yet, escort the AT-TE with ARC troopers to discourage flanking attacks. Pilots running along the AT-TE may be needed as well to help conduct repairs as the transport advances across the battlefield.

AT-AT

Size: 15 Meters Tall, 20 Meters Long
Max Speed: 60 KPH
Crew: Pilot, Co-Pilot
Armament: 2 Heavy Lasers,
2 Blaster Turrets
Faction: Galactic Empire

After reviewing the Old Republic's past successes with their AT-TE walkers, Gen. Maximillian Veers worked with Imperial engineers to resurrect the AT-AT concept. The Empire has since produced hundreds of these mammoth walkers at Kuat Drive Yards for use in ground assaults. An awe-inspiring staple of the Imperial Army, the AT-AT is perfect for moving troops into occupied areas while instilling fear in enemy forces. The AT-AT is nearly unstoppable.

TIP

Unlike the AT-TE, all of the AT-AT's weaponry faces forward, making its sides and rear open to attacks. Therefore other units and vehicles must make it their responsibility to prevent flanking attacks on this huge walker. AT-STs or IF T-TS make the best escorts, but shocktroopers can make an impact, too, especially if aerial units attack the AT-AT. On Hoth, the Rebel airspeeders pose a huge threat, especially if they wrap the AT-AT's legs with tow cable. To prevent tow cable attacks, keep both AT-ATS close together, traveling side by side.

FIGHTER CRAFT

These craft are fast maneuverable starfighters. They have forward-firing blasters and a small complement of missiles. Their purposes are to provide cover for enemy troops on the field and keep the skies clear of enemy craft. Designed for space combat, the weapons installed on each craft are the most powerful on the battlefield. Establish air superiority, then conduct strafing runs to eliminate enemy vehicles and troops.

GEONOSIAN STARFIGHTER

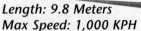

Length: 9.8 Meters
Max Speed: 1,000 KPH
Crew: Pilot
Armament: 1 Laser Cannon
Faction: Separatists

Built by Huppla Pasa Tisc Shipwrights Collective, the Geonosian starfighter is more of a stealth fighter than a frontline assault craft. Its engine produces little glow and houses its weapon systems between the beak wings that form the craft's nose. The Geonosian starfighter's design allows pilots to move and attack without giving away their position too soon. Many Geonosian pilots use the craft for ambushes in and around the asteroid field of their home world.

NOTE

On Geonosis, the Geonosian starfighters are the separatists' most valuable asset. Their powerful laser cannons can blast through the AT-TE's armor faster than any of the ground-based weapons. For this reason, the CIS forces need to protect their spawn points inside the hangar near the spire command post.

JEDI STARFIGHTER

Length: 8 Meters
Max Speed: 12,000 KPH,
Class 1 Hyperdrive Module
Crew: Pilot
Armament: 2 Laser Cannons,
Missiles (4/16)
Faction: Republic

Commissioned by the Jedi Council, the Delta-7 Aethersprite Interceptor was developed by Kuat Systems Engineering. The Jedi starfighter is a light high-performance reconnaissance ship. Pilots looking for a sleek ride with formidable firepower and defenses will find this fighter craft to their liking.

TIP

Its dual-firing missile launchers give the Jedi starfighter a huge advantage over the droid starfighter. The missiles are capable of achieving locks on enemy craft. Wait for the red diamond to stop shrinking before launching the missiles to take full advantage of their homing capability.

DROID STARFIGHTER

Length: 3.6 Meters
Max Speed: 1,180 KPH
Crew: Pilot
Armament: 2 Blaster Cannons
Faction: Separatists

Designed by fanatical Xi Char engineers, the droid starfighter was produced in massive quantities for the Trade Federation. The droid starfighter is a short-range combat craft that is often used in large attack groups to swarm enemy targets. Droid starfighters aren't the strongest fighter craft ever produced, but there are always more of them waiting to be unleashed.

TIP

Although it lacks missile launchers, the droid starfighter is still a capable and maneuverable fighter. When engaging the Jedi starfighters, stay behind them to deprive them of their missiles. The fighter's dual blaster cannons are also effective in strafing runs. Look for tight clusters of enemy infantry to maximize damage.

vehicles & turrets

X-Wing

Length: 12.5 Meters
Max Speed: 1,050 KPM
Crew: Pilot
Armament: 4 Laser Cannons, Proton Torpedoes (2/6)
Faction: Rebel Alliance

Designed by Incom Corporation in the Empire's early days, the X-wing schematics found their way into Rebel hands when several Incom engineers defected to the Rebel Alliance. The X-wing proved itself on the battlefield time and again with its high maneuverability, heavy firepower, and dedicated pilots. It became one of the most important vehicles in the Rebel Alliance's arsenal.

TIP

when it comes to ground attack, no fighters come close to matching the offensive capability of the x-wing. with its full compliment of powerful laser cannons and torpedoes, the x-wing can destroy multiple ground vehicles in one strafing run, reducing an enemy assault force to a smoldering pile of rubble. but it can only carry six torpedoes at a time, so locate the map's repair droids and make frequent stops to re-supply.

TIE Fighter

Length: 6.3 Meters
Max Speed: 1,200 KPH
Crew: Pilot
Armament: 2 Laser Cannons
Faction: Galactic Empire

Sienar Fleet Systems designed the Twin Ion Engine fighter for the Empire as a fast, maneuverable, and cheap attack craft. It is a short-range fighter craft with no frills (i.e., life support and deflector shields). TIE fighters can outrun everything, including the Rebel Alliance's X-wing. Imperial Navy commanders rely on vast numbers of TIE fighters to overwhelm enemy forces in battle.

TIP

the TIE fighter's speed and maneuverability give it a key advantage over the x-wing in dogfights. reduce speed and turn tightly to keep the Rebel fighter in front of you while blasting it with the two fire-linked laser cannons. when x-wings are present on the battlefield, take them out before conducting strafing runs on enemy ground units.

BOMBERS

Bombers are slower but more heavily armed than their fighter craft counterparts. Designed for engaging huge ships, the bombers bring a devastating array of weapons to the battlefield during planetary assaults. Use starfighters to escort them as they make bombing and strafing runs on enemy positions. When manned by an experienced pilot and co-pilot, the bombers can inflict massive damage.

Y-Wing

Length: 16 Meters
Max Speed: 1,000 KPH
Crew: Pilot, Co-Pilot
Armament: 2 Laser Cannons, Proton Bombs (24), 1 Laser Cannon Turret
Faction: Rebel Alliance

Developed by Koensayr for surgical strikes and light bombing runs, the Y-wing proved to be a highly versatile craft. Audacious Rebel fleet commanders often relied on them for everything from escort duty to reconnaissance. The Y-wing was already "old tech" in the Rebellion's early days, but its durability and heavy firepower ensured it a place in Rebel Alliance fleets long past the height of the Galactic Civil War.

TIP

the Y-wing's pilot is capable of dropping a string of five proton bombs over enemy positions. use the map to line up your targets and avoid friendly-fire incidents. the bombs drop in quick succession, up to a total of five, so make sure your flight path remains over enemy positions throughout the duration of the bombing run. meanwhile, the co-pilot's laser cannon turret is essential in keeping the Y-wing safe from fighter attacks.

TIE BOMBER

Length: 7.8 Meters
Max Speed: 850 KPH
Crew: Pilot, Co-Pilot
Armament: 2 Laser Cannons, Proton Torpedoes (4/12), Proton Bombs (10/40)
Faction: Galactic Empire

Sienar Fleet Systems designed this variant of the TIE fighter, providing a large ordnance pod and a wide array of destructive weapons. The TIE bomber is a heavy assault ship designed for strategic strikes against surface targets, as well as torpedo runs on capital ships.

NOTE

The co-pilot is responsible for dropping the TIE bomber's proton bombs, so there must be coordination between the pilot and co-pilot while making bombing runs. The pilot should look for high concentrations of enemy units and vehicles and level out over their positions while the co-pilot lets loose a salvo of 10 bombs. If the bombs hit the intended target area, the results will be devastating. In addition to the proton bombs, the pilot can fire off a few proton torpedoes for more precise strikes against enemy vehicles.

AIR TRANSPORTS

Air transports act as attack craft and troop transports in battle. They also provide limited anti-air support, but the smaller starfighters outmaneuver them. Air transports are most effective in close air-support roles, blasting enemy ground vehicles with their powerful weapons. When needed, use them to transport troops to key areas on the battlefield. This is useful in opening new fronts and staging sneak attacks on enemy command posts.

REPUBLIC GUNSHIP

Size: 17.4 Meters Long, 17-Meter Wingspan
Max Speed: 620 KPH
Crew: Pilot, Co-Pilot, 2 Turret Gunners, 1 Transport Position
Armament: 2 Laser Cannons, Rockets (4/20), 2 Wing Lasers, 2 Beam Cannon Turrets
Faction: Republic

The LAAT/I repulsorlift gunship is a heavily armed assault craft capable of recon, transporting troops across the battlefield, and low-altitude combat against ground targets. A skilled pilot in the cockpit of a Republic Gunship, developed by Rothana Heavy Engineering, can perform high-risk tactical maneuvers at speeds of more than 600 kilometers an hour or hover above the battlefield, providing cover for the clone army.

TIP

When manned by five pilot units, the Republic Gunship is durable, capable of taking heavy fire with little damage. Fully manning the gunship also allows the crew to take full advantage of the craft's impressive weapons, including the two beam-cannon turrets. Hover above the battlefield and pick off enemy troops with these powerful lasers. The gunship's rockets are effective against infantry and vehicles.

MAF

Length: 18.2 Meters
Max Speed: 820 KPH
Crew: Pilot, Co-Pilot, Turret Gunner
Armament: Rockets (8/32), 2 Beam Cannons, 1 Blaster Cannon Turret
Faction: CIS

The mechanized assault flyer is produced by Haor Chall Engineering for close-range bombardment of targets while doubling as a recon craft. The hover capability of the craft allows the MAF to sit in one place and provide cover for the battle droid army. Additionally, the MAF hosts an impressive weapons layout, including a top-mounted turret with a 360-degree turning radius.

TIP

The MAF's top turret is useful in ground attack situations, but is also instrumental in defending the craft from air attack. When attacking this transport with a starfighter, hit it from a distance with missiles, or attack from below where the turret can't hit you.

vehicles & turrets

SPECIAL CRAFT

The remaining vehicles lack specific categorization and are only on a few maps. Some are even more rare, appearing exclusively in certain game modes or only during specific battlefield conditions.

T-47 AIRSPEEDER

Length: 5.3 Meters
Max Speed: 1,100 KPH
Crew: Pilot, Co-Pilot
Armament: 2 Laser Cannons, 1 Harpoon Gun
Faction: Rebel Alliance

Incom Corporation designed the T-47 airspeeder for industrial use as a cargo handler. The Rebel Alliance adopted the T-47, modified it for military use, and further modified the design to handle various extreme climates, such as the ice world of Hoth. The T-47 airspeeder proved its worth when the Rebels used the craft's high maneuverability and tow cables to entangle Imperial walkers, slowing down the Imperial advance long enough for Rebel transports to escape.

TIP

The T-47 is only available to Rebel forces during the battle of Hoth. In this battle, they are the first line of defense against the AT-AT onslaught. While their laser blasters are capable of destroying these huge walkers, wrapping their legs with the tow cable is faster. However, such attacks require a fair amount of skill and coordination on behalf of the pilot and co-pilot. See the "Hoth: Echo Base" level for more details on tow cable attacks.

SAND SKIFF

Length: 9 Meters
Max Speed: 250 KPH
Crew: Pilot, 3 Turret Gunners
Armament: 3 Heavy Gun Turrets
Faction: All

Ubrikkian developed the sand skiff with many uses in mind. Primarily used as a cargo transport, the design lends itself well to military uses with minor modifications to the hull and a few mounted turrets. The sand skiff provides enough speed, firepower, and protection to cause trouble wherever it goes. Troopers needing a ride have never been more useful than manning the guns on a combat skiff.

TIP

The sand skiff is better used as a transport than as an assault platform. The three mounted gun turrets have limited firing arcs, plus they leave the gunners open to counterattack. Instead, load up the skiff and rush toward an enemy command post's capture radius and disembark to assault with four units at close range.

GIAN SPEEDER

Length: 5.7 Meters
Max Speed: 160 KPH
Crew: Pilot, Main Gunner
Armament: 2 Gian Blasters, 1 Laser Cannon Turret
Faction: Naboo Royal Security Forces

The Gian speeder is a modified SoroSuub V-19 landspeeder. Used by Naboo Royal Security Forces to keep Naboo peaceful, NRS forces adapted the technology for use as an assault craft. Reinforced hull plating and excellent maneuverability make the Gian speeder an excellent vehicle for patrol duties. Gian speeders are also used as quick-response craft for emergencies that crop up throughout Theed's busy city streets.

NOTE

The Gian speeder is only available to the AI-controlled Naboo Royal Security Forces on the Naboo: Theed map in the Historical campaign. However, its open-top configuration leaves the pilot and main gunner vulnerable to attacks, making this vehicle easy to steal. The speeder maneuvers like the Rebel combat landspeeder, capable of sliding around corners while keeping the twin Gian blasters aimed at enemies. The main gunner sits next to the pilot and controls the more powerful laser cannon turret on the speeder's front.

VEHICLES & TURRETS

CLOUD CAR

Length: 7 Meters
Max Speed: 1,500 KPH
Crew: Pilot, Co-Pilot
Armament: 2 Laser Cannons, Rockets (45)
Faction: All

Storm IV twin-pod cloud cars are manufactured locally by Bespin Motors and have a variety of uses, from defense to sightseeing. The Bespin Wing Guard primarily uses the cloud cars to monitor the airspace around Cloud City. Cloud cars are a fast and maneuverable atmospheric craft with pods that house two crew members. Pilots can navigate around the city buildings while the gunner handles the details. Cloud cars are lightly armored and maintain a standard weapons layout for a non-military vehicle.

NOTE

cloud cars appear on the bespin: platforms map only after an enemy command post is captured. The enemy vehicles connected to the command post explode and a cloud car spawns in their place. The cloud car is maneuverable, but its lack of armor and powerful weapons make it vulnerable to turret and starfighter attack. Like the bomber class, the co-pilot can fire a salvo of rockets, and is useful for both ground and air attacks.

CREATURES

Some factions have harnessed the capabilities of the planet's indigenous creatures to further their cause. Like the scout vehicles, creatures should be used for transportation. You can try rushing enemy command posts, but creatures aren't durable when attacked. Like any other vehicle, the enemy only needs to kill the creature to kill the rider. If injured, creatures can only be healed when a pilot unit is riding them—medical droids and repair droids have no impact on their health.

KAADU

Faction: Gungan Grand Army, Republic, Rebel Alliance

Kaadu are large bipedal animals that can traverse multiple terrains. Gungan warriors ride trained kaadu, often wielding electropoles and energy balls against enemy infantry. Kaadu are not equipped with weapons, so riders head into battle equipped only with what they are carrying.

TIP

on naboo, use kaadu to raid the enemy-held command position to capture the command post or steal vehicles.

TAUNTAUN

Faction: Rebel Alliance

The tauntaun is a large bipedal animal that can move at great speed over snow and ice. This creature is not suited for combat; it has no weapons other than those carried by its rider. Tauntauns are skittish about combat and if the rider dismounts to fight, the tauntaun may flee.

TIP

on hoth, stage a massive rush attack on the imperial-held forward camp command post using all six tauntauns on the map. The tauntauns are also great for rushing the AT-AT's legs for close-ranged attacks, using the vanguard's mines or the smuggler's time bombs.

TURRETS

Turrets play a vital role in defending command posts. These emplacements are effective in engaging infantry as well as vehicles. Man them in the early stages of the battle to prevent rush attacks on your command posts.

GUN TURRET

The gun turret is the most common type, found on several different maps. Unlike other turrets, a pilot unit must construct this one before it's operable. Scour the ground for square metal plates inscribed with a wrench icon. A few seconds under the pilot's fusioncutter and your turret is ready! Hop inside and fire a few rounds. The turret recharges itself after each shot, but keep the energy level from getting too low.

For best results, fire three quick rounds and pause for recharging before firing another volley of three. This helps maximize the turret's rate of fire and prevents long pauses when recharging. The turret also has a zoom function, magnifying targets for more precise targeting. This is useful for picking off infantry at long range. The gun turret offers the gunner protection, but its low forward-facing armor can't prevent head shots and flanking attacks. So if enemy snipers are in the area, stay out of the gun turrets—you'll just give them an easy kill.

GEONOSIAN SONIC BLASTER

These unconventional turrets are on Geonosis, used by the Separatists and Geonosians to defend the Spire and Techno Union ships. Like the Geonosian's hand-held versions, these turrets fire a cone-shaped concussive blast capable of knocking infantry off their feet and tumbling them backward for several meters. By literally pushing back the attackers, the gunner delays attacks, but does not necessarily eliminate the attackers. Other means must be used to wipe out the enemy infantry.

TOWER TURRET

The dense forests of Yavin IV call for defensive turrets that can see above the tree line. These tower turrets, sitting on high poles, fit the role well. You can find these peculiar turrets sprinkled through the Yavin: Temple map. Unlike most turrets, the rapid-firing laser cannon uses ammo, similar to blaster rifles. Each turret comes equipped with 1,000 rounds, dispensed in 200-round clips. After the turret's ammo is fully expended, it cannot be resupplied.

The high elevation of the turret gives the gunner a good view of the surrounding area, but the turret lacks magnification capability. If one of these turrets is destroyed, it respawns after several seconds—it cannot be repaired. A newly spawned turret has a fresh stock of ammo, so destroy turrets after they run out of ammo.

TIP

If you're into bird-watching, shoot the surrounding trees with the tower turret to view Yavin IV's wildlife in action.

ANTI-INFANTRY LASER BATTERY

These large white defensive turrets blend into Hoth's icy landscape near Echo Base. The rapid-firing laser is an effective anti-infantry weapon, but is also effective in damaging vehicles, particularly AT-STs. While the turret's cumbersome design keeps the gunner safe from small-arms fire, the gun rotates slowly, making it less effective in dealing with close-ranged threats. Instead, use the turret's zoom function to engage targets at long range. The Rebels should use the massive array of these turrets to hold back the infantry attack, preventing the Imperials from infiltrating the trenches at the Outpost and Bunker positions.

ANTI-VEHICLE LASER CANNON

Accompanying the anti-infantry laser batteries on Hoth are these smaller, but more powerful turrets. As the name implies, the anti-vehicle laser cannon is useful for taking out the incoming AT-STs and AT-ATs. When operating the turret, hold down the trigger for a full charge before releasing to fire. This maximizes the damage to the target. For best results, engage targets at extreme range, using the turret's magnification capability.

If enemy infantry move within close range, abandon the turret. It rotates and fires too slowly to put up a good fight against infantry. Plus it offers little protection to the gunner. When playing as the Rebels, sabotage these turrets upon retreat with mines or thermal detonators. Otherwise the Imperials can turn them against your own units, including the Shield generator.

ANTI-AIR TURRET

The anti-air turrets rule the Bespin's skies and surrounding platforms. The turret's dual turbo-lasers are designed to take out starfighters and other aerial units. But they can also be turned on infantry units, particularly at the Extractor platform in the map's center. In the fight for air superiority, these turrets are popular targets of the swarms of starfighters circling the air space over the platforms. It only takes a few laser cannon hits to wipe out these turrets, so keep pilot units nearby to conduct repairs or reconstruct them.

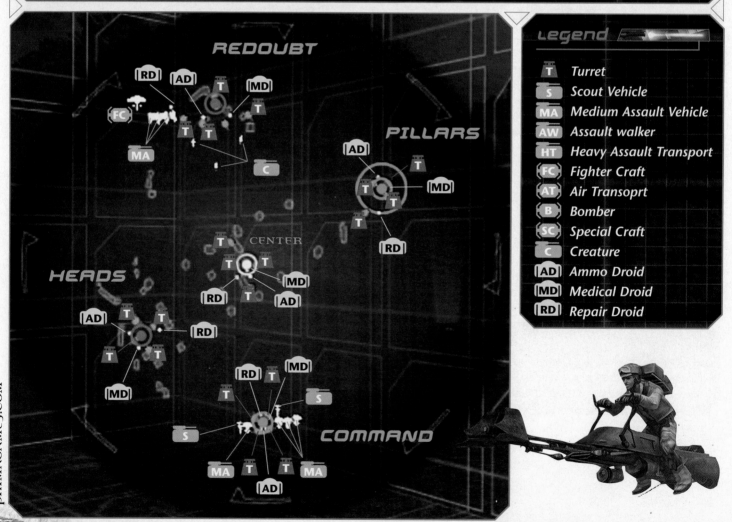

STAR WARS BATTLEFRONT™

PRIMA OFFICIAL GAME GUIDE

NABOO: PLAINS

planetary overview

An idyllic world close to the border of the Outer Rim Territories, Naboo is known throughout the galaxy for its rolling plains, green hills, and beautiful cities. The underwater Gungan settlements are a wondrous display of exotic hydrostatic bubble technology, and Naboo's river cities are resplendent with classical architecture and greenery. The natural landscape of Naboo is breathtaking, but Theed, with its canals, bridges and Royal Palace, is the pride and joy of Naboo. While the rolling plains and hills are perfect for stationing a large force, gaining control of Theed's Royal Palace is the key to claiming Naboo as a galactic trophy.

Legend

T	Turret
S	Scout Vehicle
MA	Medium Assault Vehicle
AW	Assault walker
HT	Heavy Assault Transport
FC	Fighter Craft
AT	Air Transoprt
B	Bomber
SC	Special Craft
C	Creature
AD	Ammo Droid
MD	Medical Droid
RD	Repair Droid

REDOUBT

PILLARS

CENTER

HEADS

COMMAND

naboo: plains

COMMAND POSTS

THE REDOUBT

Several ancient sculptures and ruins surround this command post.

Most attacks on the Redoubt originate from the pillars to the east.

THE COMMAND

If the Separatists want to keep spawning vehicles, they have to hold this hilltop command post.

INITIAL CONTROL: REPUBLIC CLONE ARMY/REBEL ALLIANCE

COMMAND POST TYPE: HEAVY

VEHICLES, TURRETS, & DROIDS

Unit	Count
IF T-X/Combat Speeder	3/2
Jedi Starfighter/X-wing	1/1
Kaadu	2
Gun Turrets	4
Medical Droid	1
Ammo Droid	1
Repair Droid	1

The Redoubt is the northernmost command post and acts as the main staging area for the clone army. Because all their vehicles spawn here, it's imperative to the clone army's survival that the Separatists not capture this command post. The actual command post sits in a small depression surrounded by ancient ruins, making it relatively safe from bombardment and other distant attacks.

But that also means that defenders won't have a chance to engage attackers until they're at close range. Place defenders just south of the command post so they can see approaching units. The hill to the west (where the vehicles spawn) also makes a good outlook position.

Clone pilots should construct the gun turrets around the command post early in the battle.

INITIAL CONTROL: SEPARATIST BATTLE DROIDS/GALACTIC EMPIRE

COMMAND POST TYPE: HEAVY

VEHICLES, TURRETS, & DROIDS

Unit	Count
AAT/AT-ST	4/2
STAP/Speeder Bike	2/3
Gun Turrets	4
Medical Droid	1
Ammo Droid	1
Repair Droid	1

* Galactic Civil War only

Sitting on a high hill in the south, overlooking the battlefield, the Command is the Separatists' staging area. Considering this is the command post where the Separatists' vehicles spawn, it's important that they hold it while capturing the Center to the north. The four turrets come in handy for the command posts' defense; they are easily capable of engaging all incoming targets at long range.

However, these elevated turrets (and their occupants) are ripe targets for enemy snipers. Regardless of the situation elsewhere on the battlefield, the Separatists must always rally around the Command if it comes under attack. If it falls into enemy hands, they not only lose a command post, but they also lose their vehicle spawn points.

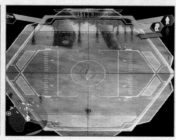

The gun turrets on the hill have a good view of the battlefield. Use them to engage enemy targets near the Center command post.

Look for this ramplike pillar just north of the command post; climb to the top to find an unconstructed turret. Build it to get a sweeping view of the command post and the surrounding battlefield. Another elevated turret is on a pillar to the south.

THE CENTER

Both sides need to rush to the Center as quickly as possible. Don't expect the enemy to give up without a fight.

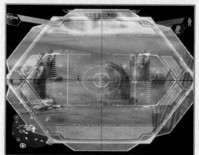

Both elevated turrets can be used to engage enemy targets at the Heads command post to the west.

INITIAL CONTROL: NEUTRAL
COMMAND POST TYPE: LIGHT

VEHICLES, TURRETS, & DROIDS

Unit	Count
Gun Turrets	4
Medical Droid	1
Ammo Droid	1
Repair Droid	1

Appropriately named the Center, this command post is in the middle of the battlefield and is often the site of intense fighting. Both sides have an equal opportunity of taking this command post first, especially when speed and coordination are used. But capturing this command post doesn't mean holding it. Unless defenders are posted around the perimeter, a captor has a tough time holding this position.

Fortunately, four turrets are available, but two of them (flanking the command post) have limited fields of view, making it difficult to engage targets at long range. The two other turrets sit atop stone columns to the north and south, offering a sweeping view of the battlefield. From these positions it's possible to hit incoming targets from all directions. Consider using these elevated turrets to assist your forces attacking the Heads command post to the west.

THE PILLARS

The Pillars command post is somewhat sheltered from the rest of the battlefield, sandwiched between a hill and a small grove of trees.

INITIAL CONTROL: SEPARATIST BATTLE DROIDS/GALACTIC EMPIRE
COMMAND POST TYPE: LIGHT

VEHICLES, TURRETS, & DROIDS

Unit	Count
Gun Turrets	5
Medical Droid	1
Ammo Droid	1
Repair Droid	1

naboo: plains

The Pillars is the second command post held by the CIS forces at the outset of the battle. It sits on a hill to the east and is one of the toughest command posts for the clones to capture. This command post is close to the Center and the Redoubt; it features five turrets, giving this position even more defensive teeth. The Separatists should use this position to spawn the droidekas needed to assault the Center at the start of the battle.

A couple of pilots should be able to construct all five defensive turrets before the enemy can stage an attack.

If the Separatists lose this command post, they have a hard time retaking it without a well-coordinated attack plan.

THE HEADS

This command post sits on an open plain, with nothing more than a few stone ruins for cover.

Situated on a relatively flat plain, the Heads command post gets its name from the ancient head-shaped sculptures surrounding the area. These heads provide some cover and concealment from an otherwise open position. Like the Redoubt, this command post is controlled by the clones at the start of the battle. They should use pilots to set up the four turrets before the droids attack.

The turrets are useful against infantry attacks, but useless against armor. For this reason, defenders must reinforce this position with armor of their own. At the very least, use anti-tank units to drive back enemy attacks. They can hide in or around the ruins and pop out to attack when enemy armor draws near.

Using cover here is extremely important, because the command post itself is extremely susceptible to bombardment by tanks and air units. This command post probably changes hands several times in the course of the battle.

The command post's gun turrets can be taken out rather easily, so use the stone ruins for cover.

Pop out from behind cover to engage enemy units, then duck out of sight before they can retaliate.

When defending, watch for fast-moving units rushing toward the command post. Deal with them before they convert it.

INITIAL CONTROL: REPUBLIC CLONE ARMY/REBEL ALLIANCE

COMMAND POST TYPE: LIGHT

VEHICLES, TURRETS, & DROIDS

Unit	Count
Gun Turrets	4
Medical Droid	1
Ammo Droid	1
Repair Droid	1

CLONE ARMY STRATEGY

The most immediate threat to a clone victory are the Separatist AATs. You must take these out quickly, but spend the first few moments of the battle securing the neutral command post. Have pilots use the two Kaadu at the Redoubt to capture the Center. When they arrive, they can construct the laser turrets. Meanwhile, send tank units to help reinforce the Heads and Center.

If your team can successfully hold the Center, the Redoubt, and the Heads, the Separatist reinforcements begin draining away. But you won't be able to hold the command posts very long if the AATs go unchallenged. The best way to deal with this threat is to attack with the Jedi starfighter. Using homing missiles, the Jedi starfighter can inflict heavy damage on the enemy armor. Your tank units should also concentrate their fire on the AATs. Combined air and ground attacks should reduce the AATs to flaming wreckage within moments.

As long as the Separatists control the Command to the south, new AATs continue to spawn. Take aggressive steps to capture this post, even if it means losing one of the central positions. Denying the Separatists their AATs tremendously increases your chances of victory.

Hit the Separatist staging area with a coordinated assault. Use the Jedi starfighter to take out the Command's turrets.

When the defenses are down, the Jedi starfighter should stay in the area and provide support while ground units move in to capture the Command.

If needed, the Jedi starfighter can land and its crew can secure the position.

SEPARATIST STRATEGY

Get to the Center as quickly as possible and secure it. A few droidekas work well for this task.

As with the clone army, the Separatists find it best to go for the neutral command post first. Use the two STAPs to get pilot droids to these positions, then follow up with droidekas to provide cover while the gun turrets are constructed. Split the AAT force between the Heads and Center command posts to deal with any clone armor that might threaten your new position. Rush the Heads with AATs and take out any constructed turrets to help secure the area before droids rush in.

Holding the Heads, the Center, and the Pillars will make containing the clones much easier. Build a solid line of AATs and droidekas across the center of the battlefield and blast anything that moves.

Expect to encounter heavy armor resistance between the Center and the Heads command posts. Use the AATs to engage the enemy tanks.

TIP When attacking the Redoubt, try to drive a wedge between the command post and the hill to the west, where the clone vehicles spawn. Preventing the enemy from reaching their vehicles increases your chances of taking over the Redoubt.

For the easiest victory, try to manage the battle so that the clone army is left with the Center command post. If you hold four out of five command posts, their reinforcements wither away while your forces squeeze them from all directions. Plus, if you capture the Redoubt, they won't have any vehicle spawn points. Instead of attacking the Center, simply hold back and defend the surrounding command posts.

naboo: plains

Rush the Heads command post with AATs and knock out all the turrets.

If the other command posts are already controlled, lay siege to the Redoubt. As the clone forces grow weak, send in droidekas and droids on STAPs to rush in and capture it.

TACTICS

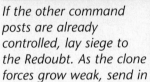
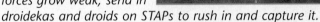

TANK BUSTING

Tank battles are common on the battlefield, particularly during the opening few minutes. After all, taking out enemy tanks should be the primary focus of your own tank units.

But infantry units can lend a hand when it comes to blowing away armor. Units like this anti-armor droid can often tilt the odds in your team's favor.

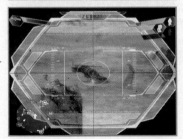

The battlefield's various gun turrets can help. Use them at long range, where you're less likely to draw the tank's attention. If the tank turns toward you, vacate the turret immediately.

To prevent command posts from being overrun by enemy armor, lay some mines. Place minefields in areas where the enemy is most likely to break through. Surrounding the command post with mines isn't a bad idea.

AIR SUPPORT

The clones' Jedi starfighter is a valuable unit, particularly when it comes to taking out enemy armor. Instead of staying low to the ground, gain some altitude before making an attack run. While climbing, use the map to keep an eye on your position over the battlefield.

Lower the starfighter's nose to begin an attack run. The high altitude gives you more time to attack, and the steep attack angle reduces your chances of being noticed by your intended target.

When you need repairs or more missiles, return to the Redoubt and land near the droid between the hill and the command post. Resupply takes a couple of seconds. Repair takes longer, depending on the extent of the damage. Damage should never be too extensive if a pilot unit is operating the starfighter.

BATTLE HINT

At the start of the battle, take the neutral Center CP right away. From the Center, launch attacks on your enemy's primary command post, either the Command or the Redoubt, and cut off their supply of vehicles. Always stay in a vehicle when engaging in combat. Even riding a Kaduu gives you a speed advantage that can be the difference between life and death. If an aircraft is available, take it and hold on to it for as long as possible. Air power is dominant in battles on this map.

by Tester James Morris

NABOO: THEED

planetary overview

The canals and bridges of Theed are the pride and joy of the peaceful planet Naboo. However, as a result of the growing galactic conflict, Theed has seen its graceful gardens transformed into a battleground. The streets of Theed vary from open avenues and plazas to narrow back streets, alleys, and cul-de-sacs. Any commander worth his salt uses the buildings as cover to set up ambushes and escapes down narrow streets to avoid direct fire from heavy combat vehicles.

Control of the Royal Palace is key to claiming the city. The large river that bisects the city is passable in only three areas—control of these bridges is essential to victory.

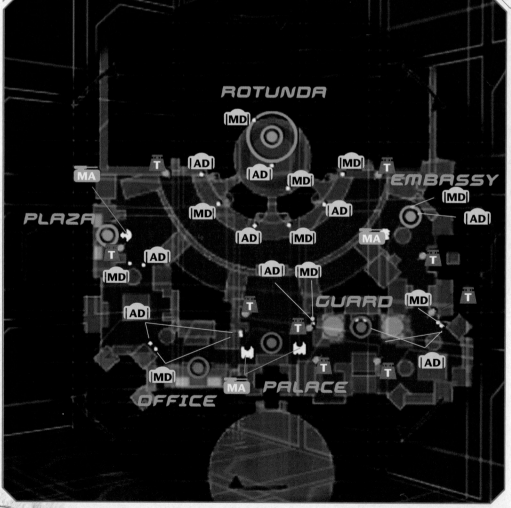

Legend

T	Turret
S	Scout Vehicle
MA	Medium Assault Vehicle
AW	Assault walker
HT	Heavy Assault Transport
FC	Fighter Craft
AT	Air Transoprt
B	Bomber
SC	Special Craft
C	Creature
AD	Ammo Droid
MD	Medical Droid
RD	Repair Droid

naboo: theed

COMMAND POSTS

THE OFFICE

The Office command post sits on this balcony, just west of the Palace.

INITIAL CONTROL: REPUBLIC CLONE ARMY/GALACTIC EMPIRE
COMMAND POST TYPE: LIGHT

VEHICLES, TURRETS, & DROIDS

Unit	Count
Medical Droid	1
Ammo Droid	1

Sandwiched between the Palace and the Plaza, the Office acts as a buffer protecting the Palace's western flank. Nothing more than a couple of droids are positioned by the large fountain, so defending this area is the job of infantry units. The clones should spawn a few ARC troopers here to hold back attacks from the west.

The fountain to the command post's northwest acts like a small barricade, slowing any armor attacks from this direction. To close off this avenue entirely, place mines on both sides of the fountain. If an AAT from the Plaza attempts to attack the Palace along this street, it runs into the mines.

The fountain to the west creates a choke point in the street. Place mines around the fountain, then take to the balcony to fire down on incoming infantry.

If enemies make it past the fountain, watch the stairway to prevent infiltration.

THE PALACE

The courtyard in front of the Palace is filled with decorative planters that attackers use for cover. Defenders should use the surrounding balconies to fire down on the incoming assault.

INITIAL CONTROL: REPUBLIC CLONE ARMY/GALACTIC EMPIRE
COMMAND POST TYPE: LIGHT

VEHICLES, TURRETS, & DROIDS

Unit	Count
IF T-X/IF T-T	2/2
Gun Turret	3
Medical Droid	2
Ammo Droid	2

Because of its central location and valuable assets, the Palace is the single most important command post on the map. Take great pains to defend or capture it. When controlled by the Clone Army, the command post spawns two IF T-X tanks. If the Separatists manage to convert it, two AATs spawn near the Palace gates, giving the droids a tremendous advantage.

The courtyard in front of the command post is relatively open, making the area easy to defend from a frontal assault, thanks to the two turrets. The side streets to the east and west pose the biggest challenges for defenders. The turret flanking the Palace gate can cover the eastern street (leading to the Embassy), but take other defensive measures as well in case the turret is destroyed.

To the west is another street that lacks defensive features, making a blindside attack from the Plaza a certainty. Defenders on this western street may want to use the surrounding balconies and fire down on the incoming attackers. Mining this passage is also a good idea; enemy units from the Plaza are likely to attack with armor.

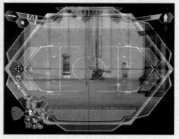

Try jumping in one of the planters for better concealment. The planter just west of the gate is a good spot for snipers covering the street leading to the Plaza.

THE GUARD

The Guard command post is in this nook just east of the Palace. Jet troopers can cover this area from the balcony to the south.

INITIAL CONTROL: REPUBLIC CLONE ARMY/GALACTIC EMPIRE COMMAND POST TYPE: LIGHT	
VEHICLES, TURRETS, & DROIDS	
Unit	Count
Gun Turret	1
Medical Droid	1
Ammo Droid	1

The Guard, like the Office command post, is a no-frills position on the Palace's eastern flank. The clones want to deploy more ARC troopers here, as well as a pilot to construct the turret to the east. This turret is the command post's only defense against droid attacks originating from the Embassy. Mines come in handy, too, especially since an AAT spawns at the Embassy.

A fountain is at a bend in the street to the east. Mine this narrow area to prevent armor attacks. The turret can repel most other attacks, but infantry support is needed too.

Man this turret to the east at all times. Pick off enemies as they round the corner near the fountain.

THE EMBASSY

A large fountain outside the Embassy provides some cover for defenders.

INITIAL CONTROL: SEPARATIST BATTLE DROIDS/REBEL ALLIANCE COMMAND POST TYPE: LIGHT	
VEHICLES, TURRETS, & DROIDS	
Unit	Count
AAT/Combat Speeder	1/1
Gun Turret	3
Medical Droid	1
Ammo Droid	1

The courtyard in front of the Embassy is bound to be hotly contested. Compared to the Palace and the Rotunda, the Embassy's defensive features are relatively light, offering only one turret within direct view of the command post. Another turret lies to the south, covering the street leading to the Guard and the Palace. A third turret sits outside the main arch to the north, but has little impact once enemy units have infiltrated the courtyard. Like the Plaza, this one spawns an AAT for the CIS forces.

The turret near the command post can be used to engage enemy units approaching from the Rotunda. Zoom in to pick them off at long range.

A second turret sits just outside the archway to the north. This is best suited for engaging enemies crossing the easternmost bridge leading from the Rotunda.

naboo: theed

THE ROTUNDA

A small river separates the Rotunda from the rest of the city.

INITIAL CONTROL: SEPARATIST BATTLE DROIDS/REBEL ALLIANCE
COMMAND POST TYPE: LIGHT

VEHICLES, TURRETS, & DROIDS

Unit	Count
Medical Droid	2
Ammo Droid	1

Sitting to the north across the river, the Rotunda presents a unique challenge to both attackers and defenders. Three small footbridges connect the Rotunda to the rest of the city. Defenders should use these bridges as choke points, concentrating their fire on these narrow passages to prevent enemy infantry units from crossing. The command post offers no gun turrets; its defense relies solely on infantry. Anti-tank infantry work particularly well, blasting enemies off the bridges with missiles and mines.

But keep an eye out for unorthodox attacks. Instead of using the bridges, the clones are likely to try an aerial assault, using their jet troopers to bypass any defensive efforts at the bridges. If the clones take control of the Rotunda, they have a slightly easier time holding it, because the Separatists have no air units. Armor is also less effective when attacking the Rotunda, which is isolated to the southern bank of the river where trees partially obstruct their view.

Mines and other explosive ordnance make crossing the bridges risky for attackers.

Clone jet troopers have the best luck infiltrating the Rotunda, bypassing the bridges altogether.

The Rotunda has only one supply droid, so defenders must back away from the bridges to stock up on ammo.

THE PLAZA

The Plaza gives the Separatists a presence on the western side of the city as well as an AAT.

INITIAL CONTROL: SEPARATIST BATTLE DROIDS/REBEL ALLIANCE
COMMAND POST TYPE: LIGHT

VEHICLES, TURRETS, & DROIDS

Unit	Count
AAT/Combat Speeder	1/1
GunTurret	2
Medical Droid	1
Ammo Droid	1

The Plaza is another staging area for the Separatist attack. Like the Embassy, this command post spawns one AAT. But the AAT might be best used to defend this command post, as there's only one laser turret within the Plaza. Like the Embassy, it has another turret, sitting outside the arch to the north. This can be used to hold back attacks along the street running parallel to the river, but it won't help repel direct attacks on the command post.

The command post sits on a balcony to the far west and can be accessed via two stairways to the north and south. Defenders may place mines at the tops of these steps to deter attackers.

Place mines at the top of the steps leading up to the balcony—attackers are less likely to see them here as they rush up the steps.

Toss another mine near the command post to surprise any jet troopers attempting an aerial assault.

Consider using the Plaza's AAT to defend against enemy attacks near this fountain to the south.

CLONE ARMY STRATEGY

Start by attacking the Plaza. Move along the street west of the Palace, but expect a firefight with a droid assault force near this fountain.

The key to pulling off a quick victory is to isolate the Separatists at the Rotunda. This means taking the Plaza and the Embassy while holding the three other command posts. Attack the Plaza along the street just west of the Palace command post. At the same time, brace for attacks at the Guard and Office command posts. Use pilots to construct the turrets and ARC troopers to lay mines.

Even if your attacks on the Plaza and Embassy are unsuccessful, the Palace must be held at all costs. Assuming the Plaza and Embassy are taken and you retain the other command posts within the city, start moving your units north, toward the Rotunda. But don't attempt to capture it. Instead, hold on the south side of the river and blast the droids as they move across the three bridges. Use armor to patrol the street south of the river and mop up any droids that break free. By containing the

droids to the Rotunda, you will inflict heavy casualties and impose a reinforcement drain. Most important, they won't have access to any tanks.

Capture the Plaza and Embassy while holding the other command posts in the city.

Keep the Separatists pinned at the Rotunda. Position sharpshooters on this balcony and pick off the droids on the opposite side of the river as they attempt a counterattack.

If your plan goes horribly wrong and the Palace is captured, consider making your last stand at the Rotunda—assuming you can capture it. The key to winning at the Rotunda is letting the attackers come to you. Mine the bridges and take cover within the Rotunda while waiting for the droids to attack. Falling back to the Rotunda takes the Separatist AATs out of the battle, effectively leveling the playing field.

To halt the reinforcement drain, try some breakout attacks using a small squad of jet troopers. There's a chance the jet troopers can convert a command post, especially if the droids are preoccupied with the siege of the Rotunda.

AATs can't cross the bridges leading to the Rotunda, but they can blast anyone that tries to cross. If stuck at the Rotunda, stay there and let the droids come to you.

naboo: Theed

SEPARATIST STRATEGY

Take the Palace first. Get a few droidekas to the Palace gate to convert the command post.

The Separatists need to move out quickly, striking the clone positions before they have a chance to fortify them with turrets and mines. Start by attacking the Palace, hitting it from the north and east simultaneously. Send units from the Rotunda south to attack the Palace head-on while moving the AAT and troops from the Embassy along the southern street. This two-pronged attack should secure the Separatists a quick victory.

Capturing the Palace gives the Separatists access to two more AATs, bringing their total to four. Use these tanks to surround the Guard and Office command posts and pound the clones into submission. While laying siege to the clone positions, make sure the other three command posts are still well defended by infantry. The clones are likely to attempt a breakout attack using jet troopers. Always make sure the AATs are occupied as soon as they spawn. If the clones manage to capture an AAT at the Embassy or Plaza, your victory is not certain.

Use the Palace as a spawn point for droidekas and keep assaulting the Office and Guard command posts until they fall.

TACTICS

ROTUNDA LOCKDOWN

Place mines on all three bridges leading to the Rotunda. One mine per bridge should be more than enough.

Watch the bridges for an attack and be prepared to place new mines as needed. Watch for the mine's red glow. If you don't see it, the mine has probably been detonated.

Anti-tank weapons like this droid's rocket launcher also come in handy for keeping the bridges clear.

BALCONY DEFENSE

Whenever possible, take the high ground. Theed is filled with balconies, including this position overlooking the main street just south of the river.

Some balconies feature high railings that can help provide cover. But you may need to crouch or drop prone to return fire.

JET TROOPER ASSAULT

The Rotunda

Jet troopers can reach elevated areas that other units can't, so put this ability to good use. When attacking the Rotunda, jump up to the rooftop of the one of the structures near one of the bridges.

NABOO: THEED

Pause on this rooftop and wait for the jet pack to recharge before making the next jump. Keep moving to avoid getting hit by the droid defenders.

When the jet pack is recharged, fly across the river and land on the Rotunda's rooftop.

When you set down on the rooftop, keep moving until you stop drawing fire. Fire down on enemies inside the Rotunda and swoop down to capture it once it's clear.

The Plaza

Jet troopers also come in handy for assaulting the Plaza. Take to the skies and bypass any droid defenses on the ground.

Watch for any mines near the command post before setting down on the balcony. A thermal detonator works well for clearing a landing area.

As soon as you land on the balcony, drop to a crouch to avoid taking fire from the ground below. Watch both stairways to the north and south to halt any counterattacks.

AAT THEFT PREVENTION

As the Separatists capture more command posts, there's a good chance a clone might try to slip past your lines and steal an AAT. To prevent this from happening, booby-trap the AAT spawn points by mining them with anti-armor droids.

For best results, move the AAT, place a few mines, then move it back over the mines; this helps conceal your trap. Mines only detonate when an enemy is nearby, so they won't explode until a clone tries to get inside the tank. The resulting explosion kills the thief and destroys the tank, preventing any of his friends from capturing it.

The same tactic can be used to prevent enemies from using your own gun turrets.

BATTLE HINT
The strategy I like to use on Naboo Theed is to spawn near a vehicle. Using a vehicle is the quickest way through the level. It gives you more protection and firepower while moving from CP to CP. As part of the Rebels in the Galactic Civil Wars, setting the combat speeder is your best bet. While as part of the Empire in the Galactic Civil Wars, setting the IFT-T is your vehicle of choice. In the Clone Wars, setting the IFT-X is the best choice as a clone trooper; while the CIS should use the AAT.
by Tester Diarmuid Bosse

BATTLE HINT
This level is tougher than the first. The Palace is probably the most important CP to take, to prevent its two vehicles from spawning in. However, take one of the outlying CPs first, so that your team can help you, as opposed to being crushed in a pincer attack.
by tester Xavier Rodriguez

KASHYYYK: ISLANDS

planetary overview

Kashyyyk is a lush world teeming with immense forests standing many kilometers tall. The planet has several horizontal levels of ecology throughout the trees; the Wookiees occupy the upper-most level and danger increases at each lower level. The mighty wroshyr trees have limbs so thickly intertwined that the Wookiees have perched cities in the natural cradle they form. Wookiee architecture uses many narrow catwalks and ladders that connect the large huts and platforms that aid in the defense of Wookiee cities.

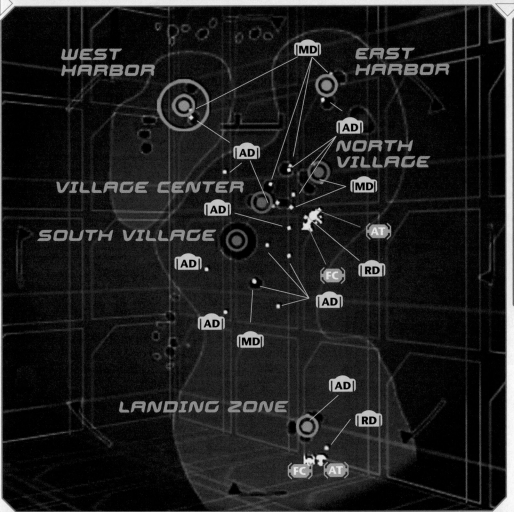

WEST HARBOR

EAST HARBOR

NORTH VILLAGE

VILLAGE CENTER

SOUTH VILLAGE

LANDING ZONE

Legend

T	Turret
S	Scout Vehicle
MA	Medium Assault Vehicle
AW	Assault walker
HT	Heavy Assault Transport
FC	Fighter Craft
AT	Air Transoprt
B	Bomber
SC	Special Craft
C	Creature
AD	Ammo Droid
MD	Medical Droid
RD	Repair Droid

COMMAND POSTS

WEST HARBOR

The West Harbor command post overlooks the Wookiee village to the southeast.

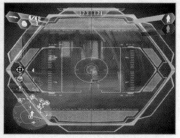

The surrounding command posts can also be covered from this position. Scour the North Village for defenders and pick them off. This helps if your team is attacking this position from the East Harbor.

INITIAL CONTROL: SEPARATIST BATTLE DROIDS/GALACTIC EMPIRE COMMAND POST TYPE: LIGHT	
VEHICLES, TURRETS, & DROIDS	
Unit	Count
Medical Droid	1
Ammo Droid	1

Droidekas should use the bridge to the east when crossing the harbor. If they're exposed to deep water, they take damage until they're destroyed.

Sitting on a hill in the northwest corner of the battlefield, the West Harbor is separated from the main island by a small stream running along its eastern side. A small bridge spans the harbor to the east, connecting this position with the East Harbor. But most attackers ford the stream rather than cross the bridge. Still, it's a good idea to mine the bridge. The high elevation of this command post provides a view of the clone-held village to the southeast, making this a great position for droid snipers. The command post itself sits in the open, between a couple of huts. The CIS forces may want to deploy a droideka nearby to defend it. Throwing some mines around the command post may deter clone jet trooper assaults too.

EAST HARBOR

The East Harbor completes the Separatist northern front, providing a good view of the North Village.

INITIAL CONTROL: SEPARATIST BATTLE DROIDS/GALACTIC EMPIRE COMMAND POST TYPE: LIGHT	
VEHICLES, TURRETS, & DROIDS	
Unit	Count
Medical Droid	1
Ammo Droid	1

From the command post's eastern side, you can fire down on attackers as they cross the stream. A droid assassin comes in handy for sniping the clones as they attempt to cross.

Its close proximity to the North Village makes the East Harbor a frequent site of intense fighting. Droid defenders should place units along the south side to prevent incoming attacks. The steep incline to the east is also a popular route for attackers attempting to flank the command post. But this position is also good for staging attacks on the village command posts. The CIS forces should use droidekas and assassin droids to provide cover fire while sending in units to attack the North Village.

kashyyyk: islands

Position a droideka on the southern side of the command post. From this spot it can fire on clone-held positions in the village while protecting the command post from attack.

Watch out for aerial assaults. The enemy may attempt to land troops on either the West or East Harbor command posts. Use anti-armor units to prevent such attacks.

NORTH VILLAGE

The North Village spawns a LAAT/I gunship and a Jedi starfighter for the clone army, making this a command post well worth defending.

INITIAL CONTROL: REPUBLIC CLONE ARMY/REBEL ALLIANCE
COMMAND POST TYPE: LIGHT

VEHICLES, TURRETS, & DROIDS

Unit	Count
Jedi Starfighter/X-wing	1/1
LAAT/I Gunship/Y-wing	1/1
Droid Starfighter/TIE Fighter *	1/1
MAF/TIE Bomber *	1/1
Medical Droid	2
Ammo Droid	3
Repair Droid	1

* Under Separatist/Empire control only

The North Village is one of the most important command posts on the map. Not only does it produce air units for whoever controls it, but, if captured by the droids attacking from the north, it also gives them a dangerous foothold within the village. Clone defenders need to reinforce the northern side of the command post using ARC troopers. Place mines in-between the wooden barricades where attackers are likely to break through.

Toss a few mines around the command post, too, including inside the nearby hut—the command post can be converted from within. Get clone troopers and sharp-shooters to the northern barricades and engage incoming attackers from the East Harbor. Watch out for flanking attacks originating from the West Harbor.

Use these wooden barricades to the north for cover. ARC troopers are useful for laying mines and attacking incoming droidekas—try to hit them before they deploy their shields.

Get the gunship and starfighter into the air quickly before the droids strafe them with their own air units.

The command post can be converted from within the nearby hut, offering some much needed cover. The droids inside can also be used to heal and resupply.

VILLAGE CENTER

This command post sits among a cluster of huts in the center of the Wookiee village.

INITIAL CONTROL: REPUBLIC CLONE ARMY/REBEL ALLIANCE
COMMAND POST TYPE: LIGHT

VEHICLES, TURRETS, & DROIDS

Unit	Count
Medical Droid	2
Ammo Droid	5

Appropriately, the Village Center command post is directly in the middle of the Wookiee village, surrounded by two huts and a fire pit. The open nature of the command post makes it difficult to defend, particularly from droideka rush attacks. For best results, place mines in the openings between the surrounding huts. Most attacks on this position originate from the West Harbor—assuming the North Village is held. Place defenders along the western side of the command post and use the wooden barricades for cover. The huts can also be used for concealment, but the small windows only offer limited fields of view.

There's no easy way to defend or attack this position, because the surrounding command posts provide plenty of reinforcements within striking range. If the droids take any of the village command posts, expect plenty of close combat in this area and spawn the appropriate units. Clone troopers, droidekas, and super battle droids can all hold their own here.

Take cover behind these wooden barricades to the west to engage attackers from the West Harbor.

Move closer to the stream to the west and ambush incoming droids with rapid fire and thermal detonators.

 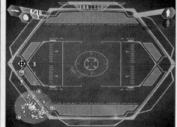

The huts near the command post make great sniping positions. Peer out the windows to pick off droids spawning at the West Harbor.

SOUTH VILLAGE

The South Village command post is located inside this large hut.

INITIAL CONTROL: REPUBLIC CLONE ARMY/REBEL ALLIANCE
COMMAND POST TYPE: HEAVY

VEHICLES, TURRETS, & DROIDS

Unit	Count
Medical Droid	1
Ammo Droid	4

Housed by a large hut, the South Village command post is relatively easy to defend. The slightly elevated hut can only be accessed via the short steps on the northern side. This means defenders have only one entrance to cover. Consider placing mines in the main doorway and around the command post. Sharpshooters can use the two windows to the south to pick off incoming attackers from the Landing Zone. But the large rectangular windows also make defenders susceptible to fire from the exterior. If defending from within, keep a low profile, especially if enemies are in the surrounding area.

Mine the entrance early in the battle to prevent rush attacks by droidekas.

The hut's slight elevation makes it useful for firing down on attackers. Use ARC troopers to wipe out droidekas before they make a run at the command post.

Turn to the west to engage droids crossing the stream. Saturating this choke point with missiles and sniper fire is a good way to repel attacks from the West Harbor.

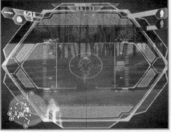

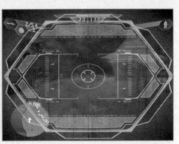

Position sharpshooters at the southern windows to pick off droids rushing the command post from the Landing Zone.

This hill to the west of the command post is an ideal sniping spot. Scan the areas in the village to find plenty of targets. It's also possible to attack enemies near the West Harbor from this position.

LANDING ZONE

The Landing Zone is the southernmost command post, providing the CIS forces a couple of air units.

Place some droidekas north of the command post. From this position they can blast any attacks from the north.

INITIAL CONTROL: SEPARATIST BATTLE DROIDS/GALACTIC EMPIRE
COMMAND POST TYPE: LIGHT

VEHICLES, TURRETS, & DROIDS

Unit	Count
Droid Starfighter/TIE Fighter	1/1
MAF/TIE Bomber	1/1
Jedi Starfighter/X-wing *	1/1
LAAT/I Gunship/Y-wing *	1/1
Medical Droid	1
Ammo Droid	1

* Under Clone Army/Rebel control only

Keep an eye on the western and eastern coastlines, too, to prevent flanking attacks.

CLONE ARMY STRATEGY

Lead an assault on the Landing Zone command post in an effort to eliminate the Separatist's southern front.

Located to the far south, the Landing Zone allows the Separatists to hit the clone positions from a different direction, equalizing pressure on the village command posts. The command post also provides an MAF and droid starfighter, giving the droids a presence in the air. These craft should be used to attack the clone air units and make frequent strafing runs on their defensive positions.

Isolated to the south, the command post is relatively easy to defend with all attacks approaching from the north. Position a droideka or two on the northern side of the command post's huts to cover this avenue of attack. A hill to the west provides a better view of the village. Consider placing some assassin droids here to pick off enemies as far away as the West Harbor.

At the start of the battle, the clones are being squeezed from all directions. Take off some of this pressure by staging an attack on the Landing Zone to the south while holding firm at the village command posts.

Hit the Landing Zone from the ground and air using the LAAT/I gunship and troopers spawned at the South Village. Use the gunship to clear out any defenders as the troopers rush in to capture the command post.

If clear, the crew of the gunship can land and secure the position. Capturing the Landing Zone eliminates the

CIS presence to the south while denying them their air units. You also gain one more gunship and an extra starfighter, which can be used for strafing runs.

Use the gunship to strafe enemy positions while your troopers hold back attacks on the ground.

Now bolster your defenses around the Village Center and North Village. With only two command posts under their control, the Separatists suffer a reinforcement drain. But this also means that their forces will be more concentrated to the north. Hold tight at your current positions and wait for the enemy units to dwindle away. Use your air units to strafe the clusters of droids rushing toward your positions.

As the Separatists weaken, send an assault force from the North Village to capture the East Harbor. Flank the command post from the east and wipe out any defenders at close range. Now you can contain the droids at the West Harbor while waiting for their reinforcements to run out.

Rush along the coastline to flank the East Harbor, then turn west to capture the command post.

Separatist Strategy

Strike the North Village with a mix of super battle droids and droidekas.

The Separatists start the battle from an advantageous position, with the clones surrounded at the village. But they need to gain a foothold inside the village before they can start dishing out serious damage. Strengthen defenses at the Landing Zone and West Harbor while assembling a strike force of super battle droids and droidekas at the East Harbor.

When air support is available, move the strike force against the North Village. Attack straight ahead with the super battle droids, while the droidekas flank the position from the east. This way they can get behind the barricaded positions and blast the defenders at close range. Keep pushing against the North Village until it's captured. This takes away the clone air units, and gives your team two more air units—an MAF and a droid starfighter.

While squeezing the clones at the village, conduct strafing runs with your air units to thin out the defenses. Target the various ammo droids, too, to hinder their ability to restock their ARC troopers with missiles.

In the village, start spawning droidekas to assault the other command posts. Try hitting the South Village with units spawned from the Landing Zone. Meanwhile, squeeze the clones at the Village Center by pressing from the North Village and West Harbor. Instead of assaulting these positions, slowly encircle them and inflict casualties as their reinforcements drain away. The clones may attempt breakout attacks using their jet troopers, so maintain a defensive presence at all of your command posts.

Spawn droidekas inside the village and use them to lay waste to defenders while slowly advancing on the remaining command posts.

Tactics

Droideka Carnage

The Separatist droidekas are absolutely devastating if they manage to infiltrate the village. For best results, they should always travel in pairs.

When danger is encountered, they should deploy their shields and begin the attack. In the thick of it, they should maintain this attack configuration.

The clone's Jedi starfighter is clearly the best craft for establishing air superiority, thanks to its missiles. Remember, you can stock up on more missiles by landing near a repair droid. There's one at the Landing Zone and another at the North Village.

Two droidekas are also great for defending command posts. This way they can cover each other's backs, helping compensate for their slow movement.

The Separatist MAF also poses a serious threat for air units. Be careful when trailing this craft because it has a top-mounted turret with a 360-degree turning radius. Keep your distance and blast it with missiles.

The clone's LAAT/I gunship is sluggish by comparison, but it's capable of carrying five troopers. Use it to open new fronts by transporting troopers and launching surprise attacks on distant command posts. The Landing Zone is a good candidate for such aerial assaults.

Of the village-based command posts, the droidekas have the best chance of taking and holding the South Village command post. Rush up the steps and clear out any defenders. Then turn to face the doorway and dare the clones to counterattack.

TIP

The clones need to strike the droidekas before they can deploy their shields. Otherwise, it's best to take cover and wait for their shields to run low on power. When the shield is down, pop out and hit them with everything you've got.

AIR SUPREMACY

Whoever makes it into the air first should make a strafing pass at the enemy's air units, with the droids hitting the North Village and the clones striking the Landing Zone.

Both factions want to make it to their air units fast and take off. Otherwise the enemy air units may blast your craft on the ground.

BATTLE HINT

AI units commandeer vehicles quickly on this level, so if you want to have air superiority, spawn at either the North Village or Landing, depending on your faction, and immediately head for a vehicle. If piloting the MAF, LA-AT, TIE bomber, or Y-wing, use the right directional D-Pad to order AI troops to fill other positions in the vehicle (e.g. co-pilot, bomber, gunner). The key command posts to capture are the Landing and Village Center. Snipers have "high ground" advantage, and thus good visibility, from either of the Harbor command posts. Several of the huts have supply droids inside, with open views of the battle—these are good "camping" spots.

by Tester Greg Quinones

BATTLE HINT

Xavier's way: Take the droideka and start from the East Harbor and capture the North Village. Once you have this, use the droideka to move inward, or respond quickly if the Wookiees get too close to the West Harbor.

Ahmad's way: Start from the Landing Zone and use one of the droid starfighters to pick off Wookiees before they get to your CPs.

by Testers Xavier Rodriguez and Ahmad Abbott

GEONOSIS: SPIRE

planetary overview

Geonosis is a ringed planet, located along the outer rim of the galaxy, near Tatooine. Its uninviting surface is marked by mesas, buttes, and barren stretches of parched desert hardpan. The rocks and sky are tinted red. The creatures that evolved on Geonosis are well equipped to survive in the harsh terrain. Geonosis is also home to sentient insectoids that inhabit towering spire-hives.

The Geonosians, as they are known, maintain large factories for the production of droids and weapons. The droid foundries and the planet's remote location make it an ideal base of operations.

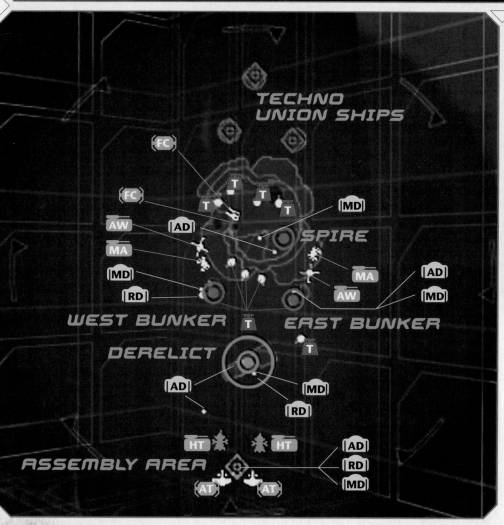

Legend

T	Turret
S	Scout Vehicle
MA	Medium Assault Vehicle
AW	Assault walker
HT	Heavy Assault Transport
FC	Fighter Craft
AT	Air Transoprt
B	Bomber
SC	Special Craft
C	Creature
AD	Ammo Droid
MD	Medical Droid
RD	Repair Droid

geonosis: spire

COMMAND POSTS

ASSEMBLY AREA

This command platform can be destroyed, denying the clones a spawn point.

INITIAL CONTROL: REPUBLIC CLONE ARMY
COMMAND POST TYPE: N/A (DESTRUCTIBLE)

VEHICLES, TURRETS, & DROIDS

Unit	Count
AT-TE	2
LAAT/I Gunship	2
Medical Droid	1
Ammo Droid	1

The Assembly Area isn't a true command post because it can't be captured. But it can be destroyed by the CIS forces. This position serves as the staging area for the clone army, meaning that their forces can spawn here throughout the battle unless the command platform is destroyed. If the platform is destroyed, the AT-TEs continue spawning nearby, but the LAAT/I gunships do not, giving the clones even more reason to secure this area. It's imperative to the clone army to keep these vehicles from falling into enemy hands.

If you want to catch a ride on a gunship, this is the place to spawn.

The command platform is tough to destroy. The droids must attack with vehicles to take it out.

DERELICT

The race is on to capture the map's central command post.

INITIAL CONTROL: REPUBLIC CLONE ARMY
COMMAND POST TYPE: LIGHT

VEHICLES, TURRETS, & DROIDS

Unit	Count
Medical Droid	1
Ammo Droid	1

The Derelict provides the clones with a good defensive buffer for protecting the Assembly Area. If this position isn't adequately defended early on, however, it can be rushed by droidekas from either the western or eastern Bunkers. Attackers must enter the hollowed-out hull of the crashed ship to convert the command post.

The most direct path into this cavernlike command post is through the western side. A small hole along the south side of the ship also provides access, giving the droids a slight advantage in the early moments of the battle. When captured, the command post is relatively easy to protect as long as defenders stay beneath the cover of the ship's hollow hull. Most attacks come from the western side, but hull breaches to the north and south should be covered too.

Defenders might try dropping prone and firing through the low openings on the ship's north side. But huddling in the cramped confines of the ship's hull makes defenders extremely vulnerable to explosive attacks, so don't concentrate too many defenders inside.

Drop prone to shoot through these openings to the north.

This narrow hull breach to the south can be used to infiltrate the command post. Defenders may want to mine this spot.

It's possible to hop up on the wrecked ship for a better view of the battlefield, but that leaves you vulnerable to attacks of all kinds.

WESTERN BUNKER

The sonic blaster is useful for keeping attackers away from the southern path leading up to the command post.

INITIAL CONTROL: SEPARATIST BATTLE DROIDS
COMMAND POST TYPE: LIGHT

VEHICLES, TURRETS, & DROIDS

Unit	Count
Spider Walker	1
Hailfire Droid	1
Geonosian Sonic Blaster	1
Medical Droid	1

This command post makes up the right flank of the CIS front lines at the start of the battle. Located at the southwest base of the Spire, this command post (along with its eastern counterpart) is likely to see heavy fighting throughout the conflict. The droids want to hold on to this position because it provides them with a spider walker and a hailfire droid that spawn to the south, just west of the Spire. These vehicles are essential in stopping the clone AT-TEs.

The command post sits on a raised spire and can only be accessed via a small ramp along the southern side. This path is partly protected by a single sonic blaster, just west of the command post. The sonic blaster is useful for pushing away enemy infantry, whether they approach from the north, south, or west; the command post's spire blocks the eastern approach. Attackers have an easy time converting this position by getting right next to the command post and dropping prone.

When attacking this position, rush up to the command post and drop prone. The surrounding rocks provide cover from incoming fire as you convert the position. But a well-tossed thermal detonator could still ruin your day.

This medical droid to the south is tucked away from the chaos of the battle-field. But avoid standing still while healing—an enemy sniper near the Spire may be using the droid as bait.

EASTERN BUNKER

A sonic blaster is positioned right next to this command post.

INITIAL CONTROL: SEPARATIST BATTLE DROIDS
COMMAND POST TYPE: LIGHT

VEHICLES, TURRETS, & DROIDS

Unit	Count
Spider Walker	1
Hailfire Droid	1
Geonosian Sonic Blaster	1
Medical Droid	1
Ammo Droid	1

The Eastern Bunker is nearly a mirror image of its western counterpart, spawning the same types of vehicles for the CIS forces. But there are some differences, mainly the location of the sonic blaster right next to the command post. From this elevated position, the sonic blaster has a clear view of the southern approach. But it can also spin around and cover the ramp to the north, preventing enemy troops from infiltrating the command post.

Unlike the Western Bunker, this one features an ammo droid, located right next the medical droid to the south. When defending, spawn anti-armor troops here and use the ammo droid to keep them replenished with rockets.

For the droids, anti-armor units are useful for shooting down the clone gunships and mining the pass to the north leading toward the Techno Union ships.

Anti-armor units, like this droid, can use this position to attack both air and ground units without worrying about running out of munitions. The ammo droid (to the south) provides an endless supply of rockets.

Attackers need to catch the defending sonic blaster operator by surprise. Otherwise reaching the command post may prove difficult.

THE SPIRE

The Spire command post can be converted from any spot inside this circular war room.

INITIAL CONTROL: SEPARATIST BATTLE DROIDS
COMMAND POST TYPE: HEAVY

VEHICLES, TURRETS, & DROIDS

Unit	Count
Geonosian Fighter	2
Geonosian Sonic Blaster	7
Medical Droid	1
Ammo Droid	1

This centrally located command post is extremely valuable to both factions. For the droids, it provides two Geonosian fighters, a key to stopping the clone AT-TEs. Denying the CIS forces access to these fighters is the main reason the clones need to capture this early in the battle—but it won't be easy.

A total of seven sonic blasters (three to the south, four to the north) surround the Spire and are capable of pushing attackers away as they attempt to gain entry. The command post is in a cavernous war room along with a medical droid and an ammo droid. This room can be accessed by ground from three separate corridors, one to the north and two to the south.

Inside the war room, a corridor to the west leads to a hangar where the two fighters spawn. The hangar opening is also a potential entry point for clone jet troopers. As a result, droid defenders want to keep an eye on each corridor. If attackers reach the war room, the command post is contested.

The holographic table in the center of the room shows a simulation of enemy vehicles on the battlefield, which doesn't reflect the actual position of vehicles. It also provides decent cover in a firefight, especially if the combatant is crouched.

Four corridors lead into the war room. Defenders may want to place mines in each, including the corridor leading from the hangar. Clone jet troopers can fly through this wide opening to the west.

The cliff to the south provides an elevated view of the battlefield. Use the sonic blasters to push back enemy troops and attack enemy air units with rockets.

TIP

The spire is also the spawn point for the Geonosians. These insectlike creatures are more of a nuisance than a threat, but the clones want to take their presence into account before staging an assault on the spire. If the clones capture the spire, the Geonosians stop spawning.

TECHNO UNION SHIPS

The three Techno Union ships are destructible spawn points used by the CIS forces.

INITIAL CONTROL: SEPARATIST BATTLE DROIDS
COMMAND POST TYPE: N/A (DESTRUCTIBLE)

The three Techno Union ships to the north are the primary targets of the clone army. These ships serve as a spawn points for the CIS forces, but they offer no vehicles, turrets, or droids to help in their defense. Still, the droids want to keep these ships safe—as long as they're intact, the CIS reinforcements cannot be drained.

The biggest threats are the clone army's AT-TEs. The LAAT/I gunships also pose a threat, so the Separatists should be ready with anti-armor droids. If the ships sustain damage during the battle, pilots can repair them, but this can often turn into a full-time job if left to one droid. Several droid pilots working together can keep the ships in tip-top shape.

Pilot units are useful for repairing the ships if they sustain damage.

When repairing the ships, use the support legs for cover.

The AT-TEs are the quickest way for the clones to destroy these ships. But moving these slow beasts across the map can be treacherous.

CLONE ARMY STRATEGY

Use the AT-TEs to take out the various sonic blasters while moving them north toward the Techno Union ships.

A clone victory relies heavily on team communication and coordination—not to mention keeping your vehicles alive. Begin by getting your AT-TEs moving, one along the eastern side, the other to the west. The AT-TEs need to make it to the Techno Union ships as quickly as possible. Along the way, use them to engage the CIS sonic blaster positions. Taking these out allows your infantry to advance on the Eastern and Western Bunkers.

Use the gunships to protect the AT-TEs from enemy vehicles. Shooting down the Geonosian fighters should be high on the priority list too.

As the AT-TEs plod along to the north, the gunships should provide close air support, taking out the CIS spider walkers, hailfire droids, and Geonosian fighters. These enemy vehicles all pose serious threats to the AT-TEs and must be taken out quickly. After you destroy these enemy units, make attack runs on the Techno Union ships and any sonic blasters harassing your troops on the ground. Remember, protecting the AT-TEs is the primary objective.

Jet troopers can infiltrate the Spire through this hangar opening to the west.

When the AT-TE moving along the western pass moves near the Spire, use it to spawn jet troopers and stage an attack on the command post. The jet troopers can gain entry through the hangar opening on the Spire's western side. Once inside, they need to clear out any defenders in the war room and convert the command post. Once the Spire is captured, it must be held at all costs, even if it means losing command posts to the south.

Pound the Techno Union ships with the AT-TEs until they're all destroyed.

If both AT-TEs make it to the Techno Union ships, the assault should go rather smoothly. Use the gunships to provide cover while the AT-TEs reduce the enemy ships to rubble. When the Techno Union ships are destroyed, backtrack to the south and use the AT-TEs to spearhead assaults on the eastern and western command posts. If those assaults go well, you can squeeze the remaining CIS forces at Derelict while their reinforcements begin draining away. Imposing a reinforcement drain is the easiest way to ensure a clone victory.

When the Techno Union ships are taken out, use the AT-TEs to capture the remaining enemy command posts. Bombard their positions while spawning troops to capture the command posts.

Separatist Strategy

Use droidekas to rush Derelict and convert the command post. Infiltrate the wreck through the southern breach.

As the defenders, the CIS forces have it much easier than the clone army. Still, the droids need to concentrate on holding their vehicle-producing command posts to push back the clone attack and prevent them from reaching the Techno Union ships. The most valuable assets to the defense are the two Geonosian fighters. Use them to attack the AT-TEs. A few strafing passes will be sufficient to take them out. Keep an eye on the clone gunships too. They can destroy the Techno Union ships on their own.

Get the Geonosian fighters in the air and start harassing the enemy AT-TEs. Once they're down, attack the Assembly Area.

On the ground, turn the sonic blasters on the incoming clone troopers to keep them away from your command posts. Anti-armor droids are also extremely effective. Use them to shoot down the clone gunships with their rockets. Also, consider mining the passes to the east and west of the Spire. These are choke points through which the AT-TEs must pass to reach the Techno Union ships.

In the meantime, use the spider walkers and hailfire droids to harass the AT-TEs and enemy infantry. Individually, the CIS ground vehicles don't stand a chance against the massive firepower of an AT-TE. Instead, coordinate your attacks on one AT-TE at a time. By protecting the Techno Union ships and the Spire, you can inflict heavy casualties on the clone army and win the battle.

Launch coordinated attacks on the AT-TEs with spider walkers and hailfire droids. For best results, attack from the side where their fore and aft guns can't target you.

The hailfire droids are also very effective against the clone gunships. Use their rockets to shoot them down.

TIP

Remember, the AT-TEs are mobile spawn points. As long as they're on the battlefield, it'll be harder to impose a reinforcement drain.

TACTICS

MINE THE PASSES

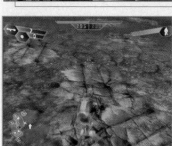

The eastern and western passes flanking the Spire are the only paths leading to the Techno Union ships. The CIS forces should use anti-armor droids to mine these narrow choke points.

Even one mine can strike a fatal blow to an already damaged AT-TE.

If no mines are laid, try rushing an AT-TE and dropping one directly in its path. Just be sure to back away before the mine explodes. Even if you don't survive, the sacrifice is well worth it.

AERIAL ASSAULT ON THE SPIRE

For the clones, capturing the Spire is the key to achieving total air superiority. Without the Spire, the droids can't spawn their fighters. The quickest way to capture the command post is by air. Load both gunships with troops at the Assembly Area. If both are filled to capacity, this gives you an assault force of 10 troopers. Take off and attack enemy vehicles along the way.

One gunship can land in the Spire's hangar to the west. It's a tight fit, but it's possible to set down just inside. Make sure the Geonosian fighters are destroyed before you land.

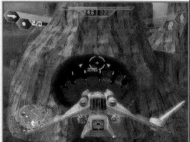

Once the gunship is inside the hangar, it won't be able to turn around to exit, so all troops should disembark and attack the command post.

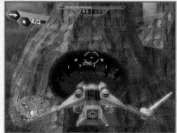

The second gunship should land at the Spire's northern entrance. Take out all four sonic blasters on the cliff below before landing.

If coordinated, troops from both ships should have no problem rushing the war room and capturing the command post.

BATTLE HINT

When playing as CIS, spawn in at the East or West Bunker command posts as a droid pilot, and jump into a hailfire droid. Take the hailfire tank to the Assembly Area and destroy the Republic's command post. Once the Assembly Area is destroyed, take out the two AT-TEs, one at a time. When playing as Republic, spawn in at the Assembly Area as a clone pilot, and jump into the Republic gunship to destroy the three Techno Union ships. Once they are destroyed, take the Spire command post, and then take the other two CIS command posts.

by Tester Ahmad Abbott

BATTLE HINT

This has been one of the tougher levels for us to finish. As a trooper, take a LAAT and destroy the Techno Union ships as fast as possible. As soon as you finish, head for the Derelict. Under no circumstances should you allow the CIS to capture the Derelict; it causes your units to spawn mostly from the Assembly Area and they usually die long before they ever reach any other CP. Your next job after securing the Derelict is to assault the West Bunker. Attempt to capture it, then immediately head for the Spire. By the time you capture the Spire, the CIS will have already taken back the Bunker, but at this point, you've started the CIS bleeding. Keep the pressure on the two bunkers, and keep the CIS from capturing anything else. If you can capture everything, or even keep and turn their last CP neutral, you'll have won the game from the bleed. You'll probably have to do a lot of running around, and don't be afraid to use the Respawn command if you don't think you can make it to your CP in time.

The key to beating this level (and most vs. the CIS) is to destroy the droidekas ASAP. If you see any, kill them first. None of your units can match this unit's offensive and defensive power.

by Tester Xavier Rodriguez

KAMINO: TIPOCA CITY

KAMINO

planetary overview

A lonely world beyond the Outer Rim and just south of the Rishi Maze, Kamino is a planet of tumultuous oceans and endless storms. Mysteriously, its entry was at one time purged from the otherwise-complete Jedi Archives. Few hints of technology mark Kamino's surface, save for massive stilt-mounted cities where the austere Kaminoans reside. Floating above the vast ocean, Tipoca City is the primary operation base for Kamino's most prized export: a clone army.

Though non-native pilots often have a difficult time navigating through the stormy climate, Tipoca City's terrace-based structural design houses many landing pads and temporary residences for visitors.

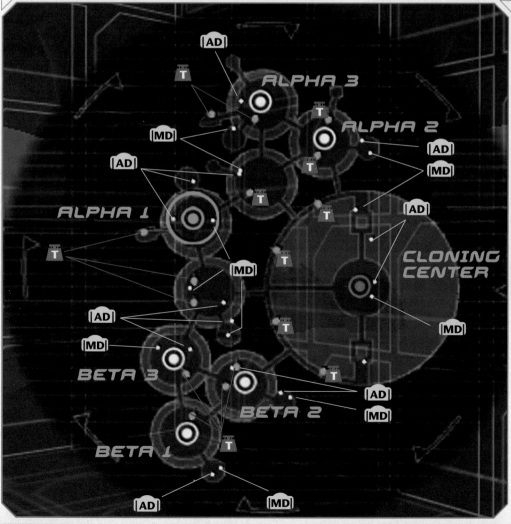

ALPHA 3

ALPHA 2

ALPHA 1

CLONING CENTER

BETA 3

BETA 2

BETA 1

Legend

T	Turret
S	Scout Vehicle
MA	Medium Assault Vehicle
AW	Assault walker
HT	Heavy Assault Transport
FC	Fighter Craft
AT	Air Transoprt
B	Bomber
SC	Special Craft
C	Creature
AD	Ammo Droid
MD	Medical Droid
RD	Repair Droid

COMMAND POSTS

ALPHA 1

Alpha 1 is the staging area for a Separatist attack.

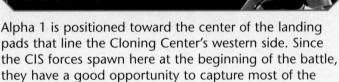

| INITIAL CONTROL: **SEPARATIST BATTLE DROIDS** |
| COMMAND POST TYPE: **LIGHT** |

VEHICLES, TURRETS, & DROIDS

Unit	Count
Gun Turret	1
Medical Droid	1
Ammo Droid	1

Alpha 1 is positioned toward the center of the landing pads that line the Cloning Center's western side. Since the CIS forces spawn here at the beginning of the battle, they have a good opportunity to capture most of the surrounding pads before the clones can.

Alpha 1 is the lowest command post, making it susceptible to attack from surrounding platforms—holding the surrounding pads is important to this position's defense. But the low elevation also has some advantages. For instance, droid defenders can use the gun turret to target enemies racing down the ramp at Beta 3. This can give droid attackers the upper hand in maintaining a presence on the platform to the south.

Construct this turret to the far west quickly. Then use it to fire on enemies attacking from Beta 3.

The bridge to the south is bound to be a bottleneck as the two factions fight for control of the platform between Alpha 1 and Beta 3. Droid pilots can be useful for repairing fellow droids as they sustain damage during the standoff.

ALPHA 2

The command post at Alpha 2 is a major point of contention because of its close proximity to the Cloning Center.

| INITIAL CONTROL: **NEUTRAL** |
| COMMAND POST TYPE: **LIGHT** |

VEHICLES, TURRETS, & DROIDS

Unit	Count
Gun Turret	2
Medical Droid	1
Ammo Droid	1

If the droids hope to capture the Cloning Center, the Alpha 2 command post serves as the best staging area. A ramp to the south provides easy access to the Cloning Center's northern entrance. But the clones aren't likely to give up without a fight, making this area particularly deadly as both sides duke it out along this ramp.

Alpha 2's southernmost turret can cover this ramp as well as the northern entrance, giving the droid attackers a slight advantage. Defenders may want to mine the southern ramp to stifle counterattacks from the direction of the Cloning Center.

If defending this command post alone, hang back in this covered area to the north. It provides more cover than the landing pad, plus there's an ammo and medical droid nearby to keep you company.

This is one of the most important turrets in the battle, allowing the droids to suppress any attacks originating from the Cloning Center.

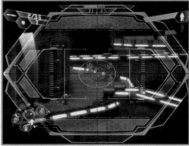

A sniper positioned in the covered area to the west can engage enemies on the neutral platform between Alpha 1 and Beta 3. The walkway on the west side of the Cloning Center can also be covered from this position.

ALPHA 3

Alpha 3 sits to the far north and is useful for maintaining control of Alpha 2.

BETA 1

Beta 1 is the southern-most platform, and both factions have an equal opportunity to capture it.

INITIAL CONTROL: NEUTRAL
COMMAND POST TYPE: LIGHT

VEHICLES, TURRETS, & DROIDS

Unit	Count
Gun Turret	2
Medical Droid	1
Ammo Droid	1

Alpha 3 is the platform just west of Alpha 2. The command post features two turrets, both along the western half of the landing platform. These are useful for defending the command post from attacks to the south and east. The droids find these emplacements most useful for repelling clone attacks on Alpha 1 to the south. Alpha 3 sits higher than the platforms to the south, allowing defenders to shoot down on their enemies.

Defenders want to construct both turrets to help suppress attacks on Alpha 1.

INITIAL CONTROL: NEUTRAL
COMMAND POST TYPE: LIGHT

VEHICLES, TURRETS, & DROIDS

Unit	Count
Gun Turret	1
Medical Droid	1
Ammo Droid	1

Located just south of the other Beta platforms, Beta 1 is the platform farthest from the CIS spawn position at Alpha 1, so the clones have a good chance of capturing it before the droids. If the clones can get jet troopers here early in the battle, Beta 1 serves as a good staging area for attacks on the rest of the platforms, particularly Beta 2 and Beta 3 to the north. The gun turret on the northern edge of the landing platform is sufficient for repelling most attacks. To further bolster the defenses, consider sprinkling mines around the command post.

BETA 3

The position of Beta 3's turret to the south makes it ineffective for preventing enemies from infiltrating the command post from the north.

Since Beta 1 sits higher than the surrounding platforms, this turret is useful for covering Beta 3 to the north and Beta 2 to the east.

BETA 2

Beta 2 is most likely to be attacked from the walkway running along the Cloning Center. Defenders must keep an eye on the bridge to the east.

INITIAL CONTROL: NEUTRAL
COMMAND POST TYPE: LIGHT

VEHICLES, TURRETS, & DROIDS

Unit	Count
Gun Turret	1
Medical Droid	1
Ammo Droid	1

Like Alpha 1, Beta 3 sits toward the center of the landing platforms. If possible, the clones should capture this spot quickly to cut off attacks on the other Beta platforms to the south. The platform to the north sits lower than Beta 3, making its turrets ineffective at engaging defenders here. But Beta 3's own turret sits too far back, making it pretty useless for covering the platform's northern side. Defenders are best off taking cover among the obstacles on the platform's north side and firing down on the incoming attackers as they try to go up the northern ramp.

INITIAL CONTROL: NEUTRAL
COMMAND POST TYPE: LIGHT

VEHICLES, TURRETS, & DROIDS

Unit	Count
Gun Turret	2
Medical Droid	1
Ammo Droid	1

Beta 2 sits between Beta 1 and the Cloning Center, making it a key defensive position for the clone army—if they can capture it. Fortunately, two gun turrets are available to help reinforce the position. Use them to cover the walkway to the east as well as Beta 3 to the northwest. Most importantly, keep an eye on the Cloning Center's western and southern entrances. For more security, place mines on the bridge to the east, as this is the path most droids take when attacking the command post.

Defenders must be prepared for attacks advancing along the northern ramp. ARC troopers are most effective for dealing with such attacks.

The command post may face stiff resistance from the walkway to the east. Pilots should man the turrets and repair them as they sustain damage.

Toss a few mines on the northern ramp to hinder enemy attacks.

KAMINO: TIPOCA CITY

If enemies occupy the platform to the north, use ARC or jet troopers to deal with the turrets.

Position snipers along the northern side of the platform to harass incoming droids.

THE CLONING CENTER

The Cloning Center is the key focus of the droid attack. The clones need to reinforce this position to make sure it doesn't fall into droid hands.

INITIAL CONTROL: REPUBLIC
CLONE ARMY
COMMAND POST TYPE: HEAVY

VEHICLES, TURRETS, & DROIDS

Unit	Count
Gun Turret	4
Medical Droid	2
Ammo Droid	2

The Cloning Center is the focal point of the battle, and it gives the occupier a strategic advantage, allowing them to flank the enemy's positions on the landing platforms. Three entrances lead directly to the command post via lengthy hallways. Defenders should focus on blocking these hallways to prevent infiltration of the command post.

The most obvious solution is mining the hallways. Try to place mines at blind corners where attackers won't see them. Anti-armor droids and ARC troopers find that rockets also work well in the tight hallways. The Cloning Center is also reinforced by four gun turrets positioned along the semicircular walkway to the west. Clone pilots

must construct and man these turrets early in the battle to help prevent the droids from gaining entry.

Use rockets and mines to blow away the attackers. The droids are most likely to attack through the northern entrance, closest to Beta 2. Set up your defenses in this hallway first.

Place mines near corners, where advancing attackers can't see them. They'll be surprised when they round the corner.

Pilots should be escorted around the Cloning Center's perimeter to construct the four gun turrets.

CLONE ARMY STRATEGY

The clones need to capture and hold their ground at the platforms, especially at Beta 3.

The clone army needs to move out quickly to gain a presence on the platforms to the west. But the clones need to hold on to the Cloning Center too. Stiffen the defenses around the Cloning Center by placing mines and constructing the turrets. Meanwhile, lead attacks on Alpha 2 and Beta 3. ARC troopers are handy for taking out the turret that covers the ramp leading up to Alpha 2, while jet troopers race to Beta 3. If Beta 3 can't be taken, get to Beta 1 and open your southern front on that platform.

KAMINO: TIPOCA CITY

Spawn at the Cloning Center and attack Alpha 2 using this ramp. Destroy the turret overlooking the ramp before advancing.

Once you take Alpha 2, do everything possible to hold on to it. Mine the bridges and ramps surrounding it to prevent droid attacks from Alpha 1 and 3. Don't bother trying to capture the remaining Alpha command posts. Just hold back and defend while your units to the south squeeze the droids on the platforms. If you hold Beta 3, you can control the other Beta platforms. The droids are left with Alpha 1 and Alpha 3 as their reinforcements drain away.

Lock down Alpha 2 by placing mines on the bridge to the northwest. This hinders droid attacks from Alpha 3.

SEPARATIST STRATEGY

Rush the Cloning Center's northern entrance with droidekas before the clones can set up defenses in the hallway.

There is no easy solution for the CIS forces, but the best path to victory is through the Cloning Center. Start by racing to Alpha 2 with droidekas. From there, advance to the Cloning Center's northern entrance. Lead the attack with a group of droidekas. They can rush the position before the clones have a chance to set up solid defenses. Get as many droids to the command post as soon as possible to convert it quickly.

Use the Cloning Center to spawn droids and flank the Beta platforms from the east.

The Cloning Center's turrets are great for halting counterattacks while providing fire support for your assaults.

If the Alpha platforms and Cloning Center are captured, the Separatists can start moving against the Beta platforms from two directions. Spawn troops at the Cloning Center to attack Beta 2. Use the Cloning Center's turrets to provide fire support while infantry rush the command post. As long as the clones are left with two command posts, their reinforcements start draining.

Let the clones hold Beta 1 and Beta 3 as you squeeze their forces from two directions. Still, keep all of your command posts well defended. Clone jet troopers are likely to try a breakout attack.

After taking Beta 2, pin the clones at Beta 3 and wait for their reinforcements to run out.

TACTICS

CLONING CENTER DEFENSE

The Cloning Center can be accessed from the platforms via four narrow bridges. ARC troopers are useful for defending these choke points. Patrol the walkway to the west of the Cloning Center and watch the map for hot spots.

kamino: tipoca city

Ideally, place one ARC trooper at each ramp. Mines are the best way to discourage high-speed breakout attacks by droidekas.

Keep pounding the defending droids until your team can secure the command post. Use the same tactic to capture Alpha 3.

◢ Jet Trooper Flanking Maneuver

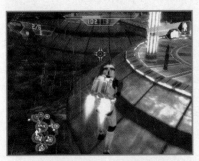

The battle between Alpha 1 and Beta 3 can often lead to a stalemate. The clones stand a chance of breaking out by using their jet troopers. From Beta 3, take off and land on the western side of the neutral landing pad to the north.

Stay on the western slope of the neutral landing pad and scan Alpha 1 for a gun turret. It's on a walkway to the far west. Use the EMP launcher to take out any droids occupying the turret. The EMP launcher destroys the droid but leaves the turret unscathed.

Before the turret can be occupied, take off and fly toward it.

Drop into the turret and use it to clear out the defenders at Alpha 1. This distraction allows your team to attack from the south.

BATTLE HINTS!

The key to this level is to capture as many neutral command posts as you can in as short a time as possible. When you start, select your fastest unit at the character selection screen. This would be the jet trooper for the Republic and the droideka for the CIS. Take the southern command posts (Beta 1, Beta 2 and Beta 3). Head north to find the remaining command posts. If you are playing as the CIS, make sure that the Cloning Center is the last CP you take. This is because the enemy will be forced into a small contained area, and the multiple entrances allow you to attack them from three different sides. When playing as the Republic, always use the clone jet trooper. His jet pack allows you to get to the roof of the Cloning Center and pick off enemy units. The jet trooper's EMP launcher in also highly effective in this level due to the narrow bridges connecting the platforms, which cause enemy units to bunch up. You can then take out these bunches with one blast.

by Tester Julian James

BATTLE HINTS!

From the Clone Center, select a jet trooper and fly from the balcony to the Beta 2. Capture this, then fly up to the Beta 1. The CIS will capture the Beta 3. Let them. You'll have height advantage when you come down to capture it. You can use the jet trooper, the sniper, or the trooper (my personal favorite) to push them off this CP. The CIS now has three CPs. You can push them off the platform just north of Beta 3, but you'll have to make sure they don't get a droideka or snipe from the turrets. Once you get your forces onto the platform across from the Alpha 1, you'll have to reinforce the Clone Center against attack. Secure the Clone Center, then push north and take the Alpha 2. It's a hard battle, but you can win it. You'll need to soldier around the middle-to-end of the battle to keep up with the CIS kill count.

by Tester: Xavier Rodriguez

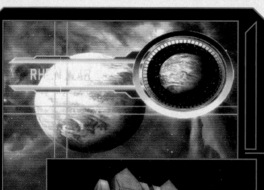

RHEN VAR: CITADEL

planetary overview

The frozen wasteland of Rhen Var was once a fertile paradise, but an atmospheric cataclysm devastated the planet's ecosystem millennia ago. It's now prone to blizzards and ice falls, and its landscape consists of icy plains, tundra, and glacier-carved mountains. Long ago, the ancient Jedi built monuments that are now buried beneath the ice. Snow-covered passages throughout the frozen wasteland allow forces to move quickly or succumb to a cold, icy conclusion.

CRYPT

TERRACE

OBSERVATORY

KEEP

RUINS

COURTYARD

WATCH

Legend

T	Turret
S	Scout Vehicle
MA	Medium Assault Vehicle
AW	Assault walker
HT	Heavy Assault Transport
FC	Fighter Craft
AT	Air Transoprt
B	Bomber
SC	Special Craft
C	Creature
AD	Ammo Droid
MD	Medical Droid
RD	Repair Droid

rhen var: citadel

COMMAND POSTS

THE OBSERVATORY

The clones begin the battle at this domed structure to the northwest.

> **INITIAL CONTROL: REPUBLIC CLONE ARMY/GALACTIC EMPIRE**
> **COMMAND POST TYPE: LIGHT**
>
> **VEHICLES, TURRETS, & DROIDS**

Unit	Count
Gun Turret	1
Medical Droid	1
Ammo Droid	1

The Observatory serves as the clone army's staging area. The map's other command posts can be accessed by the two stairways to the south and east. The southern path leads toward the Keep and the Ruins via a network of twisting paths. Take the path to the east to access the Crypt and the Terrace.

The closest turret is located outside the Observatory and covers both stairways and the command post. If defenders come under attack, they can take cover beneath the dome. There's little cover inside, but the roof and walls provide some concealment, especially if the attack comes from the high terrain to the south.

The turret can cover both stairways to the south and east. Keep the turret trained on these steps, especially if the enemy holds the Ruins or the Keep.

Use the turret to blindside attackers from the east as they rush toward the command post.

THE COURTYARD

The Courtyard command post is housed at the base of this battered four-story tower.

> **INITIAL CONTROL: SEPARATIST BATTLE DROIDS/REBEL ALLIANCE**
> **COMMAND POST TYPE: LIGHT**
>
> **VEHICLES, TURRETS, & DROIDS**

Unit	Count
Medical Droid	1
Ammo Droid	1

Appropriately, the CIS forces begin the battle on the opposite side of the map, near this ancient tower. Early in the battle, the droids should use the stairways to the north to reach the Keep and the Terrace. The western approach consists of a snowy pass that runs beneath the bridge of the Watch command post. This path can be used to mount a surprise attack on the Ruins to the far west.

The tower has four floors accessible by a set of stairs. From the fourth floor it's easy to see the Terrace, Watch, and Ruins command posts. The southern side of the Keep can also be covered from this floor. This high position is great for snipers, but it's also very obvious.

A turret sits to the north of the command post, but its slight elevation makes it difficult to spot or engage enemies attempting to enter the tower. Still, it's useful for covering the two nearby staircases. Defenders need to note that the command post can be converted from the second floor or the staircase between the first and second floors. It's a good idea to patrol these areas. At the very least, throw a few mines down.

This turret to the north can cover both stairways but is incapable of targeting enemies that manage to infiltrate the command post.

The view from the fourth floor of the tower is amazing. Use this position to attack enemies at the surrounding command posts.

The nearby staircases are the most likely avenues of attack, but defenders need to watch the area beneath this bridge to the west. Enemies might stage a surprise attack from the Ruins or Watch command posts.

THE CRYPT

Clone defenders need to mine the east and northeastern steps to prevent attacks from the Keep and the Terrace. Place the mines in blind spots where attackers are least likely to see them.

While defending, use the stone sarcophagus for cover. You can also stand behind it and lob thermal detonators into the eastern hallway.

THE TERRACE

Because of its proximity to the Observatory, the clones are likely to capture the Crypt first.

The Terrace command post sits on a high landing, northeast of the Keep.

INITIAL CONTROL: NEUTRAL
COMMAND POST TYPE: LIGHT

VEHICLES, TURRETS, & DROIDS

Unit	Count
Medical Droid	1
Ammo Droid	1

The Crypt is located between the Observatory and Terrace, along the map's northern edge. The command post is next to a stone sarcophagus in a large square room. Three main entrances into this room are all connected to the northern hallway. The hall to the west leads to the Observatory. But if the clones are defending this area, they are more concerned with the eastern entrances.

Just east of the command post is a set of steps leading to the open area between the Terrace and the Keep. Another set of interior steps are located to the northeast, leading directly to the Terrace. Clone defenders want to keep both of these passages mined to prevent infiltration.

INITIAL CONTROL: NEUTRAL
COMMAND POST TYPE: LIGHT

VEHICLES, TURRETS, & DROIDS

Unit	Count
Gun Turret	1
Medical Droid	1
Ammo Droid	1

Although the Terrace is approximately the same distance from the Courtyard and Observatory, the droids will probably reach this position first, because of the favorable terrain. The clones can reach this position, too, but the twisting hallway running along the northern side is less direct than the stairs to the south.

Whoever gains control of this command post has a great view of the Keep's eastern side. If the enemy holds the Keep, use the elevated turret to defend this command

Rhen var: citadel

post against attack. But attacks may also come along the hallway to the north, originating from the Crypt. To determine which directions need to be covered, keep an eye on the map to see which command posts the enemy holds. For more peace of mind, place some mines in the hall to the north and the steps to the south.

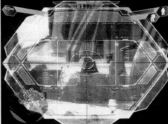

This turret is great for covering the Keep's eastern side. If the enemy holds the Keep, blast their turret protecting the eastern entrance.

Another turret poses a threat to the south. Get a teammate to this spot or take it out.

THE KEEP

The Keep is the centerpiece of the battle, and both factions should fight for its control.

INITIAL CONTROL: **NEUTRAL**
COMMAND POST TYPE: **LIGHT**

VEHICLES, TURRETS, & DROIDS

Unit	Count
Gun Turret	1
Medical Droid	1
Ammo Droid	1

Because of its central position, the Keep is extremely valuable from a strategic perspective. Not only does this command post offer an easily defensible position in the center of the map, but it also provides a staging area for attacks on the surrounding command posts. Both factions should make this command post their first priority at the outset of the battle.

The clone jet troopers can reach this spot within a matter of seconds, but the Separatist droidekas won't be far behind. Once captured, the command post must be defended. The Keep can be accessed via steps to the west, south, and east. The main entrance is on the southern side, featuring two parallel staircases leading inside the structure. Defenders want to mine and cover all four staircases to prevent enemy infiltration.

A single turret can be found just outside the eastern entrance. This can be used to repel attacks from the Terrace. But unless friendly forces hold the surrounding command posts, defenders are better off defending from within the walls of the Keep. Try hiding among the pillars and picking off attackers as they run toward the command post.

Anti-armor units can use rockets and mines to clear the staircases.

Make sure these droids (to the south) are kept in top shape. Defenders will need plenty of ammo and health to hold this command post.

Droidekas are ruthless defenders. When playing as the Separatists, use them to guard the staircases while pilot units repair them.

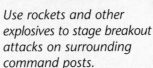

Use rockets and other explosives to stage breakout attacks on surrounding command posts.

Make sure the turret to the east is manned if the enemy holds the Terrace. This is the best option for repelling attacks from this direction. Just make sure the Terrace's turret is kept inoperable.

THE RUINS

Located on the Keep's western flank, the Ruins command post is likely to change hands several times during the battle.

INITIAL CONTROL: NEUTRAL
COMMAND POST TYPE: LIGHT

VEHICLES, TURRETS, & DROIDS

Unit	Count
Gun Turret	1
Medical Droid	1
Ammo Droid	1

The Ruins command post is partly sheltered by three thick walls. But the southern wall is missing, making the position vulnerable to attacks from the Watch. If it is held by the enemy, the Watch's turrets present a serious threat to defenders of the Ruins. These turrets (or their gunners) need to be taken out quickly to maintain a safe spawn point for your team.

Attacks from the Keep and Observatory can be held back with the turret to the east. The turret can also contribute to the chaos outside the Keep's southern entrance. Behind the command post to the west is an unprotected platform overlooking the Observatory, a fine sniping perch for covering the steps to the north.

When defending, keep an eye on the Watch command post to the southeast. Prevent the enemy from constructing turrets at this position.

The turret outside the Ruins can be used to take out the Watch's turrets and gunners.

Use this position behind the command post to cover the northern approach and to counter attacks on the Observatory.

THE WATCH

The Watch is on a platform just south of the Keep's main entrance.

INITIAL CONTROL: NEUTRAL
COMMAND POST TYPE: LIGHT

VEHICLES, TURRETS, & DROIDS

Unit	Count
Gun Turret	2
Medical Droid	1
Ammo Droid	1

The Watch's two turrets make it extremely valuable when attacking or defending the Keep. Once captured, the turrets should be constructed immediately. The western turret can be used to attack enemies at the Ruins and the Keep. Meanwhile, the eastern turret can cover the Keep and the Courtyard.

Unfortunately, the command post sits on a platform with very little cover. This leaves defenders open to attacks from all directions. Still, the command post can only be infiltrated along the bridge to the north, making it relatively easy to defend. Aerial assaults by jet troopers are more problematic, but usually originate from the Ruins or the Keep.

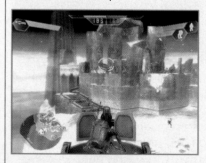

The western turret should be used to attack enemy units at the Ruins command post.

This turret is capable of hitting targets within the Keep by firing through the main entrance. It can also cover the Courtyard below.

CLONE ARMY STRATEGY

Use jet troopers to assault the Keep, via these narrow windows.

Thanks to their jet troopers, the clone army has a good chance of capturing most of the command posts before the droids can reach them. First on the list is the Keep. The jet troopers can gain quick entry through the Keep's western windows. Meanwhile, separate jet trooper squads should take the Ruins and Watch command posts while slower units advance to the north and take the Crypt. With these positions captured, concentrate on bolstering defenses at each, especially the Keep.

Launch an aerial assault on the Courtyard. Jet troopers can fly through this window on the tower's second floor.

The Courtyard command post can be contested from the second floor or the staircase leading to the ground floor. But defenders must be cleared out before it can be captured.

When all the captured command posts are stable, strike out against the Courtyard. Spawn jet troopers at the Watch and use them to assault the Courtyard from the air.

If possible, assault the command post from the first and second floors simultaneously to overwhelm any defenders. This should leave the droids with just the Terrace, causing a reinforcement drain. As the droids attempt to break out, strengthen your defenses at the Keep, Crypt, and Courtyard. Don't bother assaulting the Terrace—the battle is over soon enough if you maintain the drain on the CIS reinforcements.

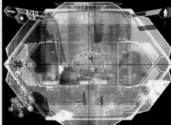

Get sharpshooters to the fourth floor of the Courtyard tower and snipe droids as they spawn at the Terrace to the north.

SEPARATIST STRATEGY

Use droidekas to rush the Keep. Push any clone defenders back out into the snow and capture the command post.

Like the clone army, the Separatists need to capture the Keep as soon as possible. Send a group of droidekas in for this task. They may not reach the Keep as fast as the clone jet troopers, but they can put up a good fight once they arrive. Use them to push the clones out of the Keep and capture the command post.

Meanwhile, send more droidekas toward the Terrace to the north and the Ruins to the west. If you can capture and hold the Ruins and the Keep, the Watch is yours for the taking. Taking the Terrace may present more problems, but if the clones are preoccupied with capturing the Keep, their defenses at this command post are probably light. If they move quickly, the CIS forces can capture all five neutral command posts within the battle's first couple of minutes.

Reinforce your defenses at the Keep with mines. Pay particular attention to the western steps.

Take to the high ground of the Ruins and fire down on the Observatory as the clones try to stage a counterattack.

The idea is to squeeze the clones at the Observatory and impose a reinforcement drain. If the clones are cornered at the Observatory, deploy droidekas and other units on the western platform behind the Ruins. From here, they can fire down on the clones as they try to break out.

Establish another blockade in the hallway to the north to stem attacks on the Keep and the Terrace. To prevent the clones from opening a new front, defend all the other command posts just in case a jet trooper manages to escape the siege.

Set up more defenses in this hallway to the north to contain the clones at the Observatory.

TACTICS

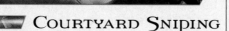

COURTYARD SNIPING

For an amazing view of the battlefield, occupy the fourth floor of the tower at the Courtyard. Turn to the north to spot the Terrace. Harass the enemy as they spawn here, particularly anyone manning the turret.

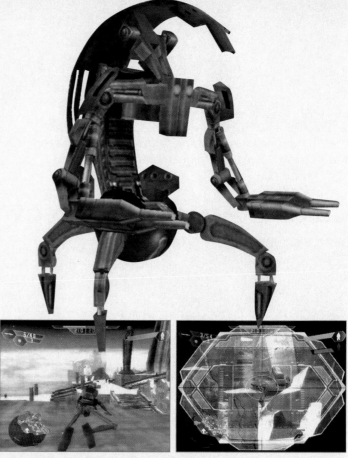

Turn to the east to spot the Ruins. Take aim at enemy units within the command post's walls.

You can also target the Keep's main entrance. Watch the steps and pick off any enemies that traverse the steps.

TERRACE ASSAULT

If the enemy holds the Terrace, attacking it from the south is unwise. Instead, hit it from behind, using the hallway to the north.

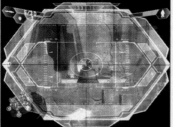

rhen var: citadel

Begin the assault by tossing a few thermal detonators around the command post, then rush in and gun down any survivors, beginning with anyone occupying the turret.

Rush in to capture the command post, but keep an eye on the steps to the east in case a counterattack is attempted.

OBSERVATORY CRUNCH

If the droids can contain the clones at the Observatory, they need to cut off all avenues of attack, including the hall to the north. Position droidekas and other units near the hall's entryway, along this platform overlooking these steps. The nearby droids provide infinite supplies of health and ammo, allowing units to maintain this position indefinitely.

Use the elevated position to fire down into the Observatory in an attempt to pin the clones inside.

TIP

Several clusters of medical and ammo droids are sprinkled across the map. For instance, these droids are located outside the keep's eastern side. Study the locations of these droids and use them as supply depots during advances. Likewise, destroy any droids that may give the enemy an advantage.

BATTLE HINT

If you are playing as the Empire or the Republic, use the dark trooper or jet trooper to take command posts quickly from the start. You can usually capture the Ruins and the Watch before the other team has a chance to get to those positions. Your A.I. teammates should take care of the Crypt for you. Once you have that set of CPs, capture the Keep and you should win every time.

by Tester Julian James

KASHYYYK: DOCKS

planetary overview

Kashyyyk is a lush world teeming with immense forests standing many kilometers tall. The planet has several horizontal levels of ecology throughout the trees; the Wookiees occupy the upper-most level and danger increases at each lower level. The mighty wroshyr trees have limbs so thickly intertwined that the Wookiees have perched cities in the natural cradle they form. Wookiee architecture uses many narrow catwalks and ladders that connect the large huts and platforms that aid in the defense of Wookiee cities.

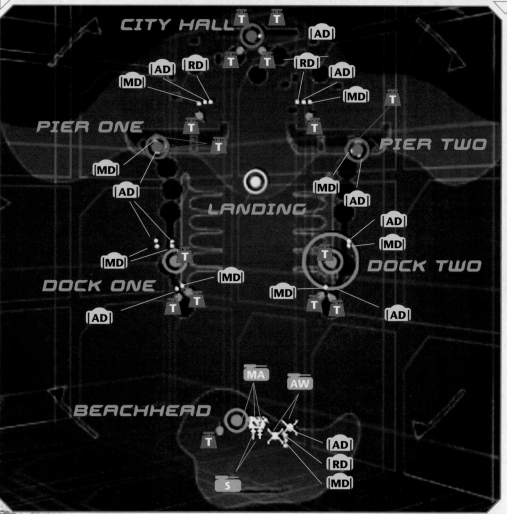

Legend

T	Turret
S	Scout Vehicle
MA	Medium Assault Vehicle
AW	Assault walker
HT	Heavy Assault Transport
FC	Fighter Craft
AT	Air Transoprt
B	Bomber
SC	Special Craft
C	Creature
AD	Ammo Droid
MD	Medical Droid
RD	Repair Droid

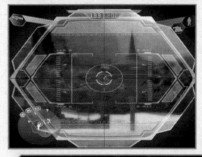

kashyyyk: docks

COMMAND POSTS

BEACHHEAD

The Beachhead is the staging area for the Separatist attack.

INITIAL CONTROL: **Separatist Battle Droids/Galactic Empire** COMMAND POST TYPE: **Heavy**	

VEHICLES, TURRETS, & DROIDS

Unit	Count
AAT/AT-ST	3/3
Spider Walker*	2
STAP*	2
Gun Turret	1
Medical Droid	1
Ammo Droid	1
Repair Droid	1

* Clone Wars Only

The Beachhead command post is the main staging area for the CIS forces, spawning AATs, spider walkers, and STAPs. A large but shallow harbor separates this command post from the clone positions to the north, requiring the droids to wade through the water to reach the mainland. This harbor makes attacking very difficult, but it acts as a good buffer when it comes to defending the Beachhead. One gun turret can be found in the high grass to the west, acting as another deterrent for would-be attackers.

Look for this turret position in the high grass and use a pilot to construct it. It can be used to defend the command post against attacks.

The turret can also come in handy for attacking clones on the southern ends of the two piers.

TIP

Unless using them for defense, don't spawn droidekas at the Beachhead. If they attempt to cross the harbor in wheel mode, they take damage as the water gets deeper, eventually leading to their destruction. The rest of the droids can wade across the harbor without getting waterlogged.

DOCK ONE

Dock One lines the western side of the harbor, sitting just beneath Pier One.

INITIAL CONTROL: **Separatist Battle Droids/Galactic Empire** COMMAND POST TYPE: **Light**	

VEHICLES, TURRETS, & DROIDS

Unit	Count
Gun Turret	1
Medical Droid	1
Ammo Droid	1

The western dock serves as a spawn point for the droids, putting them within striking distance of the mainland's command post. Droids spawning here can reach the Landing to the northeast by taking to the water and wading ashore. Advancing north along the dock eventually leads to the access ramp to Pier One.

Defenders won't find much cover on the docks, leaving them open to attacks, especially from above. Fortunately, a turret defends the command post. This can be used to engage enemies on the platforms above or stifle attacks from the north. The turret can also hit the area surrounding the Landing command post to the northeast.

There isn't much cover on the docks except for these stone stairway railings along the western side. These can provide some cover if combatants are crouched.

The turret is useful for hitting targets on the beach. But it's most beneficial for protecting the command post from attacks originating from Pier One.

PIER ONE

The Pier One command post is located in this elevated hut overlooking Dock One.

INITIAL CONTROL: REPUBLIC
CLONE ARMY/REBEL ALLIANCE
COMMAND POST TYPE: LIGHT

VEHICLES, TURRETS, & DROIDS

Unit	Count
Gun Turret	4
Medical Droid	3
Ammo Droid	3

Pier One sits on the western side of the harbor, providing the clone army with elevated firing positions on Dock One. The command post is located in a small hut on a raised platform near the coastline. This hut can only be accessed by a narrow ramp to the north. Defenders want to keep this ramp well defended, preferably with mines.

Two turrets guard the hut housing the command post, but the pier's defenses are more extensive. Two more turrets are positioned on the southernmost point of the pier, making them useful for engaging vehicles attacking

from the Beachhead. A series of ammo and medical droids also line the pier to the south, giving the clones plenty of support for attacking the dock below.

A couple of pilots should be deployed on the pier to construct all four turrets.

Be sure to construct the turrets at the southern end of the pier. These are useful for catching the incoming attackers in a crossfire as they rush the Landing command post.

Use the elevated platforms to fire down on enemies scurrying along the dock below. Make sure Dock One's turret is silenced before you stage any assaults.

LANDING

The Landing command post sits at the water's edge.

KASHYYYK: DOCKS

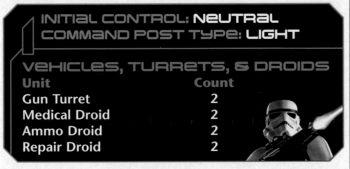

Similar to Dock One, Dock Two lines the eastern side of the harbor and serves as another Separatist spawn point.

INITIAL CONTROL: **NEUTRAL** COMMAND POST TYPE: **LIGHT**	
VEHICLES, TURRETS, & DROIDS	
Unit	Count
Gun Turret	2
Medical Droid	2
Ammo Droid	2
Repair Droid	2

The Landing command post is the only neutral position at the start of the battle. It sits on the beach, sandwiched between Dock One and Dock Two. Naturally, the droids are the most likely to capture this position because of its close proximity to their spawn points. Still, the clones should make an effort to at least mine the beach to damage the incoming AATs.

Pilots also need to construct the two turrets (one to the west and one to the east) overlooking the command post from the north. Even if the droids capture the Landing, these two turrets can dish out some serious casualties on both the Landing and the two docks.

INITIAL CONTROL: **SEPARATIST** BATTLE DROIDS/GALACTIC EMPIRE COMMAND POST TYPE: **LIGHT**	
VEHICLES, TURRETS, & DROIDS	
Unit	Count
Gun Turret	1

Dock Two is the mirror image of Dock One, except it doesn't have any support droids to provide ammo and mend wounds. But it does feature one turret at the southern tip. Defenders should use it to support attacks on the Landing and defend against attacks originating from Pier Two, just above this position. The droids can bolster the defenses of this command post by spawning a couple of droidekas. They can saturate the dock with laser fire, preventing any trooper attacks from the north.

The clone ARC troopers' missiles and mines are useful for repelling the incoming AATs.

These wooden barricades on the beach provide some cover. Crouch to prevent getting hit by laser blasts. Stay behind cover and saturate the beach with thermal detonators.

Construct the turret next to the command post and use it to hold back attacks and support the initial advance on the Landing.

A single droideka can repel most attacks advancing along the dock.

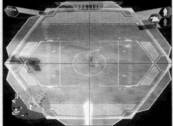

Construct both turrets overlooking the Landing and pound your enemies on the beach.

PIER TWO

Pier Two is nearly a mirror image of the pier to the west, including this command post housed by an elevated hut.

INITIAL CONTROL: REPUBLIC CLONE ARMY/REBEL ALLIANCE	
COMMAND POST TYPE: LIGHT	

VEHICLES, TURRETS, & DROIDS

Unit	Count
Gun Turret	3
Medical Droid	3
Ammo Droid	3

Almost identical to Pier One, Pier Two's elevated platforms line the eastern side of the harbor. The only major difference between them is Pier 2 has only one turret near the command post. But its position is great for covering the ramp to the north and the Landing to the west.

Other than that, the positions of the command posts, droids, and turrets are identical. By adding three more turrets, Pier Two gives the clones even more leverage in driving back the droid attack. But they must move out quickly with pilot units to construct all the turrets before the droids arrive. One pilot should be enough to get the defenses up in time. The turret near the command post should be constructed first to discourage early attacks on the ramp to the north. Then the southernmost turrets can be constructed to harass incoming vehicles from the Beachhead.

This ramp to the north is the only path leading to the command post. Defend it with mines and infantry.

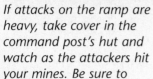

If attacks on the ramp are heavy, take cover in the command post's hut and watch as the attackers hit your mines. Be sure to replenish the ramp with new mines as needed.

If the enemy captures the Landing's eastern turret, take it out. Otherwise it can inflict heavy casualties on your teammates spawning here.

CITY HALL

The City Hall command post is located inside this hut to the north.

INITIAL CONTROL: REPUBLIC CLONE ARMY/REBEL ALLIANCE	
COMMAND POST TYPE: LIGHT	

VEHICLES, TURRETS, & DROIDS

Unit	Count
Gun Turret	4
Ammo Droid	1

Positioned to the far north overlooking the beach, City Hall is a critical command post for both factions. For the clones, this position is useful in holding the droids on the beach. The four turrets produce an awesome display of firepower, capable of shredding even the most ambitious frontal assaults.

The command post is in a slightly elevated hut, and can only be accessed via the short steps on the northern side. This entrance is covered by two hut-based turrets to the north. Wookiees also spawn around this command post, giving the clones a hand in repelling the Separatists' attack on their home world.

Despite its impressive array of turrets, City Hall is extremely vulnerable to flanking attacks. Since the two northern turrets are all positioned in huts, the gunners have difficulty challenging attacks from the east or west. To bolster the flanks, the clones should place mines in these blind spots. If the droids manage a successful assault on City Hall while holding the Landing, they'll split the clone army in two and take the Wookiees out of the battle, significantly increasing their chances of victory.

KASHYYYK: DOCKS

Defenders want to sprinkle mines around the entrance and command post to prevent a hasty droid infiltration.

The turrets to the south of the command post are useful for attacking enemy armor, but they won't last long in a toe-to-toe slugfest.

The command post's hut features four large rectangular windows useful for covering all approaches.

CLONE ARMY STRATEGY

Get ARC troopers to the beach as soon as possible and use them to mine the beach around the Landing command post. Mines are the best way to deal with the incoming armor.

As the defenders, the clones can get through the bulk of this battle without worrying about staging a major assault. First off, the Landing command post is almost impossible to capture without taking huge losses. Even if you rush it with jet troopers, the droid positions on the docks catch you in a crossfire. Concede this position to the droids at the start of the battle.

But you still want to get some ARC troopers to the beach to place mines. While the ARC troopers are busy on the beach, pilots should be busy constructing the turrets, first along the piers, then back at City Hall.

Even if the droids take the Landing, the surrounding gun turrets and ARC troopers should be sufficient to take out the enemy AATs.

When the battle is joined, the clones can expect to inflict heavy casualties on the droids as they rush the Landing. The three AATs are a major threat, but the mines on the beach and attacks by the ARC troopers and gun turrets should reduce them to rubble in short order. Use snipers and ARC troopers on the piers to deal with the droids on the docks and beach.

Try to avoid hitting areas of the beach where mines are present to prevent premature detonation. To prevent breakout attacks by newly spawned AATs, the ARC troopers need to keep placing fresh mines.

Line the piers with snipers and ARC troopers to attack droids and AATs as they rush toward the beach.

After the droids take the Landing, consider launching a jet trooper assault on the docks. Spawn at the piers and use their EMP launchers to clear out any defenders, particularly any droids manning the turrets. Then jet down to the command posts to capture them. If the jet troopers can capture and maintain control of the docks, the Landing should be easier to take.

Pound the Landing with the surrounding gun turrets while sending in jet troopers to capture the command post. If your team can capture the docks and Landing, you limit the droids to the Beachhead while imposing a reinforcement drain. Most important, they won't have a way to get their droidekas ashore.

A successful jet trooper attack on the docks can cripple the droid assault.

SEPARATIST STRATEGY

Rush the Landing with AATs and use them to provide cover while droids capture the command post.

If managed carefully, the CIS forces have the chance to wipe out the clone defenders in record time. The first objective is to take control of the Landing command post by attacking from the docks and Beachhead simultaneously. Lead the attack with the three AATs. As the AATs cross the harbor, target turrets under construction along the piers, as well as any clone units waiting on the beach. Hold the AATs at the beach until the droid infantry from the docks can catch up and convert the command post.

From the Landing, send droidekas through the high grass toward City Hall. Rush the command post and capture it to divide the clone army.

With the Landing under CIS control, the drive should continue north, toward the City Hall. The AATs should provide cover as the droids attempt to flank the command post. Droidekas can often slip by unseen in the high grass. If possible, attack from the far east or west to avoid coming under fire from the City Hall turrets.

Assault the turret positions from behind to catch the gunners off guard, then go for the command post. Eliminating the turrets also allows a more direct approach for units spawning at the Landing. Keep pushing toward City Hall until your units can infiltrate the hut containing the command post.

Use the spider walkers and AATs to pummel the pier command posts with their heavy guns.

Capturing the Landing and City Hall divides the clone army and imposes a reinforcement drain. It also takes the Wookiees out of the battle, increasing the life expectancy of your armor units. Instead of assaulting both piers, concentrate your forces

on holding the existing command posts as the clone reinforcements bleed away.

In the meantime, use the spider walkers and AATs to contain the clones at the piers. As usual, defend all the command posts and watch for breakout attacks by jet troopers.

When the clone reinforcements have dwindled, rush in and capture the two pier command posts to end the battle.

TACTICS

WOOKIEE HUNT

*The Wookiees are armed with powerful rocket launchers, posing a serious threat to the CIS vehicles.
The droids want to capture the City Hall command post to prevent the Wookiees from spawning.*

Once City Hall is captured, look for the yellow dots on the map to locate the remaining Wookiees and hunt them down.

LIKE SHOOTING FISH IN A BARREL

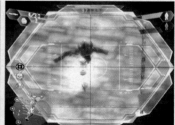

Early in the battle, the harbor becomes a shooting gallery as the droids attempt to assault the Landing command post. Clone sharpshooters can rack up multiple kills if they find a good sniping angle.

KASHYYYK: DOCKS

From the southern end of either pier, it's also possible to snipe droids spawning at the Beachhead command post. Sniper support is incredibly helpful if jet troopers attempt to attack this command post. Try to hit the droids before they can hop in a vehicle.

DROID FLANKING MANEUVERS

Instead of heading straight for the Landing, send one AAT along the eastern side of Pier Two. The AAT emerges on land near the ramp leading up to the Pier Two command post. From here it can attack the enemy turrets, helping your units that are attacking the Landing.

Consider rushing City Hall with STAPs. Maneuver to the east or west and take out the two northernmost turrets from the rear. Taking out these two turrets will make capturing and holding the City Hall much easier.

PIER PRESSURE

Both piers give the clones great firing positions to lay waste to the droids below. But they also make great attack platforms for jet troopers. Use them as staging areas for attacks on the docks below. Be sure to neutralize the turrets before assaulting.

If jet troopers take off from the southernmost platforms of the piers, they can reach the Beachhead without getting their feet wet. Upon reaching the CIS-controlled shore, they can steal unoccupied AATs and convert the command post. Denying the Separatists their vehicles definitely tilts the odds in favor of the clone army.

BATTLE HINT

When you start the game, try to capture the Landing command post as quickly as possible. This allows your troop to establish a command post at the center of the map, and easily capture other nearby command posts. The second most important command post to capture or defend is the Pier Two command post. There is only one way to enter the command post unless the other side has a unit with jet pack. If vehicles are available, get in one and support your troops when they are capturing a command post. Also, if you are a CIS or Empire, kill Wookiees to get ammo or a health power-up.

by Tester: Yobo Shen

BATTLE HINT

Ahmad's way: Use the clone trooper or jet trooper to take the outlying dock CP's. After the CIS units build their turrets, you can actually jump from the upper platforms. Time the press of your enter button so that you enter the turret instead of landing on it, and you'll take no damage from the fall!!! Capture both CPs this way, and the center CP should fall from lack of reinforcements.

Xavier's way: Being a sniper does the same thing as Ahmad's strategy, but it's slower. Droideka can be destroyed with orbital strikes. Shoot any units you see. You should keep up with the pace of the droideka kills. Don't bother trying to capture the landing point, but if you see an unoccupied tank, don't hesitate to grab it and get some kills.

by Testers Ahmad Abbott & Xavier Rodriguez

TATOOINE: DUNE SEA

Planetary overview

Tatooine is an Outer Rim world of seemingly endless desert, cooked by the intense energy of twin yellow suns. Rocky mesas, canyons, and arroyos break up the monotony of shifting dunes. The days are hot and the nights are frigid. Yet life persists on Tatooine, with a mixture of hard-working locals attempting to extract a living from the unforgiving environment and transients visiting the world for illegal ventures.

Controlled by the Hutts and their shady operations, Tatooine's few port cities attract mainly spacers, bounty hunters, thieves, and other malcontents. Anyone attempting to gain control of Tatooine is faced with the dangers of an open desert and a wretched hive of scum and villainy lurking in the city streets, looking to profit from someone else's demise.

Legend

T	Turret
S	Scout Vehicle
MA	Medium Assault Vehicle
AW	Assault walker
HT	Heavy Assault Transport
FC	Fighter Craft
AT	Air Transoprt
B	Bomber
SC	Special Craft
C	Creature
AD	Ammo Droid
MD	Medical Droid
RD	Repair Droid

TATOOINE: DUNE SEA

COMMAND POSTS

BLUFF

Most of the Alliance's vehicles, including their two X-wings, spawn at the Bluff command post.

INITIAL CONTROL: REBEL ALLIANCE/ SEPARATIST BATTLE DROIDS
COMMAND POST TYPE: HEAVY

VEHICLES, TURRETS, & DROIDS

Unit	Count
Combat Speeder/AAT	3/3
X-wing/Droid Starfighter	2/2
Gun Turret	2

The Bluff is the Rebels' major command post and produces the bulk of their attack force. Both the combat speeders and X-wings are huge assets, needed for an Alliance victory. As a result, this command post must be held at all costs. Unfortunately, the terrain and location aren't very favorable.

The command post sits between a bluff to the south and an expansive desert to the north. The Homestead command post is located to the east and the Tusken Camp to the west. Early in the battle most attacks come from the Tusken Raiders attacking from the Tusken Camp and Cistern. At the start of the battle, use pilots to build the two turrets, beginning with the one to the west. Pilots are also useful for supplying defenders with health and ammo, as there are no support droids at this command post.

Get the X-wings into the air as soon as possible. Otherwise they're vulnerable to strafing attacks by the Imperial TIE fighters.

Construct both turrets at the start of the battle, beginning with this one to the west. Man it at all times to hold back attacks from the Cistern and the Tusken Camp.

Place mines along the north side of the command post to defend against rush attacks by speeder bikes and other vehicles.

Most important, get the X-wings in the air. They're great for taking out the Imperial AT-STs.

HOMESTEAD

This local dwelling houses the Homestead command post.

INITIAL CONTROL: REBEL ALLIANCE/ SEPARATIST BATTLE DROIDS
COMMAND POST TYPE: LIGHT

VEHICLES, TURRETS, & DROIDS

Unit	Count
Combat Speeder/AAT	1/1
Speeder Bike/STAP	2/2
Gun Turret	3
Medical Droid	1
Ammo Droid	2

Located just north of the Imperial-held Dune Sea and Sandcrawler command posts, the Homestead is likely to see heavy action throughout the battle. In addition to fending off Imperial attackers, defenders must watch the pass to the southwest to pick off Tusken Raiders attacking from the Cistern. These threats all call for serious defensive measures.

Begin by constructing all three turrets near the arch to the south. These aren't very helpful in stopping the AT-STs, but they're good for repelling infantry attacks. Mining the area beneath the arch helps thwart attacks by the skiff and speeder bikes spawned at the Sandcrawler.

Back at the Homestead, place mines along the steps and near the command post to stop attackers who breach your outer defenses. When the Imperials arrive, they're likely to attack with their AT-STs, moving around the eastern side of the arch. Use vanguards to blast them with missile launchers. Notwithstanding these efforts on the ground, defenders need support from the vehicles at the Bluff, particularly the X-wings, to hold back the Empire's attacks.

Race to the arch and construct the three turrets before the Imperials arrive. Man the turrets to engage incoming attackers from the Dune Sea command post to the south.

Mine the interior of the building housing the command post. Place mines on the steps as well as around the command post.

Place more mines beneath the arch, because most Imperial attacks pass through this choke point. This is particularly useful for stopping speeder bike attacks.

When AT-STs arrive, engage them with vanguards. Try to stay behind these slow walkers to avoid their forward-firing arc.

Use the house as a bunker. Crouch on the sunken steps and fire on your enemies. This reduces your profile, making you harder to hit. But if you fall back in the house, keep in mind that it takes only a well-tossed thermal detonator to flush you out.

DUNE SEA

The Dune Sea acts as the main staging area for the Imperial attack.

INITIAL CONTROL: **GALACTIC EMPIRE/REPUBLIC CLONE ARMY**
COMMAND POST TYPE: **HEAVY**

VEHICLES, TURRETS, & DROIDS

Unit	Count
AT-ST/IF T-X	3/3
TIE Fighter/Jedi Starfighter	2/2
Gun Turret	4
Medical Droid	1
Ammo Droid	1

The Dune Sea is as important to the Empire as the Bluff is to the Rebels, producing most of its vehicles. The command post benefits from some useful defensive features, including several large rocks and four turrets. The northern turrets have a good view of the area near the arch, helping suppress attacks from the Homestead.

While the rocks provide decent cover for defenders, attackers can benefit from them as well, staying out of the turrets' line of sight while contesting the command post. To prevent such a close-range infiltration, toss some mines around the command post and patrol the areas around the rocks. Position some Shocktroopers around this position to guard against combat speeder and X-wing attacks.

Tatooine: Dune Sea

The turrets are useful for holding back infantry attacks from the north as well as for inflicting heavy damage on combat speeders attempting to rush the command post.

Place mines in the gaps between the rocks surrounding the command post. Enemies weaving around the rocks to reach the command post probably won't even notice them until it's too late.

Keep Shocktroopers around the command post at all times. Otherwise, X-wings make continuous strafing runs on the AT-STs and TIE fighters spawning here. The turrets are useful for targeting the X-wings, but they are easily taken out. Shocktroopers hiding among the rocks are much harder to spot from the air.

SANDCRAWLER

The command post is inside the front of this Sandcrawler.

The Sandcrawler is located to the west of the Dune Sea command post. Attackers from the Homestead to the north are the most direct threat to this position. But attacks from the west, by Tusken Raiders and Rebels, also are possible. The large desert to the east makes attacks from this direction unpopular—at least by infantry. Still, combat speeders spawned at the Bluff command post may flank this position, bypassing the Cistern.

To forestall any flanking maneuvers, place Shocktroopers around the Sandcrawler to lay mines and fire missiles at incoming vehicles. The command post can only be converted from within the Sandcrawler, so placing a mine or two in this cramped space is a good idea. Even better, hide defenders near the rocks to the north and make sure they have a good view of the command post so they can engage attackers.

Throw some mines in front of the Sandcrawler to prevent vehicles and infantry from reaching the command post.

Try to remain hidden near the Sandcrawler. Attackers in vehicles must dismount to reach the command post. Wait till they leave the safety of their vehicles to attack.

If you're spotted by enemy vehicles, put up a good fight with Shocktroopers. A mix of mines and missiles should be sufficient to take out incoming combat speeders.

INITIAL CONTROL: GALACTIC EMPIRE/REPUBLIC CLONE ARMY
COMMAND POST TYPE: LIGHT

VEHICLES, TURRETS, & DROIDS

Unit	Count
Skiff	1
Speeder Bike	2
Repair Droid	2

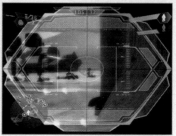

The Sandcrawler is home to the map's only two repair droids. X-wings looking to restock their missiles are likely to land nearby. Imperial defenders may want to mine the areas around these droids to prevent such resupply efforts.

From this spot, it's possible to cover the pass leading to the Homestead. Help your team attack or defend the command post from this distant perch.

TUSKEN CAMP

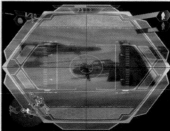

The Tusken Camp sits on a hill overlooking the Cistern.

The western side of the Bluff command post can also be covered from this cliff. Try picking off Rebels as they rush to their X-wings and combat speeders.

INITIAL CONTROL: TUSKEN RAIDERS
COMMAND POST TYPE: LIGHT

CISTERN

Because of its central location, all three factions covet this Tusken Raider-controlled position. Its control is hotly contested.

Tusken Raiders throw a curve into this battle; the hostile natives challenge both factions for control of the map's command posts. They spawn at this camp and at the Cistern to the east. The Tusken Camp offers no significant assets like droids or turrets, but its location is valuable to both sides because it offers a great view of the Cistern.

The camp sits in a narrow canyon, approachable from the east and west. Attackers must reach the camp's center to convert the command post. But they need to watch out for Tusken Raiders spawning around the various tents.

When attacking this position, always bring backup. Converting this position can be tough, especially if Tusken Raiders start spawning all around you.

Whoever controls this command post has a much easier time taking the Cistern. Position snipers on the cliff to the east and fire down on enemies below.

INITIAL CONTROL: TUSKEN RAIDERS
COMMAND POST TYPE: LIGHT

VEHICLES, TURRETS, & DROIDS

Unit	Count
Gun Turret	3
Medical Droid	2
Ammo Droid	2

Sandwiched by several command posts, the Cistern is a crossroads of carnage. Initially controlled by the Tusken Raiders, the Cistern is likely to change hands several times. The Rebels stand the best chance of capturing the position early in the game by attacking from the Bluff to the north or from the Homestead to the east. But the Tusken Raiders can stage a successful counterattack from the Tusken Camp by charging down the hill to the west.

TATOOINE: DUNE SEA

The Imperials are most likely to attack from the pass to the south. But the distance of their command posts makes an early attack unlikely unless they approach with speeder bikes or the skiff from the Sandcrawler. Whoever takes control of this position should get to work on constructing the turrets. But manning these turrets can be dangerous if enemies approach from all directions.

Make sure a teammate watches your back while you construct or man turrets. The chaotic nature of this command post makes standing still a significant hazard.

Use a fast vehicle like a speeder bike or combat speeder to rush this position. Then dismount the vehicle and use it for cover while converting the command post.

 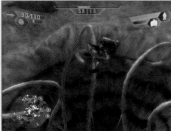

The command post's resident Sarlacc has plenty of corpses to feast on. Just make sure you don't get too close or you'll be lunch too.

REBEL ALLIANCE STRATEGY

Capture the Cistern command post quickly to halt the reinforcement drain.

At the start of the battle, each faction holds two command posts. Since no side holds a majority, the Rebel and Imperial forces begin with a reinforcement drain. The quickest way for the Rebels to remedy this problem is to take the Cistern. While strengthening defenses at the Homestead, strike at the Cistern with forces from the Bluff.

Surround the command post with combat speeders and use them to provide cover while infantry moves in to convert the position. This should halt your reinforcement drain, assuming you retain control of the two command posts you started with.

Strengthen your defenses at the Homestead and push back all Imperial attacks.

Technically, you could kick back and defend your positions while the Empire dukes it out with the Tusken Raiders for control of the Tusken Camp. But if the Empire captures the Tusken Camp, they have an easy time assaulting the Cistern. Plus, their reinforcement drain stops. Thus, it's a good idea to take the Tusken Camp to strengthen your western positions. Wipe out the Tusken Raiders completely, or they continue challenging your team for control.

In the meantime, use your X-wings to assault the Imperial AT-STs and TIE fighters. Taking out these vehicles greatly reduces the chances of a serious assault. Keep their vehicles pinned at the Dune Sea command post while their reinforcements bleed away.

Continually harass the Imperial's vehicles at the Dune Sea with your X-wings. Prevent them from breaking out and striking your command posts.

GALACTIC EMPIRE STRATEGY

Hit the Homestead with all three AT-STs at once to overwhelm the defenders.

The Empire can take the upper hand in this battle by letting the Tusken Raiders do the work. The Imperial positions to the far east face little opposition from the Tusken Raiders, so let the Rebels worry about them. Instead, launch an attack on the Homestead command post to the north. Swarm the position with all three AT-STs, then rush in with infantry on the skiff or speeder bikes to capture the command post. In the meantime, hold tight at the Dune Sea and Sandcrawler.

If you capture the Homestead, the Rebels must choose whether to attack your positions or hit the Tusken Raiders while their reinforcements drain away. Use your TIE fighters to blast their combat speeders and X-wings. Denying them these vehicles helps persuade them to go for the easier Cistern and Tusken Camp command posts. Even if they capture both command posts and wipe out the Tusken Raiders, they suffer casualties in the process. This puts your team in a good position to win the battle.

Use the TIE fighters to strafe the Rebel combat speeders and X-wings at the Bluff to hinder their offensive capabilities.

To squeeze the Rebels from the west, strike the Tusken Camp. Load a skiff with stormtroopers and attack from the south.

A more conventional approach is to squeeze the Rebels in the center. Take the Homestead as described above, but also send an attack force against the Tusken Camp. The skiff at the Sandcrawler is the quickest way to get four troops inside the camp. Approach from the south to avoid getting caught in any fighting around the Cistern. If everything goes well, the Rebels are left with the Bluff and possibly the Cistern. Lock down defenses at your command posts and wait for the Rebel reinforcements to drain away.

Hold at the Tusken Camp and fire down on the Rebels as they fight the Tusken Raiders at the Cistern.

TACTICS

TUSKEN RAIDER ERADICATION

The battle is much easier to manage if the Tusken Raiders are wiped out. To take them out of the battle you must capture the Tusken Camp and Cistern.

But taking their command posts isn't enough. You have to hunt down every last Tusken Raider to ensure that they don't gain a new foothold elsewhere. Use the map to find the remaining Tusken Raiders and wipe them out.

TATOOINE: DUNE SEA

THE ARCH

You can climb on top of the arch at the Homestead by accessing this ramp on the northeastern side. From the top, fire down on enemies approaching from the Dune Sea or Sandcrawler.

For a good view of the Cistern, keep moving west along the arch. It eventually gives way to this narrow ledge.

Keep moving along the ledge until you reach this spot overlooking the Cistern. This is a good spot for sniping.

STARFIGHTER STRAFING

The firepower offered by the X-wings and TIE fighters give both factions a major offensive boost. But you must wipe out the other side's fighters to reign over the skies. Strafe the enemy's vehicle spawn points before their starfighters can get airborne.

If the enemy gets their fighters in the air, hunt them down until you have total control of the skies.

When making a strafing run, climb high above the desert, then dive down on your target while reducing throttle. This lets you loiter longer over the target area. Remember, the X-wing has missiles, too, each capable of taking out an AT-ST.

Whenever possible, attack from the east. The system's twin suns blind troops on the ground, making your craft harder to see.

BATTLE HINT

The Tusken Raiders are tough, accurate enemies. Eliminate the threat by grabbing a speeder bike or STAP as soon as you spawn, and make a break for the Tusken Raider Camp command post. Take over this command post first, then move down the hill to capture the other Tusken-held CP, but watch out for the Sarlacc! His reach is longer than you think. Once the Tuskens are out of the way, the only thing you have to worry about is the onslaught of enemy forces.

by Tester John Shields

BATTLE HINT

The easiest (though least imaginative) way to win this battle is to start as a pilot and immediately jump into a TIE fighter. Use the TIE to destroy the combat landspeeders as soon as they spawn. You can't take down the X-wings, but they are less of a threat. With the landspeeders gone, the Rebels will have no counter to the AT-ST or Tusken Raiders, and will die very quickly.

by Tester: Xavier Rodriguez

TATOOINE: MOS EISLEY

planetary overview

Tatooine is an Outer Rim world of seemingly endless desert, cooked by the intense energy of twin yellow suns. Rocky mesas, canyons, and arroyos break up the monotony of shifting dunes. The days are hot and the nights are frigid. Yet life persists on Tatooine, with a mixture of hard-working locals attempting to extract a living from the unforgiving environment and transients visiting the world for illegal ventures.

Controlled by the Hutts and their shady operations, Tatooine's few port cities attract mainly spacers, bounty hunters, thieves, and other malcontents. Anyone attempting to gain control of Tatooine is faced with the dangers of an open desert and a wretched hive of scum and villainy lurking in the city streets, looking to profit from someone else's demise.

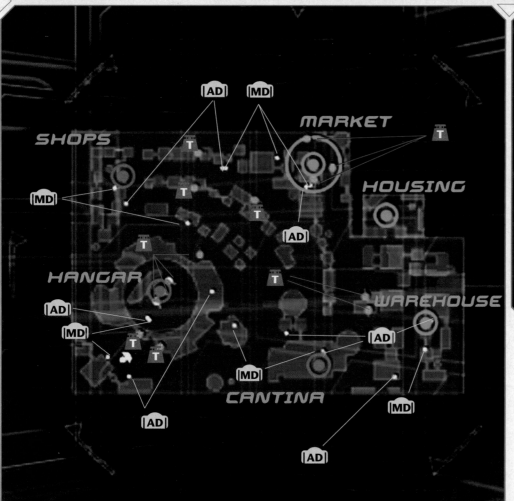

Legend

T	Turret
S	Scout Vehicle
MA	Medium Assault Vehicle
AW	Assault walker
HT	Heavy Assault Transport
FC	Fighter Craft
AT	Air Transoprt
B	Bomber
SC	Special Craft
C	Creature
AD	Ammo Droid
MD	Medical Droid
RD	Repair Droid

SHOPS

MARKET

HOUSING

HANGAR

WAREHOUSE

CANTINA

TATOOINE: MOS EISLEY

COMMAND POSTS

THE CANTINA

The Cantina's bar provides cover and concealment for defenders. Try crouching along the southern side of the bar to cover the eastern entrance.

INITIAL CONTROL: REBEL ALLIANCE/ SEPARATIST BATTLE DROIDS COMMAND POST TYPE: LIGHT

VEHICLES, TURRETS, & DROIDS

Unit	Count
Medical Droid	1
Ammo Droid	2

Held by the Rebels at the start of the battle, the Cantina is likely to see heavy fighting inside and out. Fortunately for the defenders, the command post can only be converted from the interior. This makes locking down the area much easier as there are only two entrances.

Imperial forces are likely to attack the eastern entrance, particularly in the early moments of the battle. But the western entrance should also be covered. Toss some mines around the entrances and at the command post itself to reinforce this position.

Covering the western entrance is easiest while standing behind the bar. This position allows you to hit anyone who runs in, while the bar provides adequate cover.

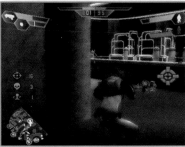

You can contest the command post from the western entrance, but watch for defenders hiding behind and around the bar. Toss a few thermal detonators to draw them out.

When assaulting the Cantina, always bring along some friends. Convert this command post quickly before more enemies spawn here. A wild firefight inside the Cantina often gets messy with thermal detonators flying everywhere. Do your best to avoid such unpredictable situations.

THE HANGAR

The Hangar's command post sits on a sail barge parked inside. Two turrets protect this wide southern entrance, but they can easily be turned inward by attackers.

INITIAL CONTROL: REBEL ALLIANCE/ SEPARATIST BATTLE DROIDS COMMAND POST TYPE: LIGHT

VEHICLES, TURRETS, & DROIDS

Unit	Count
Gun Turret	3
Barge Lasers	3
Medical Droid	1
Ammo Droid	2
AAT	1
AT-ST	1

The Hangar is the most defensible position held by the Rebels at the outset of the battle. The command post is located on a large barge inside the Hangar and can only be accessed via scaffolding on the northwest side of the vehicle. This makes the command post easy to defend and hard to convert—unless a dark trooper captures it from the air.

The outside of the building is protected by three turrets, one to the north and two to the south. Pilots should construct these quickly to prevent early rush attacks. It is wise to booby-trap these turrets to prevent them from being turned on the defenders. Simply place a mine in each turret. If an enemy tries to occupy it, the mine goes off, killing the attacker and destroying the turret.

Mines are also useful for keeping attackers at bay inside the Hangar. Place a few on the scaffolding leading up to the skiff as well as around the two entrances.

The northern turret is useful for covering the adjacent street. But if captured, it can be turned on the northern entrance and used to ambush teammates as they exit the Hangar.

The barge is equipped with three lasers, all facing east. Use these to cover both entrances.

Toss some mines on the scaffolding leading up to the barge-based command post. This scaffolding is a major choke point, but can be bypassed by dark troopers. For that reason, place a few more mines on the barge to hinder aerial assaults.

Another scaffolding is located to the north and can be used to ambush attackers rushing through the northern entrance. Crouch on this ledge and fire down on your enemies as they enter.

The Shops

This cramped courtyard is where the Shops command post is positioned. From this position, defenders can see anyone who infiltrates the courtyard.

Located in the northwest corner of the map, the Shops command post sits in a small courtyard surrounded by small buildings and low walls. The area can be accessed from both the east and the west, but attackers can easily jump over the small walls to the north too. As a result, the defenders are best holding this command post from a small nook on the southern end of the courtyard.

From here they can see anyone who attempts to infiltrate the courtyard without worrying about watching their back. The command post has no nearby turrets, but if Rebel pilots move out quickly, they can claim two rooftop turrets to the east. Both are useful for repelling attacks from the Imperial-held Market.

Keep an eye on these low walls. Attackers may try to jump over them. They're too high to shoot over, so toss thermal detonators over to engage attackers in the adjacent streets.

Race to the east to construct these two rooftop turrets. They're both extremely valuable in holding back attacks along the westbound streets.

The Market

The Market command post is on this street corner to the north.

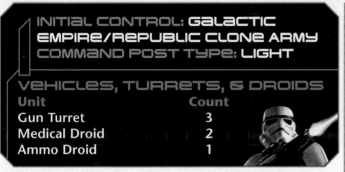

INITIAL CONTROL: GALACTIC EMPIRE/REPUBLIC CLONE ARMY
COMMAND POST TYPE: LIGHT

VEHICLES, TURRETS, & DROIDS

Unit	Count
Gun Turret	3
Medical Droid	2
Ammo Droid	1

Of the three Imperial command posts held at the beginning of the battle, the Market is definitely their stronghold. Three turrets defend this position, covering all possible avenues of attack. The turret to the north covers the northern street, capable of hitting incoming attacks from the Shops. The southern turret covers the street leading to the Cantina. A third turret sits on the nearby rooftop, just south of the command post.

From this elevated position, gunners can fire down on attackers to the south and west. It's also capable of engaging the rooftop turrets near the Warehouse. For the Rebels, capturing this command post depends heavily on taking out these turrets and preventing them from being reconstructed. Only then is it safe for infantry to move out and capture this position.

This turret covers the northern street leading toward the Shops command post. Use it to pin incoming attackers and any pilots attempting to construct the rooftop turret on the southern side of the street.

The turret west of the command post is capable of hitting targets near the Cantina to the south. As a result, this turret can shut down this street to all enemy traffic.

Located on the rooftop just south of the command post, this turret can support the other two, covering all surrounding areas. Keep an eye on the rooftop turrets near the warehouse. If they fall into enemy hands, they pose a serious threat to the Market.

Attackers can capture the command post from the rooftop to the south. Just make sure the nearby turret is destroyed or unoccupied before attempting this risky maneuver. Drop prone to avoid being spotted.

THE HOUSING

Located in another cramped courtyard, the Housing command post is best defended by flanking the two entrances on the southern side.

INITIAL CONTROL: GALACTIC EMPIRE/REPUBLIC CLONE ARMY
COMMAND POST TYPE: LIGHT

Located between the Warehouse and Market, the Housing command post offers no assets at all. Since no droids are nearby, pilots should take up residence here to help heal and resupply the defenders.

The good news is that the courtyard surrounding the command post can only be accessed via the two southern entrances. Flank these two entrances with defenders to surprise any attackers rushing in. Placing mines around blind corners is also a good way to keep the attackers out.

The courtyard housing the command post can only be accessed from these two arched entrances along the street to the south. If resources allow, defend the command post from the street and fall back into the courtyard as needed.

Camp near the archway entrances to watch enemies running along the street outside. Toss a few thermal detonators in their path to clear the street.

THE WAREHOUSE

Its close proximity to the Cantina makes the Warehouse a ripe target for Rebel attackers at the beginning of the battle. Make sure plenty of defenders spawn here to hold this position.

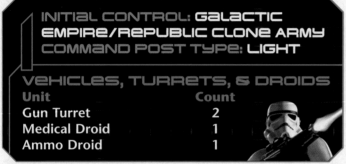

INITIAL CONTROL: GALACTIC EMPIRE/REPUBLIC CLONE ARMY
COMMAND POST TYPE: LIGHT

VEHICLES, TURRETS, & DROIDS

Unit	Count
Gun Turret	2
Medical Droid	1
Ammo Droid	1

The Warehouse is another courtyard-based command post lying along the eastern edge of the map. It can be accessed from the streets to the east or west. Because it's so close to the Cantina, early attacks are likely to be staged from the west.

The command post has no defensive features, but there are two rooftop turrets located to the west. Defending pilots should reach these turrets quickly and construct them to hold back attacks from the Cantina. The command post can be defended by infantry from the courtyard's rooftops. Use the elevation to rain down laser fire and thermal detonators on incoming attackers.

Get to this rooftop to the southwest and fire on Rebels as they round this corner leading from the Cantina.

These two turrets to the west are vital to holding back attacks on the Warehouse. Get here quickly and claim them before the enemy does.

Like the Market, this command post can be converted from the nearby rooftop. Use this position to fire on enemies attempting to counterattack.

REBEL ALLIANCE STRATEGY

Assault the Warehouse from its eastern entrance while your teammates hold the other command posts.

Because the Rebels only need to capture one command post to impose a reinforcement drain on Imperial forces, the Warehouse is the best place to start the attacks. Begin by spawning an assault force at the Cantina while the rest of the command posts are reinforced with other troops. Send your attack force along the southernmost street running along the perimeter of the map.

At the southeast corner, head north and attack the Warehouse from its eastern entrance. You're less likely to face resistance from this direction. Go to the rooftop and capture the command post while bracing for a counterattack.

Defend the Warehouse from the rooftop and suppress any counterattacks.

Consider capturing the Housing command post as well, containing the Imperials to the Market.

If you hold the other three command posts and capture the Warehouse, the Imperial reinforcements begin draining away. To fortify your position at the Warehouse, attack the Housing command post to the north.

Capturing this command post limits the Imperials to the Market, while strengthening your hold on the Warehouse and Cantina.

With five command posts captured, don't attack the Market; instead defend your current assets. The Empire may try aerial assaults using their dark troopers, so be ready for attacks at all Rebel-held command posts.

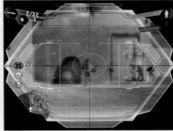

Take to the skies again and stage a joint assault on the Cantina, hitting it from the east and west entrances simultaneously.

Position snipers along the street and rooftops to prevent the Imperials from staging breakout attacks from the Market.

NOTE

The Jawas aren't linked to any particular command post. They spawn all over the map throughout the battle. They don't pose a serious threat to either side, so don't worry about shooting them.

GALACTIC EMPIRE STRATEGY

Use dark troopers to stage an aerial assault on the Shops command post.

The Empire may not start with the strongest command posts on the map, but their dark troopers allow them to perform aerial assaults, giving them the element of surprise and tremendous tactical versatility. Start by holding tight at the Market and Warehouse by constructing turrets and taking to the rooftops.

Meanwhile, assemble an assault force of dark troopers at the Market and stage an assault on the Shops command post to the west. It takes a couple of jumps to reach this position, but you should be able to drop directly in the courtyard. Once inside, blast all the defenders at close range and lock down all the entrances to prevent a counterattack. Once the command post is captured, hunt down any stragglers around the perimeter.

When the Shops are taken, assemble a second squad of dark troopers at the Warehouse. Use them to attack the Cantina's eastern entrance while the squad at the Shops attacks from the west. If coordinated, your two squads should have no problem storming the Cantina and capturing the command post. Just watch out for friendly fire when hitting the bar from both ends.

This leaves the Rebels with the Hangar. Since it's a tough nut to crack, stick to the perimeter and lay siege to the circular building. Turn its northern turret inward and blast any Rebels trying to escape. Meanwhile, cover the southern entrance from a distance, squeezing it from the east and west. Since they lack aerial units, they can't stage a breakout attack, so relax your defenses at your most distant command posts and converge on the Hangar until the Rebel reinforcements are completely drained.

Contain the Rebels at the Hangar. Turn this northern turret around to face the entrance and blast the Rebels as they try to escape. Avoid using the southern turrets in the same fashion because they're open to attacks from the barge-mounted guns.

TACTICS

HANGAR AERIAL ASSAULT

The dark trooper can bypass the Hangar's turrets and barge-mounted guns by attacking from the circular rooftop. Begin by approaching the Hangar from the northern side and fly up to the roof.

Use the stone wall on the left for cover while gunning down the defenders.

Toss a few thermal detonators down on the barge to clear out any mines or defenders you can't see from this position.

When it's clear, hop down onto the barge and crouch to convert the command post. Watch the scaffolding to the northwest for counterattacks.

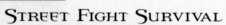

STREET FIGHT SURVIVAL

Mos Eisley's streets are extremely dangerous, particularly early in the battle as massive assault forces meet at close range. The exchange of laser fire and thermal detonators can result in some devastating massacres.

To prevent such disastrous standoffs, stay off the main streets and stick to the narrow alleyways. Also, identify the likely avenues of attack and stay away from them. The shortest path is almost always the most deadly.

The Rebel pilot and dark trooper are well suited for combat at close range. Use them in both defensive and offensive roles.

If you come face to face with an enemy turret, quickly dive out of the way and keep diving until you can reach cover. Quick lateral movements like this are the best way to avoid getting blasted.

Eliminating turrets can be a full-time job on this map. Leave it to units like this shock trooper to take out turrets before an assault.

BATTLE HINT
Jawas build turrets and repair supply droids for you. Use rooftops to attack enemies from above. Use units with jet packs to fly over hangar walls and take the CP. If the Empire captures and holds the Hangar, an AT-ST will spawn.

by Tester Justin VanAlstyne

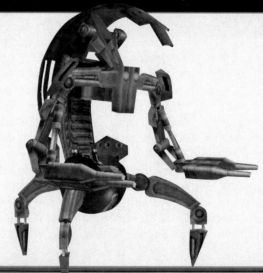

RHEN VAR: HARBOR

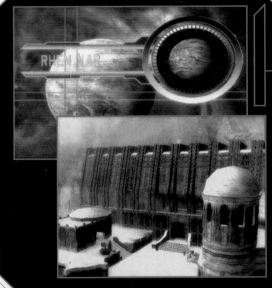

planetary overview

The frozen wasteland of Rhen Var was once a fertile paradise, but an atmospheric cataclysm devastated the planet's ecosystem millennia ago. It's now prone to blizzards and ice falls, and its landscape consists of icy plains, tundra, and glacier-carved mountains. Long ago, the ancient Jedi built monuments that are now buried beneath the ice. Snow-covered passages throughout the frozen wasteland allow forces to move quickly or succumb to a cold, icy conclusion.

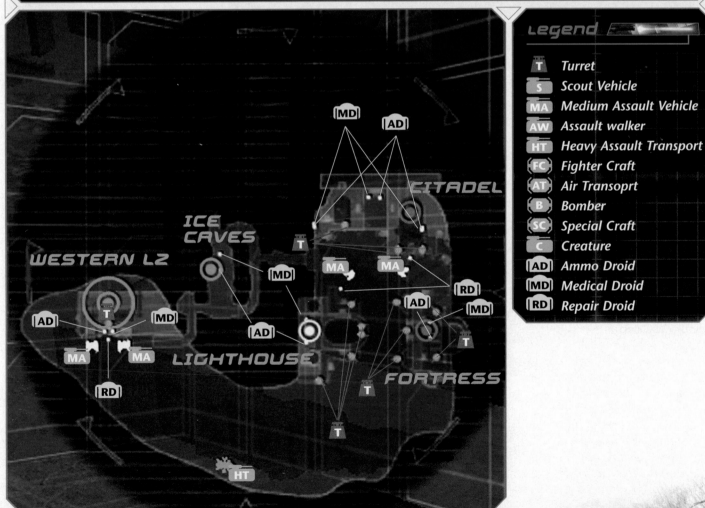

Legend

T	Turret
S	Scout Vehicle
MA	Medium Assault Vehicle
AW	Assault walker
HT	Heavy Assault Transport
FC	Fighter Craft
AT	Air Transoprt
B	Bomber
SC	Special Craft
C	Creature
AD	Ammo Droid
MD	Medical Droid
RD	Repair Droid

COMMAND POSTS

WESTERN LZ

These ruins to the far west fortify the Western LZ command post.

The pilot's grenade launcher works well for covering the entry to the Ice Caves. Lob rounds into the narrow entry to dissuade enemy advances.

Use Shocktroopers to mine the tops of the stairs. Attackers rushing up the steps are less likely to spot mines placed there.

INITIAL CONTROL: GALACTIC EMPIRE/REPUBLIC CLONE ARMY	
COMMAND POST TYPE: HEAVY	

VEHICLES, TURRETS, & DROIDS

Unit	Count
IF T-T/IF T-X	2/2
AT-AT/AT-TE	1/1
Gun Turret	1
Medical Droid	1
Ammo Droid	1
Repair Droid	1

Surround the Ice Cave entrance with mines. Although they can be taken out by attackers, they cause a bottleneck inside the cave. As attackers take steps to remove the mines, defenders have more time to fill the entrance with grenades and missiles.

The Western LZ serves as the main staging area for the Imperial assault. As expected, this command post is responsible for spawning all their vehicles, including the AT-AT. While the IF T-T tanks spawn just south of the command post, the AT-AT spawns farther east, placing it closer to the Rebel emplacements. The command post sits on a tall stone platform surrounded by three aged walls and, to the north, a steep mountain slope.

Two sets of steps line the southern side of the platform, giving attackers access to the command post. But a turret sitting on a platform between the staircases can hit both sets of steps. The turret can also be used to engage more distant targets attacking from the south. The Imperials must hold this command post, whatever the cost. If they are denied access to the AT-AT, the chances of an Imperial victory are slim.

ICE CAVES

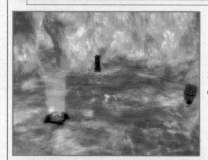

This wide chamber houses the command post as well as a couple of droids.

This position's only turret sits on top of the stone platform, just south of the command post. It's great for covering the plain to the south and the staircases on either side. But it isn't capable of hitting the western entry to the Ice Caves. Defenders should rely on other resources to cover this avenue of attack.

INITIAL CONTROL: GALACTIC EMPIRE/REPUBLIC CLONE ARMY	
COMMAND POST TYPE: LIGHT	

VEHICLES, TURRETS, & DROIDS

Unit	Count
Medical Droid	1
Ammo Droid	1

Held by the Empire at the beginning of the battle, the Ice Caves provide a welcome buffer between the Rebel positions and the Western LZ. While it's possible for the Imperials to attack from this cave, the narrow eastern entrance is a dangerous choke point, often covered by multiple turrets. The AT-AT is a much safer spawning alternative for attackers. But the Empire still wants to spawn plenty of defenders here to deny the Rebels an easy path to the Western LZ.

Train defensive efforts on the eastern entrance, using pilots and Shocktroopers to blast all incoming attackers. Deeper in the cave, place mines around blind corners to catch attackers by surprise.

Avoid using the eastern entrance as an avenue of attack. Rebels are likely to lie in wait outside with all sorts of nasty surprises. This is particularly true if the Rebels hold the Citadel and Lighthouse command posts—they have you caught in a cross fire as soon as you exit.

Defenders should set plenty of booby traps to prevent infiltration. Hide mines on walls and around blind corners.

The T-intersection is ideal for ambushes. Place mines on the walls at this narrow point in the southern passage. Then defend with troopers at the northern passage to force the attackers through your minefield. Most of the time they back into the mines while exchanging fire with your defenders to the north.

Use pilots and Shocktroopers to shut down the eastern entrance. Aim your weapons at the opening and blow away any attackers attempting to enter. Place a mine behind the ice pillar in the center of the corridor in case you need to withdraw deeper into the cave.

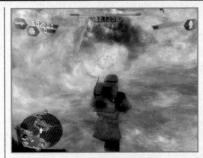

When attacking the Ice Caves, bank thermal detonators around corners to take out defenders. At the very least, a thermal detonator makes them back up.

CITADEL

The Citadel is the main focus of the Imperial assault. If defended well, it will be tough to capture.

INITIAL CONTROL: Rebel Alliance/ Separatist Battle Droids
COMMAND POST TYPE: Heavy

VEHICLES, TURRETS, & DROIDS

Unit	Count
Combat Speeder/AAT	2/2
Gun Turret	3
Medical Droid	3
Ammo Droid	3
Repair Droid	1

As the key spawn point for Rebel units, the Citadel holds a dominant position on the battlefield, sitting on a platform to the northeast. The command post is housed by a large stone building with three main entrances—one to the east and two to the west. A hole in the roof requires defenders to keep watch for aerial assaults.

The three entrances are wide, making it difficult to hide mines on the ground. Even mines placed on the walls may fail to detonate when attackers rush in. For this reason, it's a good idea to place a full-time defender within the Citadel. Hole up on the second floor and fire down on attackers as they attempt to capture the command post.

The stone platform on the northern side of the canyon compound can be accessed via three sets of steps. Three turrets lining the southern side of the platform cover all these steps. Two of the turrets sit directly south of the Citadel; the third turret sits farther to the west and can be used to cover the eastern entrance to the Ice Caves. The two combat speeders that spawn to the south can also be used to cover the steps and Ice Caves, but they're best deployed against the AT-AT.

Tucked against the northern cliff is another building that can be accessed by stairways on either end of the north side of the platform. These stairs lead to a balcony overlooking the entire compound, making an ideal nest for snipers to cover the southern approach as well as the Fortress and Lighthouse command posts.

Use pilots to construct the three turrets on the northern platform. All three should be operational before Imperial units rush in from the south and west.

The western turret is key to preventing the Imperials from escaping the Ice Caves. Simply line up the sights on the cave's opening and blast anything that exits.

Use the turrets to help engage enemy armor, too. Destroy these fast-moving tanks before focusing on the AT-AT.

Attackers can contest the Citadel command post from these steps on the western side of the building. If you are attacking alone, this is the safest spot to camp. Otherwise, enemies may spawn or counterattack from any direction.

FORTRESS

The Fortress command post is in this courtyard, surrounded by thick embattlements and several turrets.

INITIAL CONTROL: REBEL ALLIANCE/ SEPARATIST BATTLE DROIDS	
COMMAND POST TYPE: LIGHT	

VEHICLES, TURRETS, & DROIDS
Unit	Count
Gun Turret	5
Medical Droid	1
Ammo Droid	1

The Fortress is the second Rebel-controlled command post at the start of the battle. It sits on the far eastern side of the map, and spawning here gives the Rebels a good chance of capturing the Lighthouse command post to the west. Together, the Fortress and Lighthouse are the gateway to the compound's main courtyard. Controlling both of these command posts is important in holding back the AT-AT assault.

The west side of the fortress offers elevated embattlements with three turret positions. Construct these turrets quickly, before the first wave of attackers approach from the south. The command post sits in a small, open courtyard, covered by a turret to the north and another to the south. This position can be infiltrated along stairways to the south, west, and north. Southern and western attacks are most likely, but mine the tops of all three staircases. A building on the eastern side of the command post provides some upper-floor sniping spots useful for engaging attackers.

Constructing the three western turrets at the fortress should be the first priority for Rebel pilots at the Fortress. Enemy infantry spawning at the AT-AT make up the first wave of attackers approaching from the south. Use the turrets to hold back this assault.

As the AT-AT approaches, back away from the western turrets. The AT-AT's heavy lasers can wipe out the turrets and their

Rhen var: Harbor

gunners with a single shot. Fall back within the fortresses walls and await infantry attacks from the south and west. If the AT-AT's head moves past the turrets, feel free to return to the turrets and blast the behemoth's thick side armor.

These steps to the south are popular with attackers. Man this turret in the courtyard at all times, aiming at these steps—especially when the AT-AT is spawning troops nearby.

The building to the east of the command post is a good sniping position. Place snipers in front of these narrow windows and pick off enemies at the Lighthouse to the west.

The eastern building's upper level is also good for covering the southern steps.

The Lighthouse

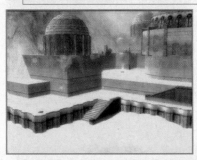

The southern side of the Lighthouse command post is relatively open, making it susceptible to bombardment by the AT-AT's heavy lasers.

INITIAL CONTROL: **NEUTRAL**
COMMAND POST TYPE: **LIGHT**

VEHICLES, TURRETS, & DROIDS

Unit	Count
Gun Turret	5
Medical Droid	1
Ammo Droid	1
Repair Droid	1

The Lighthouse makes up the compound's western flank, but the command post's neutral status gives both factions the opportunity to capture it. The Rebels are most likely to take control of this position, especially if they rush it with pilots spawned at the Fortress. But the Imperials could gain control if they rush the command post with infantry from the AT-AT or Ice Caves before the Rebels have a chance to fortify the position with turrets and mines.

The Lighthouse can be accessed from the north and south, via a series of steps. Similar to the Fortress, the command post sits in an open courtyard. But the southern approach features little protection, allowing the AT-AT to fire directly down on enemy attackers or defenders. If controlled by the Rebels, the Lighthouse's five turrets play a big role in holding back the Imperial attack. Combining these with the turrets at the Fortress and Citadel, the Rebels can focus an enormous amount of firepower on the narrow southern approach leading into the compound's main courtyard. The command post's northernmost turret can also be used to cover the Ice Caves, preventing Imperial attacks from the west.

The Rebels can gain control of this command post if they rush it with pilots spawned at the Fortress. Once it's captured, use the pilots to construct the turrets, beginning with the southernmost.

Man the turrets only when the AT-AT has moved past their positions. The AT-AT's narrow forward-firing arc makes it incapable of defending itself from flank attacks. Keep an eye on the AT-AT's feet, too, to take out the enemies that it spawns on the ground.

Four staircases lead to the command post; two to the north and two to the south. Place mines at the tops of all four staircases to lock down this position.

If the enemy holds the Fortress, take cover behind this central turret on the Lighthouse's eastern side. While using the turret for cover and conceal-ment, the Imperial pilot can launch grenades at the Fortress's western steps. It's also possible to hit the command post's courtyard from this position.

REBEL ALLIANCE STRATEGY

Storm the Lighthouse with pilots to convert the command post and construct turrets. Watch for attackers rushing up the southern steps.

Flank the AT-AT with your combat speeders and pound its thick side armor with laser fire and missiles. The combat speeders are your best answer to this menacing walker.

As the defenders, the Rebel Alliance's job is straightfor-ward—hold the Citadel and surrounding command posts against the Imperial assault. For starters, begin by taking the Lighthouse and fortifying it with mines and turrets. Meanwhile, bolster defenses at the Fortress and Citadel. Prepare for infantry attacks from the Ice Caves to the west and AT-AT and armor attacks from the south.

Use combat speeders to keep the enemy IF T-Ts from breaching the courtyard. If possible, park them near the repair droids at the Citadel and Lighthouse to get a tactical advantage while blasting the enemy tanks. When the enemy tanks are destroyed, flank the AT-AT with the combat speeders to prevent taking heavy damage from its forward-facing heavy lasers—all it takes is two hits to demolish your combat speeders.

While holding the command posts around the Citadel, attack the Ice Caves to impose a permanent rein-forcement drain on the Empire. Fighting in the Ice Caves is brutal, but taking this position fortifies the Rebel's western flank.

Holding the compound's three command posts isn't quite enough to impose a reinforcement drain on the Imperials. The drain takes effect briefly once the AT-AT is destroyed, leaving the Empire with just the Ice Caves and Western LZ. But the drain stops once a new AT-AT spawns. To inflict a more permanent reinforcement drain, stage an assault against the Ice Caves.

Assemble a mixed squad of soldiers and pilots to storm the caves and convert the command post. From there it's possible to hit the Western LZ as well. This would deny the Empire their AT-AT and IF T-Ts. A sweeping attack on the Ice Caves and Western LZ may catch the Imperials by surprise, but your main priority is to hold firm at the Citadel. Holding the Ice Caves and the compound's three command posts is sufficient to impose a permanent drain on the Imperial forces.

If the Ice Caves are under Rebel control, hit the Western LZ before the Empire catches on to your breakout assault. Strike the stronghold with infantry from the Ice Caves and a combat speeder from the Citadel. The combat speeder is useful for taking out the command post's turret. Once you capture and hold the position, you can say farewell to the AT-AT.

> ## NOTE
>
> If the Rebels capture the Western LZ and destroy the AT-AT, the balance of the battle switches dramatically. Only five command posts/spawn points remain on the map. This means your forces need to hold only three command posts to impose a reinforcement drain on the enemy.

GALACTIC EMPIRE STRATEGY

Use the IF T-Ts to escort the AT-AT to prevent flanking attacks. Pay particular attention to the Rebel combat speeders.

Rhen Var: Harbor

For the Empire, the AT-AT is the key to gaining a foothold in the Citadel's compound and maintaining a reinforcement drain on the Rebels. At the start of the battle, the Rebels begin with a reinforcement drain. Maintain it by taking the Lighthouse while holding the Ice Caves and Western LZ. Spawn stormtroopers and pilots at the AT-AT and rush the Lighthouse from the south.

When the AT-AT is within range, use it to bombard the Lighthouse command post to drive any Rebel defenders out of the area, making room for your infantry to move in. Keep watch over the Lighthouse until the infantry can maintain a solid presence and fortify it from a counterattack.

Meanwhile, use the AT-AT to take out Rebel turrets and their combat speeders. Try to prevent the speeders from flanking the AT-AT. The IF T-Ts should make protecting the AT-AT's flanks their sole responsibility.

Bombard the Lighthouse with the AT-AT from the south until stormtroopers can rush in and capture the command post.

Attack the Fortress from the south, too, using the AT-AT to bombard the command post while spawning infantry.

When the Lighthouse is firmly held by Imperial forces, move the AT-AT to the east and begin the assault on the Fortress. Move the AT-AT near the mountain in the far east, giving it a decent view of the Fortress's courtyard; fire down into it. From this southern position, spawn stormtroopers and use them to infiltrate the command post via the southern steps.

Capturing this command post may take some time, because the Rebels continuously spawn units at the Citadel and counterattack. Keep the AT-AT in place until the infantry can lock down the Fortress. Now you can contain the Rebel forces at the Citadel. Move the AT-AT within range of the Citadel's turrets and combat speeder spawn points and continually hammer them with the heavy lasers. The carnage dealt by the AT-AT and the reinforcement drain should ensure a quick victory.

When the Rebels are weak, rush the Citadel with stormtroopers and bring the siege to an end.

TIP

Don't maneuver the AT-AT between the Lighthouse and Fortress unless your team holds both command posts. Otherwise the AT-AT is open to turret and missile attacks by Rebel defenders at either position.

TACTICS

CITADEL SNIPING

Rebel marksmen want to get inside the building just north of the Citadel. Use one of two northern entrances to access the steps leading up to the balcony. From this position it's possible to see the entire compound, including the Fortress and Lighthouse command posts. Use the height advantage to pick off enemy troops to the south, including the exposed gunners in the IF T-Ts. Scan the area around the AT-AT's legs to pick off Imperials as they spawn.

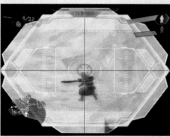

This balcony is also useful for covering the eastern entrance to the Ice Caves. Move to the west side of the balcony and fire down on Imperial troops as soon as they exit.

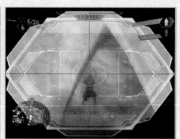

You can also cover the Ice Caves from this position just west of the Citadel command post. Drop prone and fire directly into the cave. A couple of marksmen placed at this position greatly hinder Imperial efforts to stage an attack from the Ice Caves.

FLANKING THE CITADEL

The building to the north of the Citadel also offers a potential avenue of attack for the Imperial forces. Spawn a squad of stormtroopers at the Ice Caves and immediately turn north upon exiting. Make your way to the northwest entrance and cross the balcony on your way to the Citadel.

Assault the Citadel from the eastern entrance. This is the safest path and exposes your squad to less incoming fire, especially from the nearby turrets.

Upon entry, clear out the Citadel's defenses. If the rest of your squad gets taken out, hold on these steps. Bank thermal detonators off the Citadel's interior walls to take out defenders you can't see below. Even if you can't capture it, neutralizing the Citadel denies the Rebels a spawn point, making it easier for follow-up attacks to succeed.

Dark troopers can attack the Citadel from the hole in the roof. Instead of dropping down next to the command post, hop down on the second floor and use the height advantage to eliminate defenders before moving in for the capture.

AT-AT TAKEDOWN

The combat speeders are the Rebel's first line of defense against the AT-AT. But no matter how careful you are with them, the combat speeders won't last long. So your infantry has to step up and stop this threat.

The most low-tech attack comes from the solider class. Use their concussion grenades to attack the AT-AT's armor. Unlike thermal detonators, the concussion grenades stick to the AT-AT before exploding. They don't cause much damage, but it's better than nothing.

For a more conventional option, use the vanguard missile launchers to slowly weaken the AT-AT. When possible, stand right next to an ammo droid to maintain an endless supply of missiles. If firing at close range, don't wait for the missiles to lock on. Simply fire them off as fast as possible until the walker collapses.

TIP

When controlling the AT-AT, always make sure two pilots are on board. The AT-AT takes a serious beating and requires constant repair. In addition to the pilots on board, have pilots trailing behind the walker so they can repair it from outside.

A riskier approach is to use Wookiee smugglers to attach time bombs to the AT-AT's legs. These cause significantly more damage than concussion grenades and missiles, but require the smugglers to move beneath the AT-AT, where fresh stormtroopers are likely to spawn. Use this tactic only when you can get next to the AT-AT quickly without exposing yourself to too much fire.

Then there's the orbital strike. Use a marksmen's recon droid and fly directly beneath the AT-AT. Begin calling in the strike just before you get beneath the walker. Once the strike is called in, switch away from controlling the recon droid and watch as the AT-AT takes some devastating hits from above. Multiple orbital strikes in quick succession can reduce an AT-AT to rubble in seconds.

BATTLE HINT

The CIS droideka is a powerful unit on this map. The CIS can effectively push through tunnels by rolling in fast and unfurling with the shield up, while protecting units behind it as they move through the narrow passes. The defending factions, Rebels and CIS, start this level with a slow bleed in reinforcements. Capture the center neutral CP immediately to staunch the bleed. The attacking factions, Imperials and Republic, have mobile CPs. Use the AT-AT and the AT-TE to move into the open courtyard where units can then spawn in and hold key territory.

by Tester Brianna Woodward

BATTLE HINT

Hold the Lighthouse and the Ice Caves. Take the Citadel if you like, but if you keep the CIS from taking the Lighthouse, you should be fine.

by Tester Xavier Rodriguez

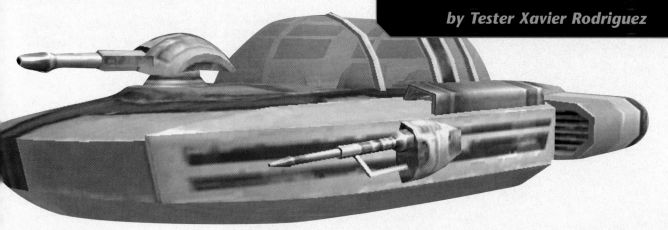

YAVIN 4: ARENA

planetary overview

The jungle moon known as Yavin IV was originally settled by Dark Lord of the Sith Naga Sadow and his minions. Over time, the descendants of Sadow evolved into the deadly Massassi warriors, who built massive stone temples throughout the jungles of Yavin IV before vanishing into legend themselves.

With few approaches through jungles full of thick brush and beautiful waterfalls, the incredibly strong Massassi temples make perfect hangars and command facilities. The Great Temple, at the crest of a great hill, is the largest of all the temples and naturally becomes the de facto HQ for any force looking to make Yavin IV a base of operations.

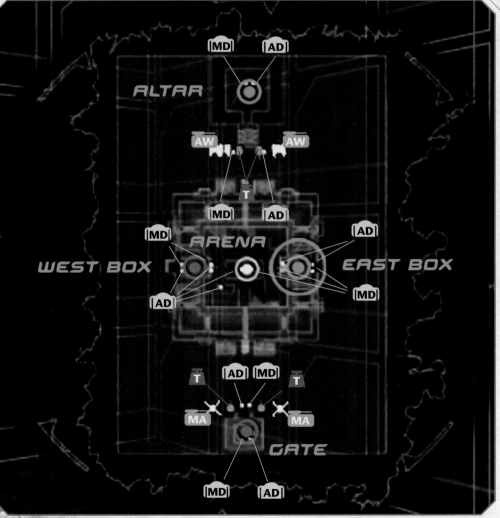

Legend

T	Turret
S	Scout Vehicle
MA	Medium Assault Vehicle
AW	Assault walker
HT	Heavy Assault Transport
FC	Fighter Craft
AT	Air Transoprt
B	Bomber
SC	Special Craft
C	Creature
AD	Ammo Droid
MD	Medical Droid
RD	Repair Droid

YAVIN 4: ARENA

COMMAND POSTS

ALTAR

The Altar is the Empire's main base of operations, spawning two AT-STs.

Place heavy weapons units like this Shocktrooper on the Altar to defend against combat speeder attacks. This allows them to fire and then seek cover while reloading. The ammo droid inside the Altar's chamber also provides an endless supply of missiles.

INITIAL CONTROL: GALACTIC EMPIRE/REPUBLIC CLONE ARMY
COMMAND POST TYPE: HEAVY

VEHICLES, TURRETS, & DROIDS

Unit	Count
AT-ST/IF T-X	2/3
Gun Turret	2
Medical Droid	2
Ammo Droid	2

Located at the north edge of the map, the Altar is a large pyramid-like structure controlled by Imperial forces at the outset of the battle. The command post sits inside an elevated chamber and can be accessed via a steep staircase on the south side of the structure. The chamber has three entrances to the south, east, and west, all of which require defenders to prevent infiltration.

Placing mines on or near the narrow entrances is the best way to lock down this position. At the base of the structure are two gun turrets as well as the spawn points for the two AT-STs. But Imperial defenders are better off defending from the Altar itself, using the height advantage to fire down on attackers. If necessary, fall back into the chamber housing the command post and cover the three entrances.

Use mines to defend the Altar from infiltration. Place the mines on the walls of these narrow entrances where they're less likely to be seen. Consider placing a mine or two at the top of the Altar's steps.

Deploy snipers near the arena to cover the Altar's long staircase. From this position you can hit attackers in the back as they rush up the steps.

WEST BOX

The West Box overlooks the arena, giving the Rebels a firm presence within the ancient structure.

The Altar's two turrets are at the base of the structure, flanking both sides of the staircase. Use a pilot to construct these early to prevent infantry attacks. But if combat speeders attack, vacate the turrets immediately and seek cover on or around the Altar.

INITIAL CONTROL: REBEL ALLIANCE/SEPARATIST BATTLE DROIDS
COMMAND POST TYPE: LIGHT

VEHICLES, TURRETS, & DROIDS

Unit	Count
Gun Turret	1
Medical Droid	2
Ammo Droid	2

The Rebels hold the West Box at the beginning of the battle, giving them the proper foothold to attain total control of the arena. But the Empire also has a presence in the structure at the East Box. The ensuing battle over these three command posts within the arena requires defenders to be on the move constantly or seek cover.

The roof overhang above the command post prevents the position from being bombarded, but snipers looking for easy kills are likely to populate the eastern side of the arena in an attempt to pick off your teammates as they spawn. The best way to counter the sniper threat is to defend with your own snipers, from within the box or from the rooftop.

A turret sits to the east of the command post, giving it a good view of the arena below and the East Box. However, gunners are prone to flanking, sniper, and missile attacks, so use this turret sparingly. While most attacks are likely to come from within the arena, some may come from outside along the two entrances to the west. Have defenders guarding and mining these entrances at all times.

 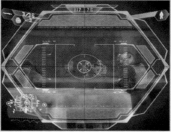

There's little cover within the West Box except for the droids positioned behind the command post. The ammo droid is just the right height for a marksman unit to hide behind. While standing, zoom in and pick off Imperials in the East Box.

If occupied by the enemy, use a marksman's recon droid to call in an orbital strike on the Arena command post.

Place mines on the northern and southern approaches to the command post. Although they can easily be seen here, their presence slows down an attack, giving your defenders more time to respond.

Also, mine the two western passages leading outside the arena structure.

Heavy-weapons troops like this vanguard should use the box's elevation to blast enemies on the arena floor. Aim for the target's feet to maximize the chance of hitting. Even if your target dodges a missile, the splash damage should inflict heavy damage.

THE ARENA

The Arena command post sits in the dead center of the battlefield and is up for grabs at the beginning.

| INITIAL CONTROL: NEUTRAL | |
| COMMAND POST TYPE: LIGHT | |

VEHICLES, TURRETS, & DROIDS
Unit	Count
Medical Droid	1
Ammo Droid	1

Because it's the only neutral command post at the start of the battle, both factions should focus on capturing the Arena. Whoever grabs it and maintains their other command posts immediately imposes a reinforcement drain on the enemy. This is incentive enough to capture and hold onto this position as long as possible. Unfortunately, it has virtually no defensive features other than a few walls, so it is likely to change hands several times throughout the battle.

Defenders on the arena floor are open to attacks from all directions, particularly from the higher elevations of the East and West Boxes. For this reason, defenders are best off patrolling the arena floor for attackers instead of camping in one particular spot. Four walls surround the command post, and all but the eastern one has an entry point. It's possible to mine the area around the command post, but in the chaotic close-quarters fighting, detonating mines may kill or injure friendly units. A mine might even go off in your face as you place it.

Once captured by your team, patrol the area around the command post. There are no safe places to camp, so keep moving to avoid being an easy kill for sniper positioned around the perimeter.

The wall to the east of the command post is high and has no entry points. Rebel defenders can huddle against this wall for temporary cover, especially if the turret in the East Box is active. Lob a few thermal detonators toward the East Box in an attempt to take out the gunner.

Mines are very effective if placed on the narrow entrances leading to the command post. Make sure your team stays away from these mined areas to prevent friendly-fire incidents during close-quarters engagements.

The mine's detonator differentiates between friend or foe, but the subsequent explosion won't, inflicting heavy damage to all units within its blast radius.

EAST BOX

The East Bunker sits directly across the arena from the West Bunker and includes identical features.

The East Box is a mirror image of the West Box, and is held by Imperials at the start of the battle. The position of the turret is the same, as are the locations of the droids—two behind the command post and two on the arena floor just below the box. Defensive tactics should resemble those mentioned for the West Box with sniper and heavy weapons units using the droids for cover.

   Imperial scouts might want to even take the box's rooftop, and fire down on Rebels scurrying about the arena floor or on other enemy snipers taking refuge in the West Box. Just as important is covering the two eastern passages leading outside the arena. Rebel flank attacks are likely to move through these passages, so place mines in these areas.

The wall on the eastern side of the Arena command post prevents this turret from getting a full view of the surrounding area. However, it's still useful for suppressing attacks and enemy movement along north and south walls.

Get on the rooftop of the box for a better view of the Arena command post. Use this position to fire missiles and lob thermal detonators down on the defenders.

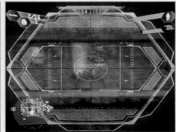

If sniping from the rooftop, always drop prone. It doesn't make you invisible, but it makes you harder to hit. This is a great position for picking off enemies in the West Box, including the turret's gunner. From this distance, sniping is the most accurate option for destroying the opposing turret.

INITIAL CONTROL: Galactic Empire/Republic Clone Army
COMMAND POST TYPE: LIGHT

VEHICLES, TURRETS, & DROIDS

Unit	Count
Gun Turret	1
Medical Droid	2
Ammo Droid	2

Don't forget to cover the two eastern passages. Place mines on the narrow entrances or hide them in the high grass. If unprotected, these passages leave the command post open to point-blank flank attacks.

GATE

The Gate provides the Rebels with two combat speeders.

Toss some mines around the command post, particularly at the top of each set of stairs. You can also catch enemies by surprise by sticking mines to the pillars surrounding the command post.

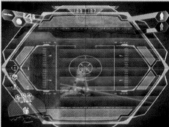

A marksman on the command post's elevated platform is essential for covering the two sets of steps on the northern side of the arena. Between marksmen and the two turrets, your team should be capable of containing enemy troops within the arena's walls.

INITIAL CONTROL: REBEL ALLIANCE/ SEPARATIST BATTLE DROIDS
COMMAND POST TYPE: HEAVY

VEHICLES, TURRETS, & DROIDS

Unit	Count
Combat Speeder/ Spider Walker	2/2
Gun Turret	2
Medical Droid	2
Ammo Droid	2

Similar to the Altar, the Gate is another ancient structure serving as the main staging area for Rebel forces. The command post sits on a high platform overlooking the southern side of the arena. This platform can be accessed via the two parallel staircases on the northern side of the structure. The area around the command post is open to attacks from all directions so defenders should use the pillars for cover.

Like at the Altar, the two turrets at the base of the Gate are useful for holding back infantry attacks, but should be vacated if AT-STs move into the area. The combat speeders should be the first line of defense against such attacks, but vanguards can lend a hand using missiles and mines.

The two turrets work well for repelling infantry attacks, but if an AT-ST approaches, jump in one of the nearby combat speeders.

REBEL ALLIANCE STRATEGY

The combat speeders dominate the area outside the arena. Use them to make frequent attacks on the enemies at the Altar, but don't stick around to duel their AT-STs, especially if both are in the area.

The chaotic situation in the arena makes for an unpredictable battle. But the Rebels can gain a slight edge if they control the action outside the arena. This involves making frequent raids on the Altar command post to the north using the combat speeders. If possible, capture the Altar to gain total control of the outer command posts.

Focus on capturing the West and East Box command posts over the lower Arena command post. The easiest way to capture the East Box is to stage an assault from one of the outer eastern entrances. This allows your assault force to hit the command post from the sides instead of crossing the arena. If both boxes are controlled, you should be able to hold the Imperials to the arena's floor. This makes it much easier to repel attacks.

Holding both boxes and the Gate is enough to impose a reinforcement drain on the Empire. Strengthen your defenses and wait for the Empire's forces to weaken before attempting to capture the remaining command posts.

Assault the East Box from the eastern entrances and overwhelm the Imperial defenders at close range. Soldiers, pilots, and smugglers are all well suited for such assaults.

NOTE

Since neither side controls half of the command posts, both factions are hit with a reinforcement drain at the start of the battle.

GALACTIC EMPIRE STRATEGY

Dark troopers are capable of capturing the Arena command post within the first few seconds of a battle.

The Imperials face the same situation as the Rebels, but the capabilities of their units allow a little more flexibility. On the outside of the arena, the AT-STs should be primarily concerned with defending the Altar. Keep them together to prevent rush attacks by Rebel combat speeders. Inside the arena, use dark troopers to continually harass the Rebel positions. A small squad of dark troopers can jump from one command post to the next with relative ease. Use them to capture the Arena command post while your other units hold the East Box.

Once captured, patrol the Arena command post with stormtroopers to avert any counterattacks. Meanwhile, send your dark troopers to attack the West Box at close range. For best results, attack from the box's rooftop and drop down to get the jump on defenders. With persistent attacks, your dark troopers should be able to drive the Rebels completely out of the arena. From there, it's just a matter of containing them at the Gate.

Lock down the arena's southern entrances with mines while your AT-STs patrol the eastern and western sides. As the reinforcement drain takes its toll, the Rebels slowly lose their strength, allowing your dark troopers to stage an aerial assault on the Gate to bring the battle to an end.

The AT-STs are well suited for covering the eastern and western sides of the arena, preventing flanking attacks on the box command posts.

TACTICS

ALTAR RUSH

The Rebels gain a huge advantage if they capture the Altar. This denies the Imperials their AT-STs and a presence on the arena's outside. One of the most unorthodox ways to capture the Altar is to rush it with the combat speeders.

Before making a run for the Altar, clear out any defenders on the ground, including the two turrets.

When the ground around the Altar is clear, simply drive the combat speeder up the steep staircase. This gets you closer to the command post chamber, limiting your exposure to fire from below.

Get the combat speeder as close to the Altar's entrance as possible before hopping out.

Once out of the combat speeder, rush into the command post chamber and mow down any defenders. The soldier and pilot classes are particularly good at such close-range combat.

While converting the command post, keep an eye on all three entrances, particularly the one to the south. If a heavy weapons unit came along for the assault, use them to mine each entrance. Hold out in the Altar's chamber until the command post is converted. Continue defending this room until more friendly units spawn, then help them clear out any defenders around the Altar's base.

YAVIN 4: ARENA

GRASS AMBUSH

The high grass surrounding the arena is ideal for setting up ambushes, especially when it comes to taking out combat speeders.

This allows you to assault the enemy's forces at close range, significantly reducing the amount of damage your squad takes en route to the command post. Take out the turret's gunner first, and then worry about the remaining defenders.

Drop prone to disappear beneath the foliage. If using a Shocktrooper, equip a missile launcher and wait for it to lock on to a target. The launcher can lock onto only one type of vehicle, indicating the presence of a combat speeder. Even if you can't see the speeder through the grass, you can hit it as long as the launcher achieves a lock.

These light command posts don't take long to convert, especially if your attack squad survives the initial assault. Still, watch for fresh units spawning in and around the box to stop any counterattacks from within. Controlling both boxes puts your team in a strong position to win the battle.

Keep firing missiles until the enemy speeder explodes. This tactic works best when an AT-ST is nearby to draw the speeder's attacks. Meanwhile, your Shocktroopers in the grass can pound away on the speeder without fear of reprisal. But remember, grass is concealment and not cover. If your position is discovered, you're not safe from attack.

TREE COVER

The combat speeder's lateral maneuverability gives it a huge advantage when engaging the Imperial AT-STs. Instead of parking in one place and dueling with an AT-ST, keep moving (particularly laterally) to dodge incoming laser blasts.

Look for trees to slip behind. Although the tree trunks are fairly narrow, they're still capable of blocking the brunt of an AT-ST's blasts. As soon as the AT-ST fires, slip back out from behind cover and fire, then move back behind the trees. Such evasive movement can increase a combat speeder's life expectancy tremendously. This is particularly important if no pilots are on board to provide repairs.

Placing mines in the deep grass is also a great way to stop speeders. Try to create small minefields in narrow areas along the eastern and western sides of the arena.

BOX FLANKING MANEUVER

Instead of assaulting the opposing team's box from within the arena, attack along either the northern or southern flanks from outside. Defenders looking for easy kills on the arena floor often neglect these avenues of attack.

BATTLE HINT
Seize the three command posts inside the Arena as fast as possible. Holding them is the key to victory, so you can get your opponent to start bleeding almost immediately. After the three inside command posts are secure, hop in a vehicle and blast your opponents as they try to retake the Arena.

by Tester Seth Benton

YAVIN 4: TEMPLE

planetary overview

The jungle moon known as Yavin IV was originally settled by Dark Lord of the Sith Naga Sadow and his minions. Over time, the descendants of Sadow evolved into the deadly Massassi warriors, who built massive stone temples throughout the jungles of Yavin IV before vanishing into legend themselves. With few approaches through jungles full of thick brush and beautiful waterfalls, the incredibly strong Massassi temples make perfect hangars and command facilities. The Great Temple, at the crest of a great hill, is the largest of all the temples and naturally becomes the de facto HQ for any force looking to make Yavin IV a base of operations.

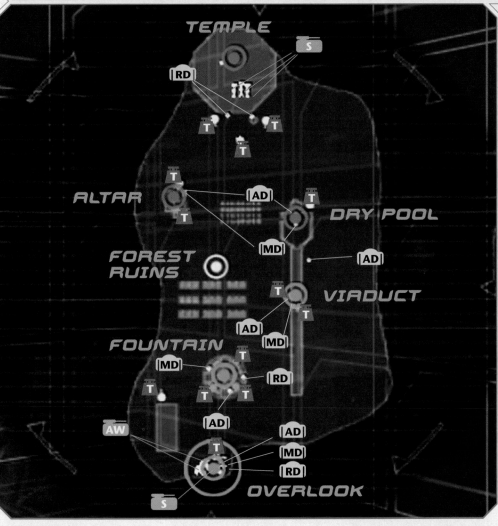

Legend

T	Turret	
S	Scout Vehicle	
MA	Medium Assault Vehicle	
AW	Assault walker	
HT	Heavy Assault Transport	
FC	Fighter Craft	
AT	Air Transoprt	
B	Bomber	
SC	Special Craft	
C	Creature	
AD	Ammo Droid	
MD	Medical Droid	
RD	Repair Droid	

TEMPLE

ALTAR

DRY POOL

FOREST RUINS

VIADUCT

FOUNTAIN

OVERLOOK

COMMAND POSTS

TEMPLE

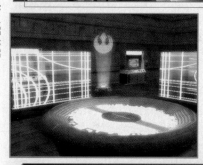

The Temple's command post is tucked away in this familiar war room at the back of the ancient structure.

Vanguards should stay near the Temple's main entrance to deal with AT-STs. Use the interior of the Temple for cover while reloading, then step out to fire.

The tower turrets outside the Temple are also useful against the AT-STs. Their rapid-firing lasers can weaken these menacing walkers quickly. But your gunners won't stand a chance in a duel, so retreat back inside the Temple if the AT-STs approach.

INITIAL CONTROL: REBEL ALLIANCE/REPUBLIC CLONE ARMY
COMMAND POST TYPE: LIGHT

VEHICLES, TURRETS, & DROIDS

Unit	Count
Speeder Bike	3
Tower Turret	3
Repair Droid	2

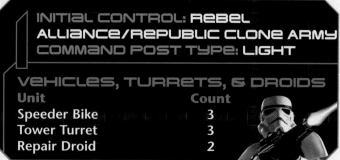

The Temple is an ancient pyramid-like structure serving as the Rebel's main base. A war room in the northern side of the structure houses the command post. Access this upper-floor room via two staircases on the east or west. These stairs lead to a catwalk providing access to the war room. Inside are tactical screens that can be used for cover by both attackers and defenders.

Rebel pilots are well suited for defending this room, using their blaster cannons at close range. The Temple can be accessed from two directions, but most attacks come through the main entrance to the south. A hole in the roof gives aerial units an alternative path. For this reason, defenders are best off holding back in the war room to intercept all potential attackers.

Use a vanguard to place mines near the war room's entrances. Mines also are useful for covering the wide southern entrance. Space out the mines to halt rush attacks by enemies on speeder bikes. The three tower turrets outside the main entrance also come in handy for repelling attacks from the south.

ALTAR

This command post sits at the top of this tall Altar—a challenge to attackers if properly defended.

INITIAL CONTROL: REBEL ALLIANCE/REPUBLIC CLONE ARMY
COMMAND POST TYPE: LIGHT

VEHICLES, TURRETS, & DROIDS

Unit	Count
Tower Turret	1
Gun Turret	1
Medical Droid	1
Ammo Droid	1

Just southwest of the Temple, the Altar's defensive features serve as a welcome buffer for Rebel defenders. A gun turret sits along the Altar's southern base, and a tower turret to the north. The gun turret can engage targets as far away as the Forest Ruins. The tower turret's range is more limited because of the thick foliage surrounding the command post, but it's still extremely effective for covering the command post.

Slap a few mines on the walls around the war room's entrances. This keeps the mines out of sight, increasing the chances of catching the enemy by surprise as they rush toward the command post.

YAVIN 4: TEMPLE

Attackers should destroy the tower turret before attempting a capture. The command post can be accessed using either ramp on the north and south sides. Alternately, dark troopers can bypass the ramp and simply fly to the top. Either way, attackers must loiter at the top of the Altar to convert the command post, making them extremely vulnerable to counterattacks. Deploy a marksman nearby for the sole purpose of covering this command post.

As usual, use vanguards to mine the command post. Place one mine at the top of each ramp. Stick another on one of the pillars flanking the command post.

The gun turret is great for engaging distant targets. Zoom in and try picking off enemies near the Forest Ruins.

The rapid-fire capability of the tower turret makes it invaluable in defending the command post and surrounding terrain.

DRY POOL

The water evaporated long ago, but this pool still serves a crucial role in the Rebel defense.

INITIAL CONTROL: REBEL ALLIANCE/REPUBLIC CLONE ARMY
COMMAND POST TYPE: LIGHT

VEHICLES, TURRETS, & DROIDS

Unit	Count
Tower Turret	1
Medical Droid	1
Ammo Droid	1

The Rebel position at the Dry Pool only strengthens their position on the hill, providing a great staging area for attackers looking to flank the Imperial positions to the south. What was once a shallow pool connected to a stone aqueduct is now a highly defensible command post. Defenders should make good use of the surrounding stone perimeter, as it provides great cover and concealment—at least from infantry.

On the other hand, the AT-ST, using its elevated weapons platform, can fire down on defenders attempting to hide in the stone ruins. Since the Empire holds the Viaduct command post to the south, Rebel defenders can expect most attacks from that direction, especially at the beginning of the battle. Use the elevated position to fire down on attackers as they charge up the hill. Lob plenty of thermal detonators in their path too. The aqueduct provides a great elevated position for covering the forest floor below.

Rebel pilots are great for defending this command post, especially if attackers infiltrate the pool. Watch the southern side of the pool and blast attackers as they storm the command post.

The tower turret on the northeast corner of the pool is also useful for defending the command post. Use it to weaken AT-STs approaching from the south, but be ready to vacate the turret if you start taking fire.

Toss a few mines in the high grass near this open corner to the southeast. Imperial attackers are likely to enter the pool at this point.

If AT-STs approach, do your best to stay out of sight. There isn't much cover within the pool, so keep a low profile until you can find a better position on the outer perimeter of the command post.

The aqueduct provides an awesome platform for covering the forest floor. Deploy troops up here, especially if your team holds the Dry Pool and Viaduct command posts.

FOREST RUINS

The Forest Ruins offer no defensive features, but the crumbling stone walls provide some decent cover for defenders.

INITIAL CONTROL: NEUTRAL
COMMAND POST TYPE: LIGHT

As the only neutral command post on the map, Forest Ruins is a key target for both factions at the start of the battle. For the quickest capture, the Imperials should attack with pilots and dark troopers from the Viaduct while Rebel pilots rush in from the Altar. Winning the foot race is less important than winning the close-quarters slugfest that is likely to ensue.

Both the dark trooper and Rebel pilot have the advantage in such engagements. Once you capture it, holding the command post won't be easy. Rebel defenders face constant attacks along the steps from the south while Imperial defenders encounter resistance from the north. Fortunately, the surrounding ruins provide some cover. Use them to crouch behind while returning fire.

When playing as the Rebels, spawn as a pilot at the Altar and rush to the south to reach the Forest Ruins. Seek cover and prepare to engage incoming attackers from the south and east.

Jump up on the western stone wall while facing south. The wall provides some cover while you engage attackers to the south from this elevated position. Zoom in to get a better view of attackers rushing from the Fountain.

For Rebel defenders, the steps to the south are a frequent path of attack by the Imperials. Toss some mines around the steps, using the high grass to hide them.

VIADUCT

The Viaduct command post sits below the large aqueduct running along the east side of the battlefield.

INITIAL CONTROL: GALACTIC EMPIRE/
SEPARATIST BATTLE DROIDS
COMMAND POST TYPE: LIGHT

VEHICLES, TURRETS, & DROIDS

Unit	Count
Gun Turret	2
Medical Droid	1
Ammo Droid	1

Of the three Imperial-held positions, the Viaduct is by far the hardest to hold. Located just down the hill from the Dry Pool, this position is susceptible to constant Rebel attack. Not only do the Rebels attack down the hill, but they may even drop down from the aqueduct above. Even the command post's two turrets have a hard time keeping attackers at bay.

For best results, the Imperials should call in an AT-ST for support. Staging a successful attack on the Dry Pool is the only way the Empire can halt the constant flow of attacks on this vulnerable position.

Spawn pilot units here to construct the two turrets before the Rebels attack from the Dry Pool. Swing the turrets to the north and engage the incoming attackers.

The command post has a relatively small capture radius, requiring attackers to approach these steps. Scatter some mines around the platform the command post sits on to prevent a quick capture by the enemy.

The Imperial pilot's mortar launcher is great for lobbing explosives in the path of the incoming attackers. Take cover behind the command post's stone platform and arc your grenades up the hill.

FOUNTAIN

The Fountain's stone pillars and three turrets make it a formidable defensive stronghold for Imperial forces.

Sitting at the base of the hill leading to the Temple, the Fountain offers multiple defensive features capable of withstanding assaults from all directions. For one, the three turrets are positioned around the command post's perimeter, providing heavy firepower support in all directions. In addition, the turrets can turn inward to blast attackers attempting to convert the command post.

Attackers must demolish each turret before even attempting an assault. Equally impressive are the stone pillars surrounding the Fountain, which provide defenders with plenty of cover. For the Imperials, the Fountain acts as a buffer between the Rebel-controlled command posts to the north and the Overlook command post to the south. It also serves as a key spawn point for infantry attacks running along the western side of the map.

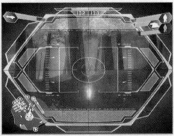

Of the command post's three turrets, the northern turret is the most effective for suppressing Rebel attacks. Zoom in and pick off enemies before they're within striking distance. It's possible to hit targets near the Forest Ruins.

Proof of the northern turret's effectiveness is the number of attacks aimed at taking it out. Keep an eye out for incoming missiles and be prepared to vacate the turret in an instant. Target heavy weapons and sniper units first—they pose the biggest threat.

To further bolster the command post's defenses, toss some mines in the Fountain, emphasizing coverage on the northern side.

INITIAL CONTROL: GALACTIC EMPIRE/ SEPARATIST BATTLE DROIDS
COMMAND POST TYPE: LIGHT

VEHICLES, TURRETS, & DROIDS

Unit	Count
Gun Turret	3
Medical Droid	1
Ammo Droid	1
Repair Droid	1

If attackers take out the turrets, fall back within the Fountain and use the pillars for cover. Stay out of sight as long as possible and engage the incoming attackers at close range.

OVERLOOK

The Overlook is the main Imperial staging area, spawning a couple of AT-STs and a speeder bike.

INITIAL CONTROL: **GALACTIC EMPIRE/ SEPARATIST BATTLE DROIDS**
COMMAND POST TYPE: **LIGHT**

VEHICLES, TURRETS, & DROIDS

Unit	Count
AT-ST/AAT	2/2
Speeder Bike/STAP	1/2
Tower Turret	2
Medical Droid	1
Ammo Droid	1
Repair Droid	1

The Imperial assault gets the bulk of its offensive power from the two AT-STs that spawn at the Overlook command post. As a result, the Imperials must hold this command post to maintain an advantage. The river to the north forms a natural barrier, discouraging a frontal assault. But the bridge to the west and the cliffside path to the east must both be defended to prevent flank attacks. The tower turret next to the command post can cover both directions, but it's a good idea to mine these areas, too.

Use the tower turret near the command post to cover the bridge to the west and the narrow cliffside path to the east.

Place some mines in the high grass on the eastern path running behind the waterfall. This is a popular route for Rebels attempting sneak attacks on the command post. The narrow path nearly guarantees that the mines are detonated as Rebels rush by.

Place more mines on the bridge to the west. To maximize coverage, place the mines in a zigzag pattern across the bridge's width. This prevents rush attacks by Rebels on speeder bikes.

Another tower turret is positioned along the northern end of the bridge. The surrounding trees obscure most angles, but the turret has a good view of the bridge and the western side of the Fountain. Use it to suppress flanking attacks on both of these southern command posts.

REBEL ALLIANCE STRATEGY

Spawn an attack force at the Altar and rush the Forest Ruins in an effort to capture the command post before the Imperials.

The Alliance begins with a superior position on the battlefield, holding the high ground of the temple and northern command posts. But simply holding these command posts isn't enough to win the battle, especially since they lack a formidable counter to the Imperial AT-STs. Start by rushing the Forest Ruins with solider and pilot units spawned at the Altar. They should be able to reach it before the Empire's forces.

Reinforce the position with vanguards, using mines and missiles to hold back the inevitable AT-ST attack. Meanwhile, launch a fierce assault on the Viaduct command post with forces from the Dry Pool. Taking this position is key in securing the Forest Ruins' eastern flank and establishing a line of defenses along the center of the map.

Launch a separate attack on the Viaduct command post, using vanguards to knock out the turrets before moving in with soldiers and pilots for the capture.

The AT-ST threat must be dealt with at the source. In the meantime, use vanguards to pound them with missiles and mines.

If your team can hold the line at the Viaduct and Forest Ruins, you begin imposing a reinforcement drain on the Imperials. But your forces don't have an easy time defending these central command posts until the AT-STs are removed from the battle. While holding the line at the center of the battlefield, assemble an attack squad at the Dry Pool for an attack on the Overlook. Advance along the eastern side of the map to reach the cliffside path running behind the waterfall. Use this narrow path to attack the Overlook from the east. Try to remain hidden and launch the attack when no AT-STs are present.

Your attack squad should be able to overwhelm the defenders and capture the command post. This limits the Imperials to the Fountain, allowing your team to squeeze them from all sides while their reinforcements bleed away.

Stage a sneak attack on the Overlook to deny the Empire access to its AT-STs.

GALACTIC EMPIRE STRATEGY

Closely coordinated AT-ST and infantry attacks are the key to an Imperial victory.

Although the Empire begins the battle with the unmatched firepower of two AT-STs, its position on the battlefield is relatively weak, occupying the lower half of the hill. This allows Rebel attackers to fire down on the low-lying Imperial positions. To prevent such attacks, the Empire must take control of the higher elevation positions, beginning with the Forest Ruins.

Spawn an assault force of dark troopers at the Viaduct and infiltrate the command post from the east. Even if they arrive late, they should be able to take control of the position by overwhelming the Rebels at close range with their blast cannons. In the meantime, move the AT-STs out, one along the western side and the other along the eastern side. The AT-STs are needed at the Viaduct and Forest Ruins to repel counterattacks.

Take the Dry Pool and Altar in an attempt to contain the Rebels to the Temple.

Using the AT-STs on the flanks of the map, slowly push the Rebel forces north. Move against the Altar and Dry Pool command posts while maintaining stiff defenses at your command posts. The Rebels are likely to stage breakout attacks using their speeder bikes to assault your positions to the rear. Once the Altar and Dry Pool fall, lay siege to the Temple and wait for the Rebel reinforcements to disappear.

Position the AT-STs on the eastern and western sides of the Temple's entrance and blast any units that attempt an escape. Containing the Rebels at the Temple is easy, because the southern entrance is the only way out. There's no need to assault the Temple's interior until the Rebel reinforcements are completely diminished. Use scout troopers to pick off any visible defenders before sending in an assault force of stormtroopers and dark troopers to capture the command post.

Lay siege to the Temple, using the AT-STs to blast any Rebels trying to escape through the wide southern entrance.

TACTICS

OVERLOOK ASSAULT

The AT-STs pose a huge threat to the Rebel forces, so consider staging an attack against the Overlook to halt their spawning. Assemble an attack squad at the Dry Pool command post, then advance south along the eastern side of the map till you come to this pool of water.

Cross the water and traverse this narrow path running behind the waterfall. Watch out for mines hiding in the high grass. Smart Imperial defenders cover this path, so be ready for anything.

Hold at the top of the hill and observe the defenses around the command post. Hold off the attack until both AT-STs vacate the area. When the attack squad is ready, and the command post's defenses are minimal, move in and begin gunning down defenders.

Circle the command post while keeping an eye open for new enemies spawning. Keep moving around the command post until it's neutralized, then stay put until it's completely converted. Prepare for immediate counterattacks along the bridge and the same cliffside path your squad just traversed. The Empire isn't likely to give up its AT-STs easily.

Opening a second front to the north can give the Empire a tremendous advantage. When playing as the Empire, consider staging a rush attack on the Temple using the speeder bike. Start by dropping down into the river to the south of the Outlook, then head east.

At the eastern edge of the map, turn north and zoom past the Viaduct and Dry Pool command posts. Rebel defenders at the Dry Pool are unlikely to see you due to the high stone walls surrounding the command post. If spotted, keep moving north. Speed is your best defense, but watch out for the trees.

Race into the Temple's entrance and run down any defenders that get in your way. But resistance is likely to be light, especially if this attack is conducted early in the battle when both factions are fighting for control in the center of the battlefield.

Ride the speeder bike up the western steps, then zoom directly into the war room. Hop off the bike and immediately gun down any defenders. Use the speeder bike and tactical screens for cover while converting the command post.

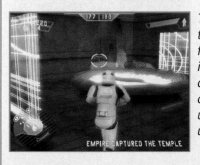

The command post doesn't take long to convert, even for one unit. Take cover inside this war room and defend against any counterattacks until more friendly units spawn here and set up more elaborate defenses.

Yavin 4: Temple

STEP DEFENSE

The steps to the south of the Forest Ruins are a hotly contested piece of territory. If they hold the command post, the Rebels are best off defending this area by using small groups of pilots to engage Imperial attackers at close range.

Their ability to heal and resupply each other makes pilots ideal for defending this area, because no droids are nearby.

FLANKING WITH SNIPERS

The center of the battlefield is extremely chaotic; both factions are constantly attacking and retreating. Obviously, this isn't an ideal area for snipers. Instead, move along the eastern and western slopes, using trees and foliage for cover.

The area to the west of the Forest Ruins is great for covering the command post. Sniping enemies around this area is great for both attacking and defending. But shift your position frequently to prevent being spotted.

THE AQUEDUCT

The aqueduct is a key feature running along the eastern side of the map. Whoever holds the Dry Pool can use it as a safe avenue of attack when assaulting the Viaduct or other southern positions. This is a great stealthy way to approach the waterfall near the Overlook.

Dropping off the aqueduct does cause some minor fall damage, but a pilot can always heal himself and teammates. If assaulting the Viaduct, try dropping off the east side and landing in the unoccupied turret below. If you enter the turret before hitting the ground, you won't take any fall damage.

BATTLE HINTS

As the Rebels or Republic, spawn at the Temple and grab a speeder bike, drive past all the action to the Overlook CP, and grab it ASAP. This eliminates their vehicles and evens the playing field. As the CIS or Empire, spawn at the Overlook, preferably as a pilot, and hop in a tank. From there, march up the east side of the map, capturing the Dry Pool CP and eventually the Temple. Don't forget that vehicles are crucial; if you see the enemy going for the Overlook CP, defend it at all costs.

by Tester Nicolas Sanford

BATTLE HINTS

The Rebel Vanguard is your unit of choice here. Start at the Dry Pool and mine the center of eastern path in anticipation of the AT-STs. Then take the Viaduct. You may want grab some extra teammates with the Follow squad command. Turn it neutral and the Empire will start bleeding. Your overall priority is to destroy the AT-STs quickly as they come up the east path. If you run out of rockets, and the AT-ST health is low, don't hesitate to run in and place a mine at their feet. You may lose a life, but it's well worth it, since one unopposed AT-ST can destroy many of your troops. Once you get the Empire below 20 reinforcements, switch to a soldier and mop up. If your teammates seem on the verge of losing the Forest Ruins, use the Respawn command and help them.

by Tester Xavier Rodriguez

HOTH: ECHO BASE

planetary overview

Hoth is the sixth planet in the remote system of the same name. Despite constant snow and ice, it supports a number of indigenous life forms, including the Wampa ice creature and the Tauntaun. The daytime temperatures of Hoth are bearable for properly equipped explorers, but the Hoth nights force even the native creatures to seek shelter. Hoth's remote location and icy surface make the planet an attractive base of operations for smugglers and other groups with something to hide, but it offers little in natural defenses against massive planetary assaults.

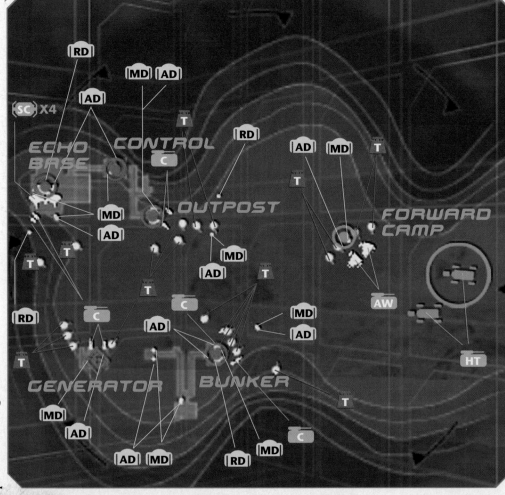

Legend

T	Turret
S	Scout Vehicle
MA	Medium Assault Vehicle
AW	Assault walker
HT	Heavy Assault Transport
FC	Fighter Craft
AT	Air Transoprt
B	Bomber
SC	Special Craft
C	Creature
AD	Ammo Droid
MD	Medical Droid
RD	Repair Droid

HOTH: ECHO BASE

COMMAND POSTS

FORWARD CAMP

The Forward Camp is the Empire's staging area for the assault.

Rebel Tauntaun rush attacks are likely to occur early in the battle. Keep troops positioned near the trench to deal with these attacks. The anti-infantry laser batteries are best suited to taking out these threats at long range, but infantry has to finish the job once the Rebels close in on the command post. Remember, killing the Tauntaun kills its rider, too.

INITIAL CONTROL: GALACTIC EMPIRE
COMMAND POST TYPE: LIGHT

VEHICLES, TURRETS, & DROIDS

Unit	Count
AT-ST	2
Anti-Infantry Laser Battery	2
Anti-Vehicle Laser Cannon	2
Medical Droid	1
Ammo Droid	1

At the base of a large hill to the east, the Forward Camp gives the Imperial forces a solid presence on the battlefield, spawning troops and two AT-STs near the Alliance front lines. Because it's their only command post at the start of the battle, the Empire needs to defend this position.

The site comes equipped with adequate defenses, but the turrets rotate too slowly to engage incoming Tauntauns, so consider deploying stormtroopers along the trench to defend against such rush attacks. The hill to the north also makes a good defensive position. Place some scouts on this hill to snipe incoming attackers. Holding the Forward Camp is also important in protecting the AT-AT spawn points to the southeast. If the Rebels take this command post, they can use the turrets to attack AT-ATs as soon as they spawn.

Consider keeping one AT-ST near the Forward Camp until you capture another command post. Infantry units are capable of holding the position, but the AT-ST guarantees its possession.

NOTE

The two AT-AT spawn points to the east are not linked to the Forward Camp. The AT-ATs spawn there continually throughout the battle, whether the Rebels hold the Forward Camp or not.

BUNKER

Bristling with turrets, the Bunker makes up the right flank of the Rebel frontline defenses.

Use the westernmost anti-vehicle laser cannon to target some of the Bunker's turrets. Take out their anti-vehicle laser cannons first, as these pose the biggest threat to your AT-ATs and AT-STs.

INITIAL CONTROL: REBEL ALLIANCE
COMMAND POST TYPE: LIGHT

VEHICLES, TURRETS, & DROIDS

Unit	Count
Tauntaun	2
Anti-Infantry Laser Battery	4
Anti-Vehicle Laser Cannon	3
Medical Droid	2
Ammo Droid	3
Repair Droid	1

The Bunker is the first Rebel position the Empire is likely to attack as the AT-ATs make their way to the Generator to the west. Rebel defenders should get to the turrets as soon as possible and start pounding away on the thick armor of the approaching AT-ATs. Don't neglect the AT-STs. They can wipe out the turrets quickly and fire down on infantry taking cover in the trenches.

The command post sits in a small bunker, flanked by two anti-infantry laser batteries. Use this small room as a defensive position too, allowing vanguards to fire on incoming attackers while using the nearby ammo droid to replenish their missiles. Mining this room is a good idea, in case the Imperial forces manage to infiltrate the outer defenses.

The crooked passage to the west leads to the Generator. If the Bunker is compromised, fall back into this passage and defend it. Otherwise, Imperial infantry have a direct path to the Generator.

 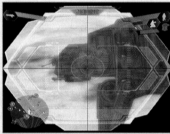

The anti-vehicle laser cannons play a huge role in weakening the armor of the two AT-ATs. One turret causes little damage, but if all the turrets at the Bunker and Outpost focus on one AT-AT, it suffers heavy damage.

The anti-infantry laser batteries are great for taking out the AT-STs. Unlike the anti-vehicle laser cannons, these enclosed turrets can rotate faster and provide some protection for the gunner. If an AT-ST begins returning fire, be prepared to jump out. The turret can only take a couple of direct hits before exploding.

The Bunker housing the command post should be mined to prevent infiltration. Place mines at the north and south entrances, sticking them on the walls to make them less

visible to attackers. Consider mining the western passage leading to the Generator as well.

Even if the turrets are all destroyed, keep up the attack on the AT-ATs using the vanguard's missile launcher.

OUTPOST

A series of trenches and turrets bolster the defenses of the Rebel-controlled Outpost.

INITIAL CONTROL: REBEL ALLIANCE
COMMAND POST TYPE: LIGHT

VEHICLES, TURRETS, & DROIDS

Unit	Count
Tauntaun	2
Anti-Infantry Laser Battery	4
Anti-Vehicle Laser Cannon	3
Medical Droid	2
Ammo Droid	2
Repair Droid	1

The Outpost completes the Rebel frontline defenses, lining the northern side of the battlefield with an impressive array of turrets. Unlike the Bunker to the south, a large hill to the east protects this position from an early assault by the Imperial walkers, giving defenders more time to establish defenses. However, Imperial infantry are likely to attack this command post by traversing the same hill to the east—the Forward Camp is on the other side.

Use the anti-infantry cannons to blast enemy troops, and occupy the eastern trenches to deny the attackers any cover. Turn the turrets on the walkers as they move within range, helping turn attackers away from the Bunker. If the Outpost comes under heavy assault, take cover inside the command post bunker and hold back infantry attacks. Turning this command post over to the Imperials gives them a direct path to the Control and Echo Base command posts via the tunnel system to the east.

нотЬ: Есно Ваѕе

The anti-infantry laser batteries come in handy for picking off attackers to the east and AT-STs swarming the Bunker to the south.

The ammo droid near the Outpost offers decent cover while providing an endless supply of munitions. Use this spot to attack the AT-ATs with vanguards. Or consider using a marksman's recon droid to call in orbital strikes.

Prevent the Imperials from gaining a foothold on the facility's main access tunnel by making a last stand at the Outpost. The elevated position gives defenders the upper hand in gunning down enemy troops as they rush the northern and southern entrances.

CONTROL

This small room houses the Control command post within the base's main facility to the northeast.

INITIAL CONTROL: REBEL ALLIANCE COMMAND POST TYPE: LIGHT	
VEHICLES, TURRETS, & DROIDS	
Unit	Count
Medical Droid	1
Ammo Droid	1

The Control command post is located along the tunnel corridor running between Echo Base and the Outpost. Protecting the command post presents a unique challenge, because defenders sit in a cramped room surrounded by computer consoles. Other than the consoles, there's no real cover. The room can be accessed from the east and west, so defenders need to keep an eye on the map to determine from which direction an attack is most likely to occur. Instead of clogging the room with defenders, spread your forces out along the tunnel, using blind corners and mines to set up ambushes.

Pilots and heavy weapons units are useful for defending the Control command post and the connecting tunnels. The pilot's blaster cannon is devastating at close range, while the vanguard's missile launcher and mines are capable of filling the narrow tunnels with powerful explosions.

Place mines in unexpected places such as this ice pillar near the command post.

Stick more mines to the walls of the nearby tunnels, placing them around corners where attackers can't see them till it's too late.

If an attack is likely, take to the tunnels and set up an ambush near one of the 90-degree turns. The pilot or dark trooper's blaster cannon can inflict massive damage on unsuspecting enemies as they round the corner. To deter such ambushes when attacking, toss a thermal detonator around a corner before rounding it.

СНО ВАЅЕ

The Echo Base command post is in this hangar, where the Rebel airspeeders spawn.

INITIAL CONTROL: REBEL ALLIANCE
COMMAND POST TYPE: LIGHT

VEHICLES, TURRETS, & DROIDS

Unit	Count
Tauntaun	2
T-47 Airspeeder	4
Anti-Vehicle Laser Cannon	2
Medical Droid	2
Ammo Droid	2
Repair Droid	2

Holding Echo Base is key to a Rebel victory, because it spawns the four T-47 airspeeders needed to confront the AT-AT threat. The command post is deep within the hangar surrounded by the airspeeder spawn points, a few droids, and a very familiar Corellian transport. These objects provide plenty of cover for defenders, as does the auxiliary hangar to the west.

The hangar can be infiltrated through the main hangar entrance to the south or through the western tunnel leading to the Control and Outpost command posts. The hangar also boasts some external defenses in the form of two anti-vehicle laser cannons useful for protecting the Generator to the south.

At the start of the battle, spawn pilots at Echo Base to get all four airspeeders in the air. Don't take off until you have a co-pilot—you need someone to fire the tow cable when going against the AT-AT walkers.

 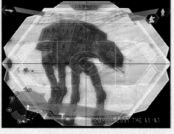

If waiting for an airspeeder, head outside the hangar and take control of one of the anti-vehicle laser cannons to help defend the Generator. A combined effort with surrounding teammates can drop an AT-AT before it inflicts too much damage.

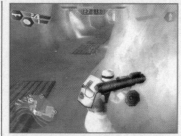

If the Outpost and Control command posts fall, prepare for an assault along the western tunnel. Position defenders in the auxiliary hangar and place mines around corners.

When playing as the Imperials, consider stealing some airspeeders before capturing Echo Base. They come in handy for strafing the Rebel positions at the Outpost and Bunker. Plus, they're the fastest option for hunting down any stragglers wandering around the battlefield when you're close to declaring victory.

GENERATOR

The Generator is tucked away in a valley to the south, defended by a few turrets.

INITIAL CONTROL: REBEL ALLIANCE
COMMAND POST TYPE: N/A
(DESTRUCTIBLE)

VEHICLES, TURRETS, & DROIDS

Unit	Count
Tauntaun	2
Anti-Infantry Laser Battery	2
Anti-Vehicle Laser Cannon	2
Medical Droid	1
Ammo Droid	1

Because it's a destructible spawn point, the Empire can't capture the Generator. But destroying it denies the Rebels a spawn point, tilting the odds in favor of an Imperial victory. Therefore the Rebels should devote some resources to defending this position. The hill to the west protects the area from an immediate attack, but if the Empire makes it past the Bunker and Outpost, the

HOTH: ECHO BASE

Rebels must concentrate their efforts on pushing back the attack.

The AT-AT's heavy lasers pose the biggest threat to the Generator, but AT-STs and frequent orbital strikes can also weaken it. If overrun, the Imperial infantry may even turn the position's own turrets against the Generator. It's best to keep the Imperial units out of the valley altogether. If the AT-ATs make it this far, a Rebel victory is unlikely, because the Imperials spawn infantry within striking distance of Echo Base and its connecting command posts.

By the time the AT-ATs reach this position, they should be in bad shape. Use the anti-vehicle laser cannons to finish them off.

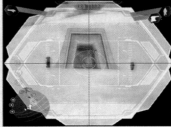

Keep an eye on the tunnel entrance to the west, the link to the Bunker. If the Bunker falls, infantry pours out of this entrance, attempting a flanking attack on the Generator. Use the anti-infantry laser batteries to cover this entrance to contain the enemies to the tunnel.

If the Generator comes under attack, move around to the south side to conduct repairs. This keeps you out of harm's way. But if attacked by an AT-AT, you should abandon your repairs and focus all efforts on bringing down the heavy transport.

REBEL ALLIANCE STRATEGY

Get the airspeeders in the air and attack the AT-ATs, trying to wrap their legs with tow cables to prevent them from reaching the Generator.

An Alliance victory largely depends on the skill and persistence of Rebel pilots in dealing with the AT-AT threat. Taking out the AT-ATs quickly not only deprives the Imperials of two awesome weapons platforms, but it also wipes two of their spawn points off the map, causing a temporary reinforcement drain on their forces.

Begin by assembling your team's best pilots at Echo Base and getting the airspeeders into the air. Focus the rest of your resources at the Bunker and Outpost, manning the turrets to weaken the AT-ATs and AT-STs. Instead of blasting away at the AT-ATs' armor with the airspeeders, use the tow cables to entangle their legs. A skilled pilot and gunner crew can cripple an AT-AT in seconds.

Strafe the enemy positions at the Forward Camp, then launch a ground assault against the position. This gives your team four turrets within attack range of the AT-AT spawn points.

Once the AT-ATs are down, use the airspeeders to attack the AT-STs as well as the Imperial positions at the Forward Camp. Try to stage an assault on the Forward Camp before a new pair of AT-ATs spawn to the east. Unfortunately the AT-ATs can't be taken out of the battle completely, so continually patrol their spawn point and wrap their legs with tow cables as soon as they appear.

By containing the Imperial forces to the east of the Bunker and Outpost, you can continue inflicting heavy casualties while imposing a reinforcement drain. Hold the front lines and keep your airspeeders on the prowl to ensure a lopsided victory.

If your airspeeders take damage, use the repair droids on the front lines to keep them in the battle. Repair droids are located at the Bunker, Outpost, and Echo Base command posts. Even if two pilots are on board, the repair droid can mend serious damage faster.

GALACTIC EMPIRE STRATEGY

During the advance, keep the AT-ATs close together. This makes tow cable attacks extremely difficult for the Rebel pilots

The AT-ATs are the lifeblood of the Imperial assault. Keeping them protected and repaired should be the primary focus of the whole team, at least till Imperial troops can establish a foothold within the Rebel base. Begin by spawning defenders at the Forward Camp, using them to repel any Rebel rush attacks. Meanwhile, start moving the AT-ATs west, keeping them side by side to discourage tow-cable attacks by the Rebel airspeeders.

Use the AT-ATs' heavy lasers to systematically demolish all the turrets at the Bunker and Outpost. Escort the AT-ATs with the AT-STs and Shocktroopers to engage the airspeeders with lasers and missiles. Push past the Bunker and Outpost, then veer south to engage the Generators. While their flanks are exposed, use the AT-STs to suppress the turrets at the Outpost and Generator command posts. If both AT-ATs are in place, they can destroy the Generator quickly.

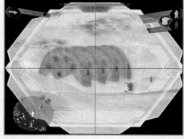

Get the AT-ATs within visual range of the Generator and blast it with heavy lasers until it explodes.

With the Generator destroyed, commence the assault on the Rebel base. Send one AT-AT toward the Echo Base hangar while sending the other to assault the Outpost. Use them to pound the Rebel defenses, then spawn troops to assault both command posts. Hitting these two command posts simultaneously forces the Rebels to split their defenses, increasing your chances of successfully infiltrating the base.

With Echo Base and the Outpost under Imperial control, squeeze the Control command post from the eastern and western ends of the tunnel. If your team maintained control of the Forward Camp throughout the battle, this leaves the Rebels with the Bunker. Lay siege to this position with the AT-ATs and AT-STs until the Rebel forces are eliminated.

Storm the Rebel base from the east and the west, squeezing the Control command post in the center.

TACTICS

AT-AT ESCORT

Protecting the AT-ATs is key to an Imperial victory. Since they're vulnerable to flanking attacks, surround them with units like this Shocktrooper to fire missiles at incoming airspeeders.

The AT-STs also play a big role in supporting the AT-AT advance. Use them to blast any airspeeders that attempt to wrap the AT-AT's legs with their tow cables. The AT-ST's co-pilot has the best chance of scoring hits on the slow-moving airspeeder.

AT-STs are also useful for taking out the turrets at the Bunker and Outpost.

TOW-CABLE TAKEDOWN

The quickest way to destroy an AT-AT is to wrap its legs with an airspeeder's tow cable. Begin by grabbing an airspeeder at Echo Base and make sure you have a gunner in the back to deploy the tow cable.

Start your attack run by skimming the ground at high speed. Level the wings and fly along one of the AT-AT's sides, parallel to the legs. As you fly past the AT-AT, reduce throttle and

Hoth: Echo Base

slowly bank inward in an attempt to circle its legs. It's at this point that your rear gunner has the best chance of attaching the tow cable to one of the AT-AT's legs.

If the cable attaches, maintain your low speed and circular flight pattern. The hardest part is maintaining a constant altitude. If you fly too high (above the legs) the cable breaks. If you fly too low, you slam into the ground.

On your first pass, stay directly beneath the AT-AT's head. If you swing out too far, its guns may blast your airspeeder out of the sky.

Keep circling the AT-AT, and try to maintain a constant altitude. The pattern with which the cable entangles the legs illustrates how level your attack is. Closely wrapped cables indicate a level flight path—maintain this same altitude. But cables that span the height of the legs show instability—try to level out around the AT-AT's knees.

It takes three passes to complete your attack run. As soon as you pass the leg your tow cable is attached to for the third time, the tow cable automatically detaches and the AT-AT tumbles to the ground in a flaming wreck.

If you feel real confident, consider teaming up with a buddy and double-wrapping an AT-AT's legs.

To make things harder, fly in opposite directions. This means you have to dodge your buddy's airspeeder in addition to maintaining a

steady altitude and circular flight path. Sure, it's a waste of resources, but you can't put a price on the intimidation factor.

TRENCH WARFARE

All the Rebel external positions feature trenches carved into the icy landscape. These give the defenders an advantage, especially during frontal assaults. Avoid hitting them head on; instead, move along their flanks and fire down on the defenders. Use thermal detonators, too. Your enemies may have a hard time vacating the trench before it explodes.

The AT-ST is the best option for clearing trenches. Its elevated guns make quick work of cowering Rebels.

 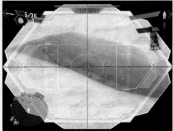

Position scouts on the nearby hills and fire down into the trenches. This immediately robs the defenders of their advantage while providing you with plenty of targets in a small, confined space.

REPAIR SQUAD

Next to the airspeeders, the Rebel's next best option for taking out the incoming assault walkers are the various turrets surrounding the exterior positions. But all of these turrets can be destroyed with a single blast from the AT-ATs heavy lasers. So you need a team of pilots to repair and reconstruct damaged and destroyed turrets.

Travel in pairs to decrease the time it takes to reconstruct a turret. If the position is under attack, one pilot can act as an escort, protecting the reconstruction efforts.

Pilots are a must when it comes to repairing the Generator. Like the Techno Union ships on Geonosis, repairing this mammoth structure can turn into a full-time job. So keep a pilot ready to counter damage dealt to the Generator if it comes under attack.

ALTERNATE AT-AT ATTACKS

If your airspeeders are ineffective and your turrets are constantly destroyed, consider assaulting the AT-ATs by other means. Rush toward the AT-AT's legs with vanguards and throw mines ahead of it. Its lack of maneuverability almost guarantees it hits the mines, but they won't do too much damage. Be extremely careful when doing this, and stay clear of the AT-AT's feet. If you get too close, the mine detonates as soon as you toss it on the ground, doing significantly more damage to you than to the AT-AT.

If you like close assaults, the smuggler's time bomb is a much safer option. Use a Tauntaun to rush the AT-AT and stick bombs to its legs. You can place a new time bomb once the previous bomb reaches "6" on its countdown. Back away before the bombs explode.

The safest and most effective option is to use the marksman's recon droid to call in an orbital strike. Find a safe place on the battlefield, preferably next to an ammo droid. Rush the AT-AT's feet with the recon droid and call in the strike once you're directly beneath the walker. Use an ammo droid to grab another recon droid and repeat the attack continuously until the AT-AT explodes.

TIP

Imperial scouts attacking the Generator can also use orbital strikes. camp near the ammo droid to the east of the Generator and call in continual attacks while sniping defenders. To inflict the most damage, fly the recon droid to the top of the Generator before calling in the strike.

Battle Hints

The key for a Rebel victory is taking the Empire's Forward command post and neutralizing the AT-AT presence. Accomplish this with an all out Tauntaun rush on the Forward Camp CP. You can usually surprise the enemy with this quick strike. For the Empire, the key to victory relies on getting the two behemoth AT-AT units across the map to the Shield Generator. This allows you to bring the ground-shaking power of their main guns to bear on the Rebel's Shield Generator. The best way to keep the AT-AT walkers alive is to maneuver them parallel to each other. By walking together, side by side, you prevent snowspeeders from using their tow cables.

by Tester Heath Sutherland

BESPIN: CLOUD CITY

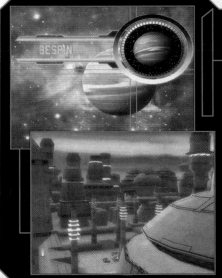

planetary overview

The planet of Bespin is actually a large gas giant, covered by huge billowing clouds and an array of colorful vapors. Bespin has no land but its core is liquid. A band of temperate breathable air exists in the upper atmosphere, where colonists have established floating colonies such as Cloud City. Since it was founded, Cloud City's primary industry has been mining tibanna gas, which can be used as a hyperdrive coolant or as an energy source for blasters and other weapons.

Under the direction of Baron Administrator Lando Calrissian, Cloud City developed a small tourist industry that includes casinos and luxury resorts. Those trying to escape the turmoil gripping the galaxy can find sanctuary here.

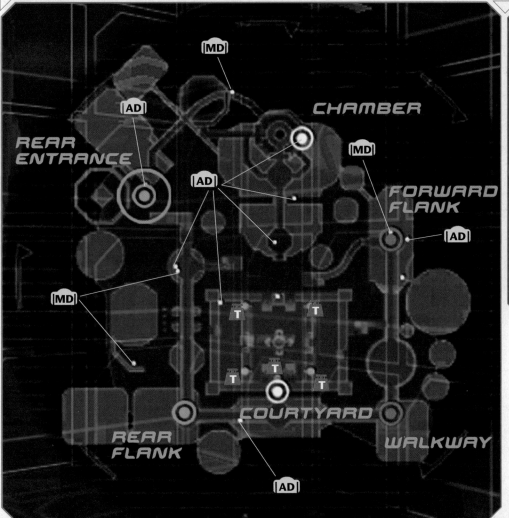

Legend

T	Turret
S	Scout Vehicle
MA	Medium Assault Vehicle
AW	Assault walker
HT	Heavy Assault Transport
FC	Fighter Craft
AT	Air Transoprt
B	Bomber
SC	Special Craft
C	Creature
AD	Ammo Droid
MD	Medical Droid
RD	Repair Droid

COMMAND POSTS

REAR FLANK

The Rear Flank command post provides the Rebels with a presence on the upper levels of the city.

INITIAL CONTROL: REBEL ALLIANCE/REPUBLIC CLONE ARMY
COMMAND POST TYPE: LIGHT

Unlike the Empire, the Rebels begin with only one upper-level command post at the start of the battle, in the form of this L-shaped junction connecting the elevated walkways that encircle the map. The position comes with no droids, so consider keeping a pilot here to help supply and heal defenders.

The most direct threat comes from the Imperial-held Walkway command post to the east. In fact, your marksmen can use their rifles to pick off enemies spawning at this eastern command post. But Imperial scouts can do the same from their position, potentially making the southern walkway a dangerous alley of sniper fire. Keep defenders away from the eastern passage and deal with attackers at close range. Meanwhile, position marksmen along the northern walkway to snipe enemies around the Courtyard.

 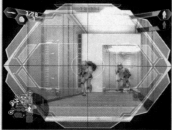

Use marksmen to cover the southern walkway. Drop prone and zoom in on the narrow corridor to pick off incoming attackers approaching from the Imperial-held Walkway command post to the east.

Because of the high traffic in the other passage, use the walkway to the north to snipe enemies down in the Courtyard. The gunners in the turrets make easy targets.

Instead of placing mines in front of the eastern entrance, stick them to the nearby slanted walls. This makes them invisible to attackers attempting to infiltrate the command post from the east. Do the same on the northern entrance to further lock down the position.

REAR ENTRANCE

The Rebel-controlled Rear Flank is located in this open area in the northwest corner of the map.

INITIAL CONTROL: REBEL ALLIANCE/REPUBLIC CLONE ARMY
COMMAND POST TYPE: LIGHT

VEHICLES, TURRETS, & DROIDS

Unit	Count
Ammo Droid	1

The Rebel's second starting position is on the ground floor of the city, offering a quick path to the Chamber. But the command post sits in the open, making it vulnerable to attacks, particularly from the nearby ramp to the south. Defenders should occupy this ramp leading to the upper level, especially if the Empire takes control of the Rear Flank command post.

Another overlooked path of attack is the vacant and often quiet alley to the south. Attackers can creep up on the command post from this direction and assault at close range. If resources allow, deploy defenders along the western side of the map to prevent such attacks. At the very least, patrol this area frequently. Finally, there's the path to the Chamber. If the Chamber falls into enemy hands, immediately cover this passage just north of the command post.

If defending alone, hide in this small nook to the northwest. From here you can stay out of sight and still spot any attackers approaching the command post. If a thermal detonator finds its way into your hiding spot, move fast.

bespin: cloud city

Take the high ground along this ramp to the south. Not only is this a great spot for covering the command post, but it's also useful for stifling attacks moving along the upper western walkway.

This passage presents a serious threat if the enemy takes control of the Chamber. Stick mines to the outside of the entrance to catch attackers by surprise.

The Chamber passage can also be covered from the ramp to the south. A vanguard or Shocktrooper firing missiles down into this narrow passage can wipe out any attack force. Use the ammo droid in the round upper-level room to the south to replenish your missiles.

CHAMBER

Carbon-freezing chambers like this one play a significant role in Cloud City's economy.

```
INITIAL CONTROL: NEUTRAL
COMMAND POST TYPE: LIGHT
```

VEHICLES, TURRETS, & DROIDS

Unit	Count
Medical Droid	1
Ammo Droid	2

This carbon-freezing Chamber is one of two neutral command posts, making it an early destination for both factions. Located on the north side of the map, it's also the only command post positioned beneath the city, and is accessed via two descending passages. The passage to the south exits on the northern side of the Courtyard. The other passage runs to the west, exiting near the Rear Flank command post.

This passage to the west gives the Rebels a good chance of capturing this position early in the battle. The command post is on an elevated platform along the eastern side of the chamber. This can be accessed from the chamber's central platform or along a ramp running along the northern side. However, the command post can be captured from beneath the platform as well by standing near the ammo droid. Defenders need to patrol the floor, platforms, and connecting passages to root out attackers.

Because the command post can be captured from below the platform, consider placing a mine or two around this ammo droid to surprise sneak attackers.

The color and lighting of the central platform makes mines hard to see. Place one on the platform next to the steps leading up to the command post.

The western passage can be covered from this elevated platform accessed from the Chamber's western steps. This is useful for ambushing Rebels attempting attacks from the Rear Flank. Fire down on them as they rush across the narrow catwalk, or toss thermal detonators into the western passage. It's possible to jump down on the catwalk below, but you suffer some light damage—unless you're playing as a dark trooper or jet trooper.

FORWARD FLANK

Imperial forces must protect this cramped upper-level junction to maintain a strong presence on the upper-level walkways.

INITIAL CONTROL: GALACTIC EMPIRE/ SEPARATIST BATTLE DROIDS
COMMAND POST TYPE: LIGHT

VEHICLES, TURRETS, & DROIDS

Unit	Count
Medical Droid	1
Ammo Droid	1

The Forward Flank is tucked away in the northeast corner of the map, providing the Empire with one of two upper-level spawn points. A ramp to the west leads down to the ground level near the north side of Courtyard. This ramp must be covered with mines and defenders to dissuade Rebel attacks from the Rear Entrance.

Fortunately, the high ground gives the Imperial defenders a tremendous advantage, allowing them to lob thermal detonators and grenades down on would-be attackers. The southern passage presents a bigger threat, especially if the enemy holds the Walkway command post. If this happens, consider positioning a forward defense force along the eastern walkway.

While defenders keep attackers at bay, position scouts along both walkways to fire down on enemies scurrying around the Courtyard. Their recon droid also provides the option of calling in orbital strikes on the turret positions below. Use the ammo droid near the command post to grab new recon droids and keep calling in new strikes on the enemy positions.

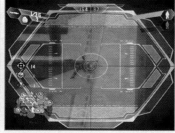

This large window to the south of the command post is a prime sniping position. Pay particular attention to the northern side of the Courtyard, picking off Rebels moving from the Rear Entrance and Chamber command posts.

Defend this western ramp with a mix of units. The Imperial pilot's mortar launcher is great for lobbing grenades down on the Rebels. Keep pounding the area on the north side of the Courtyard. This is a high-traffic area, where Rebels from the Rear Entrance and Chamber are most likely to enter the battlefield's center.

WALKWAY

The Walkway command post is another sparse upper-walkway junction held by the Imperials at the start of the battle.

INITIAL CONTROL: GALACTIC EMPIRE/ SEPARATIST BATTLE DROIDS
COMMAND POST TYPE: LIGHT

Along with the Rear Flank, consider the Walkway a frontline position at the start of the battle. Held by opposing factions and separated by only a narrow corridor, these two positions are bound to see plenty of action.

Like the Rebel's command post on the other end of the hall, scouts at the Walkway can focus their sniper rifles on incoming attackers from the west as well as enemies spawning at the Rear Flank. But the rounded part of the northern passage provides a better sniping spot for scouts looking to cover the Courtyard below.

Dark troopers spawning at this command post have a good chance of reaching the Courtyard command post before any other units. But non-flying units can also reach the same spot quickly by simply dropping off the upper level. The fall damage is minimal, and if pilots are used, they can heal themselves and begin constructing turrets once they reach the command post.

Bespin: Cloud City

The corridor leading to the Rear Flank is a hotly contested piece of territory. Advances and retreats are common, especially at the start of the battle. Explosive munitions such as thermal detonators and missiles are particularly deadly in these close-quarter battles, offering little room for evasive maneuvers. So exercise extreme caution when using these weapons.

A scout should always support an advance along this corridor. They're capable of picking off enemy defenders at great distances, including opposing Rebel marksmen covering the passage from the Rear Flank command post.

COURTYARD

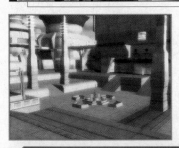

The Courtyard sits at the center of the map, making it a key location to capture, but a difficult one to hold.

| INITIAL CONTROL: NEUTRAL |
| COMMAND POST TYPE: LIGHT |

VEHICLES, TURRETS, & DROIDS

Unit	Count
Gun Turret	5
Ammo Droid	1

Usually central command posts are a huge asset, but as the lowest and most open position on the map, the Courtyard is a funnel for sniper fire, making it extremely difficult to defend. Even its five turrets do little to ease the 360-degree sniper threat.

But if your team already holds the high ground, the Courtyard can be a strong addition to your collection of command posts. The turrets are extremely effective in dealing with attacks from the Rear Entrance and Chamber. But if the enemy grabs one of the upper-level command posts, consider withdrawing to the east or west, using the cover of the upper walkways to hide from snipers. From these flanking positions, watch the command post and engage any attackers who approach it.

This position can be captured from the Courtyard floor, just beneath the command post. This spot provides a bit more cover from sniper fire coming from the Rear Flank or Walkway command posts.

Keep moving while constructing the turrets surrounding the Courtyard. Enemy snipers are probably watching these spots, waiting for a stationary target. Strafing left and right can prevent you from becoming an easy kill.

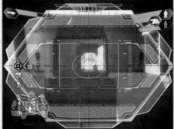

The southern turret is great for suppressing attacks from the Rear Entrance and Chamber. Zoom in to pick off enemies inside the Chamber's southern entrance on the opposite side of the Courtyard.

REBEL ALLIANCE STRATEGY

Capture and fortify the Chamber early in the battle, but watch for Imperial attacks approaching from the south. Holding this position strengthens the Rear Entrance, helping prevent point-blank attacks along the western passage.

With only one command post on the upper levels, the Rebels begin the battle with a slight disadvantage. But the Rear Entrance's close proximity to the Chamber gives the Rebels an edge in reaching this northern command post before the Empire. Rush this position early in the battle with pilots and vanguards using the connecting passage next to the Rear Entrance. The Courtyard can also be taken quickly by a pilot or two spawning at the Rear Flank.

Instead of using the ramps, simply head east and drop off the walkway—pilots can heal themselves to offset the fall damage. While capturing the Courtyard command post, construct the southernmost turret, then use it to defend the position from eastern attacks.

Commence the attack on the Walkway by using a vanguard unit to fire a few missiles down the narrow corridor.

Meanwhile, push toward the Walkway command post to the east with a mixed force of marksmen and soldiers from the Rear Flank. The idea is to contain the Imperials to the Forward Flank command post while imposing a reinforcement drain. No matter how effectively you lay siege to this command post, you have to defend your existing command posts to prevent breakout attacks by dark troopers. The Rear Entrance and Chamber are likely targets for such attacks.

Contain the Empire to the Forward Flank and use the Courtyard's turrets to blast incoming attackers as they charge down the adjacent ramps.

GALACTIC EMPIRE STRATEGY

A single dark trooper spawned at the Walkway can capture the Courtyard faster than any other unit on the map.

Although the Empire has a dominating presence on the city's upper levels, their starting positions aren't particularly close to any of the neutral command posts. However, quick attacks by dark troopers can remedy this problem. Strike out at the Courtyard with dark troopers spawned at the Walkway command post—a quick jump or two should

be adequate to reach it within the first few seconds of the battle.

The Chamber can also be reached early by spawning more dark troopers at the Forward Flank. Fly them to the west and enter the Chamber's northern entrance. The Rebels may already be present, but a squad of dark troopers attacking simultaneously from multiple points should be able to overwhelm any defenders and capture the command post.

After capturing the Chamber, use this western passage to assault the Rear Entrance.

For a truly wicked finish, gradually pull back your defenses from the Courtyard and let the Rebels capture it. In the meantime, move against the Rear Flank and Rear Entrance. If you can capture these western positions, you can contain the Rebels to the Courtyard, squeezing them from all directions with sniper fire and the occasional orbital strike.

Because the Courtyard provides little cover, your scouts have the jump on new units as soon as they spawn. Guard the ramps leading to the second level and keep pounding the Rebels till their reinforcements are completely wiped out.

Try containing the Rebels to the Courtyard, to give your scouts plenty of target practice.

TACTICS

COURTYARD SNIPING

One of the best sniping positions on the map is located in the southern upper-level walkway, just above the Courtyard's command post. An energy barrier blocks this passage from movement, but it's still possible to shoot through it.

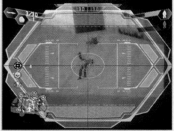

For best results, drop prone. This reduces interference from the energy barrier while making you harder to see and hit.

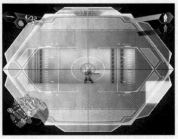

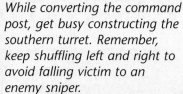

While converting the command post, get busy constructing the southern turret. Remember, keep shuffling left and right to avoid falling victim to an enemy sniper.

While you're prone, it's possible to see the entire northern side of the Courtyard. This spot is beneficial if the enemy holds the Rear Entrance and Chamber command posts. Rebel marksmen may want to take this position early in the game to countersnipe Imperial scouts at the Forward Flank. Suppressing the Imperial snipers is an important step in capturing or simply traversing the Courtyard.

As soon as the command post is captured, hop inside the turret and swing its gun to the east to engage the incoming Imperial attackers. You should be able to hold back the initial assault with the turret, giving your team more time to reach the Courtyard and construct the remaining turrets.

REAR ENTRANCE SQUEEZE

Despite its lack of decent cover, the Rear Entrance can be one of the hardest command posts to assault—especially if it's one of the last command posts the enemy holds. But a coordinated attack from the south and east should send defenders running. Begin by attacking along the western passage leading from the Chamber.

ROOFTOP AMBUSH

The Imperial dark trooper and Republic jet trooper can reach all sorts of elevated positions on this map, useful for catching your enemies by surprise. Try camping above the ramps. These are narrow high-traffic areas—perfect for assaulting with thermal detonators.

Meanwhile, get units on the upper-level ramp overlooking the command post. From up here they can snipe defenders or call in an orbital strike. Maintain this position to keep the enemy distracted.

Seek out the rooftops just above droid locations. By standing on a roof above a medical or ammo droid, you can heal yourself or stock up on more thermal detonators.

While the upper-level units draw the defenders' attention, sweep in from the Chamber passage and assault at close range. Rush the command post and convert it quickly before fresh enemy units spawn.

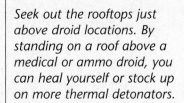

This flat rooftop above the Chamber's northern entrance is great for picking off unsuspecting enemies distracted by the chaos of the battle. If they catch on to your presence, simply fly elsewhere.

COURTYARD RUSH

If the Imperial dark troopers fail to recognize their ability to quickly capture the Courtyard, the Rebels stand a good chance of taking it early. Spawn a pilot at the Rear Flank and head east, dropping off the upper-level platform. Heal yourself while rushing toward the command post.

BATTLE HINTS

Spawn at any CP on the upper structure and be any character with a blaster rifle (clone trooper, super battle droid, Rebel soldier, or stormtrooper), and then take all CPs on the upper structure (it will take a few lives to do so). After you take the upper structure, players can spawn in as any character they want to be. Work your way back to the Rear Flank CP. You will save lives if you stay on the upper structure, as it is easy to get distracted cutting through the Courtyard. Then continue toward the Rear Entrance CP. Next take the Carbon Freezing Chamber. After this is done, your bot count will be low. The player can usually just take the Courtyard at his point and await victory.

by Tester Jeff Diaz

STAR WARS BATTLEFRONT™

BESPIN: PLATFORMS

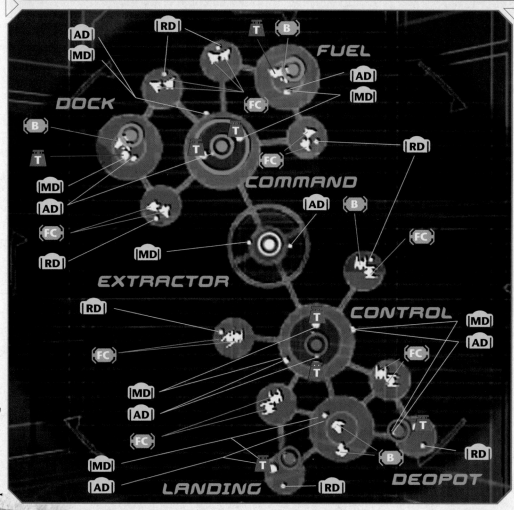

planetary overview

The planet of Bespin is actually a large gas giant, covered by huge billowing clouds and an array of colorful vapors. Bespin has no land but its core is liquid. A band of temperate breathable air exists in the upper atmosphere, where colonists have established floating colonies such as Cloud City. Since it was founded, Cloud City's primary industry has been mining tibanna gas, which can be used as a hyperdrive coolant or as an energy source for blasters and other weapons.

Under the direction of Baron Administrator Lando Calrissian, Cloud City developed a small tourist industry that included casinos and luxury resorts. Those trying to escape the turmoil gripping the galaxy can find sanctuary here.

Legend

T	Turret
S	Scout Vehicle
MA	Medium Assault Vehicle
AW	Assault walker
HT	Heavy Assault Transport
FC	Fighter Craft
AT	Air Transoprt
B	Bomber
SC	Special Craft
C	Creature
AD	Ammo Droid
MD	Medical Droid
RD	Repair Droid

COMMAND POSTS

DOCK

The Dock's sphere of influence encompasses these two northwestern platforms.

INITIAL CONTROL: REBEL ALLIANCE/REPUBLIC CLONE ARMY
COMMAND POST TYPE: LIGHT

VEHICLES, TURRETS, & DROIDS

Unit	Count
X-Wing/Jedi Starfighter	2/2
Y-Wing/LAAT/I Gunship	1/1
Cloud Car*	1
Ant-Air Turret	1
Medical Droid	1
Ammo Droid	1
Repair Droid	1

* Under Galactic Empire/Separatist battle droid control only

The Rebel-held Dock platforms to the northwest spawn multiple air units needed to rush the Empire's positions to the south. At the start of the battle, get the fighters and bomber into the air before the Empire conducts strafing runs. Most important, get a unit to the anti-air turret on the western side of the platform. This turret must be manned and fully operational at all times to prevent enemy craft from strafing or landing to capture the command post. Keep a pilot stationed here to repair or reconstruct the turret as it sustains damage.

Rush to the X-wings and Y-wings and get them in the air as soon as possible before they become strafing targets for incoming TIE fighters.

Man the anti-air turret and engage the swarms of enemy fighters and bombers circling the skies above. But watch your fire to avoid hitting friendly units.

If the Extractor falls into enemy hands, turn the anti-air turret in its direction and begin pounding it with laser blasts. Even if you can't see specific enemies, bombarding the Extractor platform is likely to inflict massive damage on enemy forces—just watch the map and make sure your teammates are clear of the target area.

The anti-air turret can also be turned against the two TIE fighters on the platform to the south, just west of the Control building.

Position a marksman near the command post and scan the same enemy platform to the south. Zoom in and pick off enemy pilots as they rush to the TIE fighters.

FUEL

These two northeastern platforms are the Fuel platforms.

INITIAL CONTROL: REBEL ALLIANCE/REPUBLIC CLONE ARMY
COMMAND POST TYPE: LIGHT

VEHICLES, TURRETS, & DROIDS

Unit	Count	
X-Wing/Jedi Starfighter	2/2	
Y-Wing/LAAT/I Gunship	1/1	
Cloud Car*	1	
Anti-Air Turret	1	* Under Galactic
Medical Droid	1	Empire/Separatist
Ammo Droid	1	battle droid
Repair Droid	1	control only

The Fuel command post covers the Rebel eastern flank with more air units and another anti-air turret. Along with the Y-wing on northeastern platform, this command post spawns the two X-wings on the platform to the west. As with the Dock, get pilots to the fighters, bomber, and turret early in the battle.

Defend the platform with vanguards and pilots. The vanguards can fire missiles at enemy spacecraft while the pilots can man the turret and conduct any repairs.

Scatter some mines around the command post's platform to discourage enemy air units from landing.

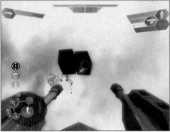

Like the Dock's turret, turn this one on the Control's eastern platform and blast enemy air units before they can get off the ground. Keep an eye on the skies, too, blasting any TIE fighters that fly within range.

COMMAND

At the Command, the X-wings spawn on the two platforms to its east and west.

Holding the Command position allows the Rebels to prevent an infantry incursion on the northern platforms. Therefore it's necessary to hold all enemy advances at the narrow covered bridge connecting to the Extractor. If the enemy pushes across the bridge, they can infiltrate the command post at close range, since one of the Command's entrances is adjacent to the bridge.

Mines and the two anti-air turrets can be used to hold the enemy at bay, but soldiers are required to do most of the heavy lifting, defending the bridge and command post. The best defensive option for the Command is to hold the Extractor to the south, providing an extra buffer.

The two anti-air turrets can engage enemy units at the Extractor, but support beams prevent them from getting a clear view. Still, both turrets working together should be capable of bombarding most of the platform.

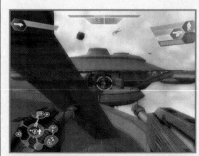

Both anti-air turrets are likely to come under attack. Keep a pilot nearby to reconstruct them. Maintaining these guns is essential to deter aerial assaults on the northern platforms.

The southern entrance to the Command building is the most likely entry point for attackers. Lay a zigzag pattern of mines across this entrance to prevent quick infiltration. The attackers must destroy the mines first, buying your teammates in and around the building more time to pick them off.

Either the eastern or western flanking platforms can be used to cover the bridge to the south. Use vanguards and marksmen to fire at attackers through the windows.

bespin: platforms

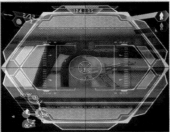

A marksman on one of these flanking platforms can also hit the northernmost anti-air turret gunner at the Control command post. It's not an easy shot, especially if the turret is moving. But your pilots will thank you for silencing this threat.

EXTRACTOR

The Extractor's neutral status and central position make it a major point of contention throughout the battle.

INITIAL CONTROL: NEUTRAL
COMMAND POST TYPE: LIGHT

VEHICLES, TURRETS, & DROIDS	
Unit	Count
Medical Droid	1
Ammo Droid	1

Sitting directly in the center of the map is a large platform called the Extractor. Unlike the surrounding platforms, this one has a large roof, sheltering it from the chaotic air battle above. Two covered bridges on the northern and southern sides of the platform connect this command post to the rest of the facility. On the eastern and western sides of the platform are two ramps, both leading up to the ring-shaped catwalk surrounding the roof.

This can be used by snipers and other defenders to suppress attacks on the command post or strike out at the surrounding platforms. Since it's the only neutral position at the start of the battle, both sides should race toward the Extractor with infantry. Whoever captures this command post gains not only a central spawn point, but also a welcome buffer that helps protect their half of the map from infantry assaults.

Rush the Extractor with your main attack force at the very beginning of the battle. If it's captured by the enemy, it's hard to take.

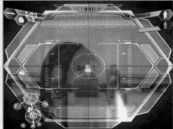

Use the eastern or western ramps to access this elevated catwalk ringing the platform's rooftop. From this elevated position it's possible to pick off enemies around the Command or Control command posts. Rebel marksmen can also use this position to pick off the northern anti-air turret gunner at the Control command post to the south.

If the Empire takes control of the Extractor, a scout can lie prone near the northern bridge and engage enemies inside the Command building and beyond. This makes Imperial infantry assaults on the Command much easier. It also helps prevent attacks on the Extractor.

CONTROL

The Control command post contributes three TIE fighters and a TIE bomber to the Imperial's squadron of air units.

INITIAL CONTROL: GALACTIC EMPIRE/ SEPARATIST BATTLE DROIDS
COMMAND POST TYPE: LIGHT

VEHICLES, TURRETS, & DROIDS

Unit	Count
TIE Fighter/Droid Starfighter	3/4
TIE Bomber*	1
Cloud Car**	2
Anti-Air Turret	2
Medical Droid	3
Ammo Droid	3
Repair Droid	1

* Galactic Civil War only

** Under Rebel Alliance/Republic clone army control only

Although Control looks similar to the Rebel's Command position to the north, there are some significant differences between these two command posts. For one, this command post spawns three fighters and one bomber on the platforms to the northeast and northwest. The Control's entrances and turrets are also oriented differently—the turrets face north and south, and the entrances are positioned on the eastern and western sides.

These side entrances make the command post easier to defend against infantry attacks approaching from the north, because attackers must circle halfway around the building before gaining entry. But the north-facing turret also comes in handy for blasting enemy units at the Extractor. Rebel units want to take this turret out early and often to prevent it from targeting friendly air units and troops.

The northern anti-air turret is one of the most devastating on the map, offering an unobstructed view of the skies and the Extractor. If the enemy holds the Extractor, use this turret to soften their defenses before launching an infantry attack.

Both the northern and southern turrets can be rotated to cover the ramps leading up to their elevated positions. If the command post is captured, be prepared to take out infantry attacking along this narrow path.

Consider defending the command post with pilots positioned along these same narrow ramps. If they hover between the upper and lower levels, they can cover both entrances with their mortar launchers while staying in close proximity to the turrets should they need repair.

LANDING

The Landing command post is on the southwest platform, where most of the nearby air units spawn.

INITIAL CONTROL: GALACTIC EMPIRE/ SEPARATIST BATTLE DROIDS
COMMAND POST TYPE: LIGHT

VEHICLES, TURRETS, & DROIDS

Unit	Count
TIE Fighter/Droid Starfighter	2/2
TIE Bomber/MAF	1/1
Cloud Car*	1
Anti-Air Turret	1
Medical Droid	1
Ammo Droid	1
Repair Droid	1

* Under Rebel Alliance/Republic clone army control only

Like the Rebel-held platforms to the north, the Landing command post influences the spawning of nearby vehicles, particularly the two platforms to the north and east. While the northern platform spawns two TIE fighters, the eastern platform spawns two TIE bombers. But the Landing is only responsible for spawning the TIE bomber in the center—the one to the south is spawned by the Depot command post.

Defensively, the Landing is best guarded by its anti-air turret. Make sure this is manned and operable at all times. Otherwise the Rebels attempt to land here. Keep an eye on the Depot to the east as well and blast any Rebel craft that attempt to land there. The turrets at both positions must help cover each other to deal with the constant swarm of approaching craft.

Like the rest of the platforms, make sure the anti-air turret is always manned. But a second teammate on the platform is a good idea, to help prevent ground attacks the turret might miss while scanning the skies.

If an enemy fighter attempts to land, let it. Then take out the pilot as soon as he gets out and tries to capture the command post. This gives you an enemy fighter to fly against unsuspecting foes. Use this opportunity to take out the enemy turrets without worrying about immediate return fire. But the enemy units eventually catch on, so maximize damage to enemy forces while the disguise still works.

Depot

The Depot completes the Empire's presence on the southern platforms.

Along with the two TIE fighters on the platform to the north, the Depot also spawns the southernmost TIE bomber on the large platform to the west. If the Rebels capture the Landing or Depot, it doesn't mean both TIE

bombers disappear altogether. An anti-air turret helps bolster the command posts defenses, but infantry support may be necessary, especially if the Rebels infiltrate one of the surrounding platforms. Place mines at the top of the ramps and use the turret to fire on incoming attackers.

Shocktroopers work well as secondary defenders. Their missile launcher is capable of locking onto enemy craft as well as blasting any infantry attackers who may wander up one of the two ramps.

To prevent enemy aerial incursions, throw some mines around the platform. If there's an enemy presence on the surrounding platforms, place a mine at the top of each ramp as well.

If the Depot is captured, be aware that the turret is likely to be manned by enemy forces. Still, it's possible to pick off the gunner with a standard weapon like a blaster pistol. This is often faster than taking out the entire turret with missiles. When making such an assault, use the railings on the ramp for partial cover and concealment.

REBEL ALLIANCE STRATEGY

Rush the Extractor and prevent the Empire from reaching the platform by containing the enemy to the southern bridge.

In addition to getting their starcraft in the air, the Rebel's main objective is to take the Extractor. If the Empire captures this, they have a solid foothold on the center of the map and a strong chance of scattering troops north. So rush the Extractor with pilots and soldiers. When they arrive, use the surrounding pillars for cover to push back the

Imperials. Slowly take control of the Extractor platform and hold your defenses on the southern side at the covered bridge.

The Y-wing's two-man crew makes it ideal for aerial assaults. Blast the platform's turret, then land and capture the command post quickly.

Meanwhile, conduct frequent air assaults on the Landing and Depot. Clear a path with X-wings, then land a Y-wing with a crew of two to quickly capture the command posts. If your air units are quick and decisive, you can take both the Depot and Landing before your ground troops secure the Extractor. Try to contain the Imperials to the Control command post, using the turrets at the Depot and Landing to blast their TIE fighters before they get off the ground. Depriving the Imperials of their air units make them easier to lock down at the Control, but you still need to watch out for breakout attacks by dark troopers.

Once they're captured, use the Landing and Depot's turrets to suppress attacks from the Control command post. Begin by targeting its southern turret.

TIP

While it's fun to play around with the star-fighters, the real battle is on the ground. Don't get distracted with dogfights and strafing runs. The team that loses focus and ignores the command posts is likely to lose.

GALACTIC EMPIRE STRATEGY

Get to the Extractor quickly using dark troopers. They can usually capture it before the Rebels can even set foot on the platform.

The Empire's strategy shouldn't differ that much from the Rebels', but they may have an easier time taking the Command than the Rebels have taking the Control. This makes a full-on ground assault worth a try. Like the Rebels, begin by assaulting the Extractor. Dark troopers' flight capability may give the Empire the needed edge to reach this position first. Once there, position scouts on the northern side and snipe Rebels on the northern bridge and inside the Command. Sniper support makes it easier for stormtroopers and dark troopers to move along the northern bridge and infiltrate the Command.

Cover the northern advance with scouts. Use them to pick off defenders on the northern bridge and within the Command building.

Inside the Command building, blast the defenders at close range while capturing the command post. But don't approach the side ramps leading up to the anti-air turrets. Instead, stay on the ground floor and lob thermal detonators up at them. This is the safest way to destroy the turrets from within. Next, fortify the position against counterattack, especially the northern entrance. Consider mining both entrances and covering them with shock troopers.

Containing the Rebels to the Dock and Fuel command posts can be tough, but it also means that all their spawn points are outside, making them vulnerable to strafing runs by your TIE fighters and TIE bombers. Hold out at the Command and your other command posts until the Rebel reinforcements have bled away.

In the Command building, toss thermal detonators and concussion grenades into the upper level to unseat enemy gunners in the anti-air turrets. Whatever you do, don't rush up the ramp—you won't win the duel.

TACTICS

BRIDGE WALK

The northern and southern covered bridges flanking both ends of the Extractor are deadly tunnels filled with constant blaster fire and explosions.

To avoid walking through these tunnels, jump up on the sloped sides to reach its roof, then simply run across.

This is a good way to bypass the constant fighting below, but it leaves you open to other attacks. Rebels want to make sure the Control's north-facing turret is destroyed before attempting such a maneuver. Otherwise you may get blown off the bridge—and on Bespin, it's a long fall.

DIVE & DITCH

Landing at enemy command posts is extremely dangerous because the craft must hover before setting down, leaving it open to all sorts of air and ground attacks. Spawn a pilot and get in your craft of choice. Then make a low-level pass at an enemy command post's turret. Make sure it's destroyed before proceeding.

While still moving toward the platform, reduce your speed and get as close to the surface as possible.

Instead of landing, simply jump out. If you're low enough, you won't take any fall damage, but your craft crashes and explodes—preferably a fair distance away. If you capture the command post, you won't be needing it anyway. Remember, dark troopers and jet troopers don't take fall damage, so they can bail out at much higher altitudes.

While converting the command post, rush to the turret you destroyed earlier and repair it. Then use the turret to defend your new command post from counterattacks.

TIP

When strafing turrets, try to attack from the east. The sun has a blinding effect on gunners in this direction, making it harder to see and hit your craft.

COMMAND JUMP

Conducting a top-down assault on the Command building is a great way to catch defenders by surprise. But such attacks are only possible with aerial units like dark troopers. Begin by taking off from the catwalk encircling the Extractor's roof. Take off from the very edge, just above the northern bridge, or you might not make it.

BESPIN: PLATFORMS

While in the air, veer to the left or right to choose which side you'll attack from. This decision is easier to make if you know which anti-air turret is destroyed. If neither turret is destroyed, do your best to be discreet and sneak by. If the gunner in the turret spots you, your attack is over.

Descend the ramp while scanning the command post's floor below. The dark trooper's blaster cannon makes quick work of any defenders. If you coordinate with teammates and attack simultaneously from both sides, this attack can be devastating.

THE CLOUD CAR

The famous Bespin cloud cars are not available at the beginning of the battle. These peculiar craft spawn only after your team has captured an opposing faction's command post. Upon capture, any enemy craft linked to the command post explodes and a cloud car appears a few seconds later on one of the associated platforms.

Compared to the starfighters zooming over the map, the cloud car is slow and weak. But it's also extremely agile, capable of flying circles around the competition. It's most maneuverable at high speeds, so keep the throttle slammed forward at all times—don't worry, it's not that fast.

The cloud car's co-pilot has access to a missile launcher, capable of firing a salvo from the belly of the craft. These are useful for attacking large clusters of ground troops or attacking turrets—they're much more destructive than the craft's weak lasers. You have only 24 missiles to start with, and they disappear really fast. But you can always restock at one of the map's repair droids.

The cloud car's weak armor and armament make it a liability to its crew. It's best used as a transport for staging two-man sneak attacks on distant platforms. To avoid the frequent dogfights, fly below the platforms. This also makes you less susceptible to attacks from the anti-air turrets.

Battle Hints

The key to controlling the command posts are the anti-aircraft turrets. The turrets at the Command and Control can fire out to the other CPs and their turrets to keep the other faction from claiming them, and they can even fire at the Extractor in the middle of the map. It's very difficult to take out the turrets with anything other than a rocket or fighter blast. The turrets can shoot down unwary starfighters in only eight hits, so if you're a pilot, you'd be wise to destroy the guns on the opposite team as soon as possible. Once this is done, you have a much better chance of landing and capturing the outlying CPs.

by Tester Xavier Rodriguez

ENDOR: BUNKER

planetary overview

Endor and its moon are often confused with one another. Endor itself is a gas giant, lying in the Unknown Regions, with a massive gravitational shadow that complicates any direct hyperspace jumps. The forest moon of Endor (one of nine orbiting the giant) is covered by woodland, savannas, and mountains. Sometimes called the Sanctuary Moon, it is inhabited by a wide range of intelligent creatures, such as the Ewoks.

The trees where the industrious Ewoks build their sprawling villages can reach thousands of meters in height. Endor's remote location, forest terrain, tree villages, and dense vegetation provide many places to hide and would be a good location to house a secret facility.

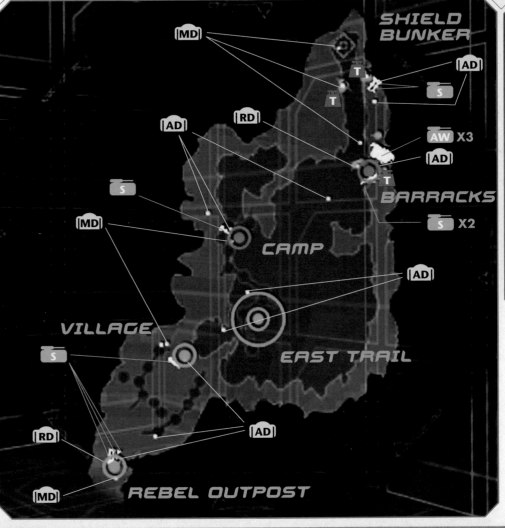

Legend

T	Turret
S	Scout Vehicle
MA	Medium Assault Vehicle
AW	Assault walker
HT	Heavy Assault Transport
FC	Fighter Craft
AT	Air Transoprt
B	Bomber
SC	Special Craft
C	Creature
AD	Ammo Droid
MD	Medical Droid
RD	Repair Droid

COMMAND POSTS

REBEL OUTPOST

Although this command post sits to the rear of the front lines, the Rebels need to position defenders nearby to repel enemy rush attacks.

Keep a few vanguards positioned nearby to deal with any AT-STs that wander within range. Try to stay concealed within the foliage of the forest and keep moving to prevent the AT-ST from tracking you.

Marksmen are an asset for defending the Rebel Outpost. Hide in the nearby bushes and keep watch over the command post. The lengthy conversion process buys you plenty of time to pick off multiple attackers.

| INITIAL CONTROL: **Rebel Alliance** | |
| COMMAND POST TYPE: **Heavy** | |

VEHICLES, TURRETS, & DROIDS

Unit	Count
Speeder Bike	3
Medical Droid	1
Ammo Droid	1
Repair Droid	1

Located to the far south, the Rebel Outpost is a key command post valued by both factions. For the Rebels, it provides three speeder bikes useful for staging rush attacks on the Shield Bunker and other enemy-held positions to the north. But if the Empire captures this command post, they open a second front, allowing them to squeeze the Rebel forces in the center of the map from the north and south. So the Rebels need to defend this position throughout the battle.

Begin by tossing mines to the north and around the command post. Mines are the best way to defend against rush attacks by enemy speeder bikes. Consider deploying some marksmen in the surrounding area. This heavy command post takes some time to convert, requiring attackers to remain within its radius for several seconds. Use this opportunity to pick off them off from a distance.

Toss a few mines around the command post and across the open path to the north. This helps stop enemy speeder bikes from rushing the command post.

VILLAGE

Surrounding Ewok-constructed catwalks and platforms overlook this Rebel position.

| INITIAL CONTROL: **Rebel Alliance** | |
| COMMAND POST TYPE: **Light** | |

VEHICLES, TURRETS, & DROIDS

Unit	Count
Speeder Bike	1
Medical Droid	1
Ammo Droid	1

The Village command post is flanked by several large rocks, providing some cover to both defenders and attackers. But the Rebel defenders can best watch this position from the nearby U-shaped network of catwalks and platforms to the south, east, and west. These elevated positions are great sniper spots, allowing marksmen to pick off any attackers who wander within the command post's radius. Placing vanguards on the platforms is also a good idea to help deal with the AT-STs. Keeping vanguards nearby is also useful for placing and replenishing mines around the command post.

The rocks around the command post cut off certain angles of attack. Place mines in the gaps between, making the command post impervious to speeder bike attacks.

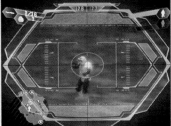

Deploy marksmen on the high catwalks and platforms surrounding the command post. The entire network of upper-level walkways provide a great view of the Village and surrounding areas.

Engage AT-STs from the upper-level platforms. While the AT-ST approaches, use the tree growing through the center of the platform for cover and concealment. Wait for the AT-ST to pass before attacking at close range.

If it turns, circle back behind the massive tree trunk for cover. Keep circling and firing until the AT-ST crumbles to the forest floor.

EAST TRAIL

This hilltop meadow may look serene now, but it's one of the frontline positions in the battle and a highly coveted piece of territory.

The East Trail command post sits on a hill between the Village and the Camp, serving as the Rebels' frontline spawn point at the start of the battle. Although it offers no vehicles, this command post must be held at all times to prevent the Empire from staging flanking attacks on the Village.

More important, the East Trail provides access to a catwalk meandering north toward the Camp. This path can be used to attack the Camp, but it can also be used by the Empire to attack the East Trail. So position troops along this catwalk and consider throwing some mines along it. Its elevation gives defenders a great view of the area surrounding the command post. Soldiers, marksmen, and vanguards all make good choices as defenders here.

Position soldiers and marksmen along the nearby catwalks and platforms to the defend the command post. But watch for attackers moving along the catwalks themselves. Attackers from the Camp may try to take the high path to reach the East Trail.

Hide mines in the thick undergrowth surrounding the command post. Even the most cautious attackers won't be able to see them until it's too late.

The platforms and catwalks give vanguards an elevated firing position, helping maximize the splash damage caused by their missiles. Aim for your target's feet and fire away.

It's also possible to cover the Village command post from the southern end of the catwalk. This is a good spot for marksmen, but vanguards can also come in handy by launching a few missiles at attackers huddling between the rocks next to the command post.

INITIAL CONTROL: REBEL ALLIANCE
COMMAND POST TYPE: LIGHT

VEHICLES, TURRETS, & DROIDS

Unit	Count
Ammo Droid	2

CAMP

The Imperials have overrun this Ewok Camp in the center of the map, giving them an edge for capturing the remaining Rebel-held positions to the south.

INITIAL CONTROL:
GALACTIC EMPIRE
COMMAND POST TYPE: LIGHT

VEHICLES, TURRETS, & DROIDS

Unit	Count
Speeder Bike	1
Medical Droid	1
Ammo Droid	2

To the Imperials, the Camp is a counterpart to the Rebels' East Trail—the frontline position. Even with the high ground of the catwalk nearby, this position is tough to hold, with the Rebels (and Ewoks) conducting constant attacks from the East Trail. To better defend the command post, consider deploying an AT-ST from the Barracks to provide support fire.

Keep an eye on the east near the downed hollowed-out tree. Rebel attackers and marksmen are likely to move and attack from this direction. The catwalk is also a favorite avenue of attack for Rebels spawning at the East Trail. Capturing the East Trail significantly reduces attacks on this command post, but until then, keep an AT-ST nearby to repel the constant assaults. Just make sure the AT-STs steer clear of the two Ewok log booby traps to the west and southwest. If an AT-ST walks between them, the logs swing free and slam the walker's turret, instantly demolishing it and killing its crew.

Get a Shocktrooper near the command post as soon as possible and throw a few mines around it. Then move to the high ground of the catwalk and watch as enemy speeder bikes explode attempting rush attacks.

The catwalk is great for blasting enemies approaching from the east. But if the Rebels manage to infiltrate the command post, you have to get down on the ground to contest it before it's captured. This requires a quick response because a group of Rebels can convert the position within a few seconds. Move within the command post's radius quickly and keep circle-strafing while blasting the attackers at close range.

 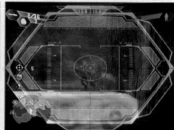

Position a scout behind the ammo droid to the far west. The droid provides some decent cover and an endless supply of ammo while the scout snipes Rebel attackers to the east. The droid is also located away from the high traffic areas, reducing the chances of getting blindsided.

Two log-based booby traps on the southwestern side of the Camp are capable of demolishing any AT-STs that stumble between them. These traps are triggered automatically as soon as a walker moves within range, causing the two suspended logs to crash together, smashing the AT-ST from both sides. If triggered, the traps eventually reset automatically, making this western path extremely treacherous for the AT-STs throughout the battle. Maneuver around them to keep your AT-STs alive.

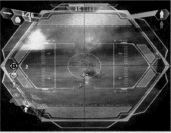

endor: bunker

BARRACKS

The Barracks supplies the Empire with multiple vehicles making it a popular target for Rebel attackers and thieves.

INITIAL CONTROL:
Galactic Empire
command post type: LIGHT

vehicles, turrets, & droids

Unit	Count
AT-ST	3
Speeder Bike	2
Gun Turret	1
Medical Droid	1
Ammo Droid	1
Repair Droid	1

The AT-STs spawned at the Barracks give the Imperials a tremendous tactical advantage over the Rebels. Therefore, the Barracks must be constantly protected against Rebel attacks. Begin by placing mines around the command post and make sure the AT-STs are manned at all times. Capturing even one could tilt the odds in favor of the Rebels, especially if they use it to assault the defensive turrets outside the Shield Bunker.

The Barracks has a turret of its own, and it should be constructed early and manned at all times. This turret is extremely useful for repelling frontal assaults in the event the Camp falls into Rebel hands. But most attacks are likely to come from the cover of the forest to the east and west. To defend against such sneak attacks, use your own troops to patrol the surrounding woods.

Maintain a constant presence of varying units near the Barracks to defend it from Rebel capture. A pilot is necessary to construct and repair the gun turret while Shocktroopers are useful for placing and replenishing mines around the command post. But standard stormtroopers are best for dealing with the close- to intermediate-range infantry attacks launched by Rebels from the forest.

Hide scouts in the forest to the east and west. Since the command post provides no cover, attackers have to stand in the open to convert it. If they take aim quickly, the scouts can kill the attackers before the command post is neutralized.

SHIELD BUNKER

This Shield Bunker houses the shield generator responsible for protecting the second Death Star from starfighter and capital ship attacks. The Rebels must take it out!

INITIAL CONTROL: Galactic Empire
command post type: N/A
(DESTRUCTIBLE)

vehicles, turrets, & droids

Unit	Count
Speeder Bike	2
Gun Turret	2
Medical Droid	2
Ammo Droid	2

The Shield Bunker sits at the north end of the map and is guarded by two gun turrets flanking both sides of the entrance. The Imperials want to construct these turrets early in the battle to prevent frontal assaults. Once constructed and manned, these turrets can cover the southern approach as well as the thick forest to the east and west.

But further efforts must be made to prevent attacks. Use Shocktroopers to place mines at the Bunker's entrance and within the main walkway leading to the shield generator. The turrets are likely to discourage frontal assaults, so consider placing stormtroopers or scouts in the thick foliage to the east and west to help spot and engage flank attacks. Unlike the other command posts, this one can't be converted. But if it's destroyed, the Empire loses a spawn point, potentially tilting the odds in favor of a Rebel victory.

Use a pilot to construct both turrets early in the battle. These are needed to prevent frontal assaults. If the gunner zooms in, it's possible to engage enemy targets as far away as the Barracks command post to the south. This allows the gunners to keep Rebel infantry at bay.

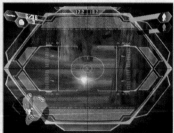

Position a scout on top of the Shield Bunker's rooftop to better cover the southern approach. The scout, like the turrets below, can engage targets near the Barracks, but with much greater accuracy and lethality.

Use Shocktroopers to heavily mine the Shield Bunker's exterior and interior. The mines probably won't surprise any attackers, but they force the enemy to slow down, giving your team more time to spawn and bring in defenders. Place a couple around the front entrance. Even if the attackers don't set them off, they have to take time to destroy them before entering. Inside, stick some more mines on the vertical support beams lining the walkway leading to the shield generator. Once again, this is more of a delaying tactic. You still need plenty of defenders to root out the attackers if they gain entry. Just make sure you minimize collateral damage to the generator during any interior firefights.

TIP

Like droids and vehicles, the shield generator can be repaired by pilots if damaged during an attack. make regular visits to the generator to inspect its status, and repair as needed.

REBEL ALLIANCE STRATEGY

Assault the Barracks from the east. But wait for all the AT-STs to leave before launching the assault on the command post.

For the Rebels, the surest path to victory is through the Barracks command post to the north. Denying the Empire their AT-STs evens the odds, making a Rebel win much more likely. But first, fortify the southern command posts to ensure they don't fall. Place the appropriate number of mines and marksmen nearby to keep the Imperials out.

Meanwhile, assemble at the East Trail an attack squad consisting primarily of soldiers. A pilot and vanguard can come in handy, too. Begin the assault by circling wide to the east where you're less likely to encounter the enemy. When you reach the eastern side of the Barracks, stay in the forest and monitor the situation—make sure all AT-STs are gone before launching the attack. Start by taking out the gunner in the turret, or the whole turret if a vanguard is in the squad. Then rush the command post while blasting any defenders.

Use vanguards to knock out the two turrets outside the Shield Bunker before assaulting.

Once the Barracks are captured, the Imperial forces are cut in two, providing direct access to the Shield Bunker to the north. Immediately fortify the Barracks before attacking any other command posts. Make sure the turret is operational and that mines are placed. Then begin some probing attacks on the Shield Bunker, using vanguards to knock out the two turrets.

Meanwhile, send another attack squad (this time with at least two smugglers) around the eastern side of the Bunker. Once the turrets are down, infiltrate the Bunker with your attack squad. Secure the interior, then post soldiers at the entrance to prevent counterattacks by Imperial troops spawning outside.

The quickest and safest way to destroy the generator is with the smuggler's time bombs. It takes four bombs and they must be placed one at a time. This means it takes a minimum of 40 seconds to take out the shield generator, but plan on holding out for a full minute. The attack squad must hold out at least this long while the smugglers demolish the generator. Once the generator is destroyed, you can contain the Imperials to the Camp while bleeding their reinforcements until the battle is won.

Storm the Shield Bunker with a mixed force, including smugglers. The smuggler time bomb is the most effective weapon for demolishing the generator.

GALACTIC EMPIRE STRATEGY

Rush the Rebel Outpost with speeder bikes and capture this southern command post to open a new front.

While the AT-STs give the Empire a tremendous advantage, the Rebels still present a serious threat and must be dealt with quickly. Start off by moving the AT-STs toward the Camp, but consider keeping one at the Barracks. Holding these positions is critical.

While the Rebels are busy attacking the Camp and Barracks, assemble a speeder bike attack squad at the Shield Bunker—your team possesses five at the start of the battle, spread out among the three command posts. Once they're assembled, race the speeder bikes south along the less-traveled eastern edge of the map toward the Rebel Outpost. When the squad arrives, stay on the eastern side and try to spots mine around the command post.

Use thermal detonators and blaster fire to wipe out the mines, then rush the command post. It takes a while to convert, but five units should be able to capture it within a matter of seconds.

Assault the Village with infantry from the south and AT-STs from the north.

After capturing the Rebel Outpost, start moving north toward the Village command post. Meanwhile, get your AT-STs moving south in an attempt to simultaneously attack the Village. No matter how strong the Rebel defenses are, they won't be able to withstand a combined infantry and AT-ST attack at the Village from two sides.

Instead of attacking the East Trail, fortify your existing command posts and hold them while the Rebel reinforcements drain away. Keep one AT-ST deployed at the Barracks, Camp, and Village command posts to help prevent breakout attacks. Place the bulk of your infantry forces on the northern and southern flanks at the Rebel Outpost and Shield Bunker. Once the Rebels weaken, move in on the East Trail and capture it to end the battle.

Wait until the Rebels are weak, then move in to capture the East Trail. Meanwhile, keep the AT-STs positioned at the surrounding command posts to prevent breakout attacks.

TIP

The ewoks are more of a nuisance than a serious threat, so deal with the Rebels before turning your weapons on these creatures. They spawn around the village and East Trail, as well as the Camp if it comes under Rebel control. Avoid moving into large swarms of ewoks because their rocks and spears can cause serious damage at close range. Blast them from a distance before moving within their short attack range.

TACTICS

SHIELD BUNKER DEMO TEAM

It only takes four time bombs to destroy the Shield Bunker, so a relatively small force can take it out. For instance, a smuggler and a pilot are more than capable of making the strike, especially if it's not well defended. Use speeder bikes to rush the Bunker early in the game to immediately deprive the Empire of a spawn point.

Circle around the Bunker and attack from the north, preferably dropping off the roof and immediately gaining entry. Once you're inside, the exterior gun turrets don't pose a threat.

ENDOR: BUNKER

The smuggler should place the time bombs while the pilot provides cover and extra ammo. Stick the time bombs to the console and back off to wait for it to explode. Placing more than one time bomb at a time can be risky—when the first time bomb explodes, it may destroy the second, hindering its full detonation power. Instead, place one time bomb and wait for it to explode before placing the next one. It takes a while, but it is the safest way.

Since it takes four time bombs, and the smuggler only carries three, the pilot must resupply the smuggler before the last bomb is placed. Once the forth bomb is in place, back off and wait for it to deal the final blow to the shield generator.

COMBINED ASSAULTS

Carefully coordinated assaults with infantry and AT-STs can wipe out the Rebel command posts in record time. Lead attacks with AT-STs infantry posted on the flanks or rear.

The AT-ST can't capture command posts by itself, and if the crew gets out, the walker is prone to capture. So be sure to move in with infantry once a walker has suppressed a particular command post. Dark troopers are useful in this role, thanks to their unparalleled speed and mobility.

In some instances, infantry can simply stay put in a safe place and convert the command post while the AT-ST provides cover. This is possible at the Village command post by sneaking along the outside of the rocks.

AT-ST THEFT

When playing as the Rebel Alliance, instead of capturing the Barracks, use it as a source to supply your own team with AT-STs. Begin by reaching the eastern side of the Barracks with a speeder bike. Hold on the eastern perimeter until a new AT-ST spawns, and stay out of sight.

As soon as an AT-ST appears, rush in from the east and get as close to the walker as possible before jumping off.

Hop off the speeder bike and jump directly into the AT-ST. Begin by blasting the defenses around the Barracks, including the gun turret. Continue suppressing enemy troops at the Barracks until friendly units can move in to capture it.

Next, head north and assault the two gun turrets at the Shield Bunker. Clearing these turrets out allows your team direct access to the Bunker. Once the Bunker is destroyed, use the AT-ST to attack other enemy positions or any surviving walkers still held by the Imperials. Just make sure it's kept in top-shape at all times. It may be the only walker your team has the chance to get—and one AT-ST can make a huge difference in this battle.

Battle Hints

The Barracks is the most tactically significant command post on Endor. The Empire will only be supplied with AT-STs when holding this position, so the Rebels must do all they can to take this CP and quell the vehicular onslaught. Once this CP has been claimed by the Rebels, they have a perfect location to launch their final assault on the Shield Bunker. The Empire must do all they can to hold the Barracks, as vehicle dominance is their biggest asset on the battlefield.

by Tester Zak Huntwork